Representation, Meaning, and Thought

Representation
Meaning
and Thought

GRANT GILLETT

CLARENDON PRESS · OXFORD
1992

Oxford University Press, Walton Street, Oxford OX2 6DP
Oxford New York Toronto
Delhi Bombay Calcutta Madras Karachi
Petaling Jaya Singapore Hong Kong Tokyo
Nairobi Dar es Salaam Cape Town
Melbourne Auckland
and associated companies in
Berlin Ibadan

Oxford is a trade mark of Oxford University Press

Published in the United States
by Oxford University Press, New York

British Library Cataloguing in Publication Data
Data available

Library of Congress Cataloging in Publication Data
Gillett, Grant, 1950–
Representation, meaning, and thought / Grant Gillett.
p. cm.
Includes bibliographical references and index.
1. Semantics (Philosophy). 2. Mental representation. 3. Meaning
(Psychology). I. Title.
B840.G54 1992   121'.68—dc20   92-15170
ISBN 0-19-823993-9

Typeset by Graphicraft Typesetters Ltd., Hong Kong

Printed in Great Britain by
Biddles Ltd, Guildford & King's Lynn

For Shirley

ACKNOWLEDGEMENTS

I SHOULD like to thank numerous people who have been directly involved with this work and others who have played a major part in my development and its production.

First I must acknowledge an enduring debt to Kathy Wilkes, who took me on in my philosophical infancy and patiently trained me in those practices of argumentation and analysis that I have followed ever since. In this task she was ably helped by many others but notably by Paul Snowdon, who also read large chunks of this manuscript and offered helpful comments and criticisms.

I should also like to thank Tony Grayling, whose encouragement initiated this study at a time when many of the ideas were nascent, even inchoate. He then followed up his original support by reading the entire manuscript and offering advice and criticism at crucial points.

Jim Tiles has also read the entire manuscript and made many helpful suggestions which have served to clarify the argument, iron out various points about which I was mistaken in early drafts, and render the whole into a form where the development of the discussion is now in some semblance of order. I cannot speak too highly of his encouragement and critical perspicacity.

Individual chapters have been read and criticized by friends at Oxford and elsewhere. I should like particularly to mention David Novitz (University of Canterbury, New Zealand), David Wiggins (University College, Oxford), Julie Jack (Somerville College, Oxford), Peter Hacker (St John's College, Oxford), Kathy Morris (St John's College, Oxford), Martha Klein (Reading University and Exeter College, Oxford), and Sir Peter Strawson (Magdalen College, Oxford). I must also record my appreciation of Olav Gjelsvik (University of Oslo), an astute and interesting interlocutor with whom I am increasingly finding a valued convergence in my thinking in many areas. He has been an inspiration to me in pressing me on to complete this study.

The project was made possible by the fellows of Magdalen College, Oxford, who had the generosity to appoint me to a Fellowship by Examination just prior to my embarking on it. Oxford is a delightful place to study and Magdalen is, I believe, one of the most inspiring settings that it provides, and I hope that, to some extent, this manuscript reflects the deep indebtedness I owe the University and the College. The completion of the project is also indebted, in no small way, to the University of Otago Medical School, who have encouraged their Medical Ethics teacher to sustain an active interest in pure philosophy.

I have dedicated this book to my wife Shirley, not merely because of my feelings for her, but also because she has challenged me more deeply and more often than anybody else to think about "life, the universe, and everything".

CONTENTS

NOTES ON REFERENCES

BBB L. Wittgenstein, *The Blue and Brown Books* (Oxford: Blackwell, 1972).

CPR I. Kant, *Critique of Pure Reason*, tr. N. Kemp Smith (first pub. 1787; London: Macmillan, 1929). (I shall give references in the text using the B pagination, where applicable, from this edition.)

EAE D. Davidson, *Essays on Actions and Events* (Oxford: Oxford University Press, 1980).

HE C. Peacocke, *Holistic Explanation* (Oxford: Oxford University Press, 1979).

IFP M. Dummett, *The Interpretation of Frege's Philosophy* (London: Duckworth, 1981).

Ind. P. F. Strawson, *Individuals* (London: Methuen, 1959).

ITI D. Davidson, *Inquiries into Truth and Interpretation* (Oxford: Oxford University Press, 1984).

LI G. Frege, *Logical Investigations*, ed. P. Geach (Oxford: Blackwell, 1977).

MA P. Geach, *Mental Acts* (London: Routledge & Kegan Paul, 1957).

OC *L. Wittgenstein, On Certainty*, tr. G. E. M. Anscombe and G. H. von Wright (Oxford: Blackwell, 1969).

PI L. Wittgenstein, *Philosophical Investigations*, tr. G. E. M. Anscombe (Oxford: Blackwell, 1953).

PR L. Wittgenstein, *Philosophical Remarks*, ed. R. Rhees, tr. R. Hargreaves and R. White (Oxford: Blackwell, 1975).

SC C. Peacocke, *Sense and Content* (Oxford: Oxford University Press, 1983).

TEC C. Peacocke, *Thoughts: An Essay on Content* (Oxford: Blackwell, 1986).

TGF G. Frege, *Translations from the Philosophical Writings of Gottlob Frege*, ed. P. Geach and M. Black (Oxford: Blackwell, 1980).

TO A. Woodfield (ed.), *Thought and Object* (Oxford: Oxford University Press, 1982).

TOE M. Dummett, *Truth and Other Enigmas* (London: Duckworth, 1978).

VR G. Evans, *Varieties of Reference*, ed. J. McDowell (Oxford: Oxford University Press, 1980).

Introduction

REPRESENTATIONS re-present. In effect they relate a present situation to former situations so that the resulting information can be analysed and repeatedly used in organizing the activity of the subject. The strategies used by higher animals seem to derive from their relating present situations to actual past situations or to possible variants of those situations. In order to describe and explain these complex strategies we speak of such creatures as having mental representations of both general features of and particulars within an environment which extends beyond the present range of their sensory capacities.

We often conceive of mental representations as events within the individual's head which reflect events outside it. Although this picture has seemed obvious to many philosophers, it raises serious problems about the relation between thought and the world. The subject is said to know about the world because of the inner events which represent the world as being thus and so, or comprise ideas and impressions of that world, or are deliverances of his sensory experience in that world. All these formulations aim to capture the nature of thought, but all of them entail that the subject has no experience of his world distinct from the representations or ideas that he happens to form. Therefore it seems that he could *never* have a substantial notion of misrepresentation because he has no access to anything which can be compared with his representational world.

This raises a problem for epistemology. How is it that the mind has contents which stand in some relation to the world of the thinker who thinks them? In that our thoughts aim to represent the world, we do aspire to representations that are faithful to it. Now, if we humans were like cameras or fossils and carried information about the world solely in virtue of its causal effect on us, then we could defend the thesis that our brains causally register the impingements of the world and thereby carry causally produced representations of it. A causal sense of 'represent' would then be central in the analysis of thought. I will argue against this seductively simple view.

In Plato we find an account of the way in which the elements of thought relate to everyday physical things. He claimed that the forms—ideals apprehended by the mind but reflected only imperfectly by their worldly instances—structured our thoughts. The problem is that it is hard to relate the forms of the intellect (and thus true knowledge) to earthly experience in any way that illuminates the semantic contents of thoughts.

Descartes conceived of thought as occurring in a *res cogitans*. This interacted with physical things and received information about the world via the nerves and the brain. Descartes claimed that subjects had incorrigible knowledge of their own ideas which were on the nearer side of an interface between mind and nature, a view which has set the agenda for philosophy of mind to the present day. Following Descartes, Locke and Hume both accepted that the mind received impressions or sensations from the world and that these formed the basis of knowledge. Thus they captured the intuition that there must be some way in which the impingement of the world figures in a specification of what the subject is thinking about. They also sharpened the problem of forging a relation between the representations in the mind and the external world. Their approach almost guaranteed that we will gravitate towards an account of the way that sensory systems give rise to events which culminate in conscious experience, a view I call the empiricist representational theory of mind (ERT). It holds that sensory events are produced in a subject by the causal impingement of the environment and that the processes and causal transactions thereby set in train constitute propositional attitudes and conscious thoughts. An incidental and historically important feature of Hume's version of this theory is the conception that mental states and events such as *the belief that p*, which we now call propositional attitudes, are dual entities comprising an item of content and a relation between the subject and that content (i.e. ⟨p⟩ and ⟨believing⟩).

Kant made an initial assault on this 'great redoubt' of empiricist epistemology by arguing that all knowledge and indeed all contentful experience involves rule-governed intellectual activity. He claimed that experience is essentially conceptual in nature and that concepts are based on functions of judgement obeying normative (rational) constraints. Such rational tools exclusively belong to conscious beings, who are distinct in important ways from the causal order that surrounds them. Their essential difference is evinced by the fact that they obey an 'ought' (or a number of 'oughts') determined not by causal dispositions but by the "apodeictic" norms of reason operative in theoretical and practical knowledge. He implied that any theory of mind giving primacy to the causal impingements of nature was fundamentally misconceived and formulated transcendental idealism to account for the fact that human beings are members both of an order of causal transactions and of an order of rational or intellectual operations governed by the oughts of reason, morality, and aesthetic judgement. Kant regarded psychological causes as "pathological" intrusions or distractions within the realm of rationality. I will draw on Kant but temper his analysis by a healthy regard for everyday human life and activity.

I begin, in Chapter 1, with concepts and give an account in which judgement plays an essential role in their analysis. The emphasis on judgement and the rules governing it raise problems for an internal (Cartesian) or 'narrow' view of mental content. I argue that concepts are abstractions from the notion of grasping a concept and dependent on rules operating within human activity. To grasp a concept is to master a principled way of responding to the world involving techniques of selected attention and directed search for criterial information which reveals whether a presentation instances the concept in question.

The present view sees the subject of experience quintessentially as a concept-user. This has implications for accounts of personal identity and suggests a modified reading of Kant's "synthetic unity of apperception" as the key to understanding that issue (Chapter 2).

Mental explanation is a major challenge for any account of content; it is often held to concern states within the agent which antecedently cause human actions. The present account of content (Chapter 3) suggests that such an analysis of action is mistaken. It shifts the focus from the events comprising an action to a structural analysis of the way in which the activity is engaged with the conceptual system of the subject and thereby with the subject's environment via an articulated system of rule-governed practices.

The basic tenets of the present position are then clarified further, in Chapter 4, via a discussion of cognitive development and cognitive science. The acquisition of concepts is a process in which the child is a novice in the art of making sense of the world. He is introduced to the meaningful world of others by learning the *tools* which unlock the secrets of that world, namely the concepts used in adult thought. I will also discuss some developments in cognitive neuroscience and relate them to the favoured analysis of concepts. The brain is portrayed as an information-gathering tool with partially 'plastic' arrays of processing equipment which register presentations and are shaped in the way that they retain information by both the things in the world and the conceptual system in which they develop. Chapter 4 also discusses the problem of Robinson Junior (the solitary thinker).

Chapter 5 discusses the implications of the present view for a doctrine of representation in which the structure, intentionality, and normativity of content are linked to the analysis of concepts and the resulting account contrasted with those of Fodor and Peacocke.

Linguistic meaning and mental content can both be elucidated by the fact that thoughts are expressed by and internally related to the understanding of utterances in a natural language. In Chapter 6, Frege's requirement that thought be tied to truth is used as the key to the account. The relation between thought and language in the present work focuses on rules for the use of terms and is compared and contrasted to Davidson's radical interpretation model of meaning and understanding. Chapters 7 and 8 address the problems that cluster round identity statements and singular thoughts. Various methodological solipsist accounts of cognitive significance are criticized *en route* to a view which draws on the human practices (where the uses of expressions are governed by rules). Singular thoughts, involving the use of demonstratives and the recognition of particulars, also provide difficulties for methodological solipsism, but singular-thought theorists are often caught short trying to explain the relation that Russell called "acquaintance". Chapter 8 offers a plausible account of this relation.

The implications of the present position for sceptical idealism are spelt out in Chapter 9. It is argued that responses to scepticism which rely on scheme and content (or some version thereof) or upon a privileged range of contents within the totality of 'conscious percepts' are unsatisfactory. The favoured response draws

on the intentionality of perception and the place of applications
and prescriptive norms in the grasp of a concept.

The present view aims to use an account derived from Wittgenstein's later philosophy to link a number of disparate topics in
philosophy of mind, epistemology, philosophy of language, and
philosophical psychology so as to present a workable theory of
mental content.

I

Concepts and Generality

THOUGHTS are about things such as frogs, numbers, cars, and relations, but thinkers only think about some of the things which they encounter. As soon as we consider a thought such as ⟨that frog is green⟩ it is clear that it is formed by combining concepts, here ⟨frog⟩ and ⟨green⟩. Without grasping the requisite concepts the thinker cannot frame the thought, and in order to think about a given thing the thinker needs to have concepts which might apply to that thing. (We could say, along with those who analyse thoughts with some attention to the predicate calculus, that a simple paradigm of a thought concerns an object, say a, and a concept, say F, and could be shown as ⟨Fa⟩ or ⟨a is F⟩.) But if thought in general is an activity involving concepts, what is a concept and what is the relation between concepts and conceptions of objects like a?

Concepts, *inter alia*, group objects according to whether they count as instances of this or that. Therefore they link different experiences by capturing common features, such as the occurrence of ⟨red⟩ or ⟨dog⟩. In fact we have a number of characterizations of concepts:

1. Concepts are ways of grouping objects.
2. Concepts capture general properties of things which may or may not be instanced by a given particular.
3. Concepts correspond to universals.
4. Concepts are functions based on acts of unity in judgement (*CPR* B93).
5. Concepts are the senses of predicates (*TGF* 43).
6. Concepts are functions mapping objects on to the True (*TGF* 28 ff.).
7. Concepts are unsaturated or incomplete (*TGF* 115).
8. Concepts are rule-governed ways of directing our interest (*PI* I. 570).
9. Concepts are compositional elements of thoughts.
10. Concepts are elements of a theory.

A successful attempt to unify these diverse characterizations would make significant inroads into the relations between representation, meaning, and thought.

In what follows it will become clear that I regard the notion of having or grasping a concept as primary and the notion of a concept as an abstraction from that. Let us accept, for the minute, that the grasp of a concept allows a thinker both to group certain objects in a principled way and to be able to reason about that grouping. This has two elements: (1) one applies a concept to actual things and (2) this enables one to relate those things to other things and to features of the world through principled transitions in thought. These transitions in thought involve discursive contents such as ⟨that is a bee⟩ and ⟨bees move⟩ and make use of the elements appearing in those contents. Thus the structure of thoughts and also their relation to a public world of things with regular properties falling under distinct kinds both depend on concepts.

1.1. Concepts, Functions, and Judgements

Hume and later empiricists often neglect to discuss concepts, or else they treat them as emergent from the input to the organism, arguing that principles of grouping or assimilation are passively acquired. The underlying thesis is that the organism is caused by inputs from the world to form representations in the mind. I have called this the empiricist representational theory (ERT). It pictures the operations of the mind as (1) arising from causal impingement by the world and (2) involving internal states and events which represent the world. It gains much of its appeal from the footprint or photograph analogy in which a thing carries information in virtue of its causal origins.

It is instructive that Kant's ideas do not appear in this picture. This is a clue to difficulties which the ERT theory usually skirts. Kant realized that human experience is conceptual and as such involves a structured system of representation. This entails that the content of any representation is determined by the conceptual structure in which it is formed. He also realized that to apply a concept is to judge that something counts as being of a certain type. Once an item is related to a conceptual structure in this way then it can figure in discursive thought.[1] In fact judgement has a dual role in mental representation:

1. a thinker can judge whether a thought (made up of concepts) is true; and
2. a thinker judges whether a concept properly applies in a situation when framing thoughts about that situation.

Merely reacting to a situation is not applying a concept because there are rules which determine whether the situation does instance the concept in question. Thus one's tendency to apply a given concept can be well or ill grounded, and in using a concept one acknowledges and is answerable to a norm which governs whether one is right or wrong in applying the concept in question. Norms also govern the judgements in which a thought (comprising conceptual elements) is assessed for its truth. The subject judges that an item counts as an instance of a concept—say, ⟨cloud⟩—he is using and also judges whether the conceptually framed thought— say, ⟨that cloud is menacing⟩—is true. In both cases the judgements implicitly answer to prescriptive norms.[2]

Contra Frege, I would argue that both uses of 'judgement' are justified because both involve the *possibility* of asking whether the situation fulfils norms of representation governing the concepts concerned. When one responds to the situation by using the concept ⟨C⟩, one can, in principle, ask 'Ought I to use ⟨C⟩ here?' or 'Is this use of ⟨C⟩ warranted?' This is similar to being inclined to think one is being approached by a green dragon but asking 'Ought I to think that?' or 'Is this true?' Frege does not take this view:

we may distinguish:

1. the apprehension of a thought—thinking,
2. the recognition of the truth of a thought—judgment,
3. the manifestation of the judgment—assertion. (*LI* 7)

In a footnote, he remarks: "It seems to me that thought and judgment have not hitherto been adequately distinguished." He limits judgement to the assessment of the truth of a thought which can

---

[1] The rule according to which an item has conceptual form may be informal and inexpressible; for instance, it may pick out 'things the same as x' where 'x' is an object or property selected from a normatively constrained range given by using that rule but not describable in any other way.

[2] I am narrowing our attention to thoughts expressed in assertions and descriptions for the moment.

be expressed in an assertoric sentence.[3] He therefore identifies one of the truth-related operations of judgement, but does not see that concepts are based on "functions of unity in our representations" (Kant).

Kant observes that thought (in which concepts order experience) is permeated with judgement because judgements do figure *both* in the application of concepts (according to norms of representation) and in the "acknowledgement of the truth of a thought".[4] The elements from which truth-assessable thoughts about the world are composed themselves rest on rules of the understanding in that the thinker must grasp that his use of concepts is answerable to norms. Kant expresses this as follows: "Everything in nature works according to laws. Only a rational being has the capacity of acting according to the conception of laws."[5] He is, in this passage, discussing the moral law, but elsewhere applies the relevance of the 'ought' governing reason much more widely (in the discussion of freedom in the First Critique). I shall return to the Kantian distinction when I compare following a rule and conforming to a rule.[6]

Kant also made a major contribution to the understanding of concepts by introducing the notion of a function:

Whereas all intuitions as sensible rest on affections, concepts rest on functions. By "function" I mean the unity of the act of bringing various representations under one common representation ... Now the only use which the understanding can make of these concepts is to judge by means of them. (*CPR* B93)

Kant uses the term "intuition" to denote the content of perceptual experience.[7] Despite his "inward-looking" view of perceptual content this passage makes some important points about concepts:

First, it states that concepts are based on functions of judgement which represent items of experience for discursive thought. These

[3] Or a statement symbolized by, for example, ⊢ *x* is *F* (*TGF* 34).
[4] Note that I have avoided the claim that every use of a concept involves a conscious judgement. But, in principle, it could do, and therefore a place must be found for this in the analysis. The stronger position results in an implausible intellectualism about concept-use.
[5] I. Kant, *Foundation of the Metaphysic of Morals*, tr. L. W. Beck (first pub. 1785; New York, 1959). [6] §1.6 below.
[7] For Kant experience was the primary datum for the rational subject and comprised intuitions—sensory matter structured according to the forms of space and time.

functions unify different experienced situations by bringing them "under one common representation". This allows an articulated or structured body of knowledge to be generated in which conceptual connections between different situations can be discursively traced. "The knowledge yielded by understanding, or at least by the human understanding, must therefore be by means of concepts and so is not intuitive but discursive" (CPR B93).

Second, the subject actively categorizes experience in terms of a conceptual structure apt for reasoning and language. Items in the world do not come furnished with labels: the subject judges that this or that element of experience counts as an instance of a particular concept (although correct application may be fairly automatic once a concept is mastered).

Third, Kant claims that concepts range over representations. For him the given "matter" of sensibility is ordered to form intuitions (inter alia, by the forms of space and time). These intuitions (or internal representational entities) then interpose between the world and discursive thought (CPR B33–4). I accept that "Thought can also be of what is not the case" (Wittgenstein, PI I. 95) and that this may appear to support Kant. I will, however, claim that concepts range over the objects, events, and features of the world so that "We—and our meaning—do not stop anywhere short of the fact" (PI I. 95). This creates an obligation to explain how it is that thoughts essentially involve objects and yet "can also be of what is not the case".

Setting aside for the minute Kant's "inward-looking" or Cartesian view, he clearly identifies the active nature of the mind in applying concepts to experience and determining its content.[8] Experience does not simply impinge upon the subject as a 'given' or a set of 'stimulations'; rather it involves conceptual judgements which should appear in an adequate account of thought and its content.

Kant sheds light on the discussion of judgements, concepts, and functions in Frege and contemporary theories of thought. The theoretical links from Kant to Frege are unclear but tantalizing: Kant remarks: "Thought is knowledge by means of concepts . . . as predicates of possible judgments" (CPR B94). For Frege, the subject–predicate combination is the bearer of truth and the content of a judgement. I will try to give Frege his "pinch of salt", but

---

[8] I shall pursue the sceptical problem in Ch. 9.

I will not address any of the major (and fraught) exegetical issues surrounding Frege's views. Instead I will focus on selected points concerning concepts and thoughts.

Dummett remarks:

the notion of a universal derives, in the first place, from the linguistic practice of predication: this . . . is made fully explicit by Frege's doctrine that a concept is unsaturated and in need of completion. But this does not mean that the concept is . . . a constituent of the objects falling under it: to make reference to a concept, it is enough to have something that can be predicated of objects whether or not it can be truly predicated of any. (*IFP* 171)

He also quotes Frege as saying:

I do not start from the concepts and put together the thought or the judgment out of them but I attain to the parts of thought by decomposing the thought . . . The expression of the judgeable content must . . . be articulated, in order to be able to be thus analysed. (*IFP* 40)

This view hinges on the idea of judgeable content and its structure or articulation. In a simple case (cf. the observational case of Peacocke, p. 66 below), a subject grasps a concept when he can judge whether a meaningful term can be applied to something presented to him. But this claim may go too far towards a strong linguistic thesis. A weaker claim is that the grasp of a concept is an ability to respond to an item in a rule-governed way (the ability may be well or ill developed). This can be linked to Frege's claim that "A concept, as I understand the word, is predicative" by recalling that a concept essentially applies to a series of items. On this view, combining a conception of an object and a general concept yields a thought which can be judged as true or false according to whether or not the concept is instanced by the denoted object. The point could also be expressed in terms of functions and arguments.

A function yields a determinate value when it is completed by an argument and in this sense is "incomplete". When all the possible arguments for a function are surveyed a complete range of values for the function are generated and if the function has the form of a statement such as '$x < 3$' rather than a form such as '$3x + 2$', then substitutions for x will result in one of two values, namely true or false.[9] According to Frege, concepts as functions of the former

---

[9] The two types of function are not always clearly distinguished by Frege.

type yield truth values by taking as arguments the objects to which they are applied.[10] The possible extension of the concept comprises the range of arguments yielding a determinate value (whether true or false) when substituted in the argument place.[11] If some subset of all the objects which could be combined in judgements with a given concept yield true thoughts, the concept has an actual world extension. I will pursue Frege's claim that concepts are inherently "incomplete" or "unsaturated" (as evident in the function '. . . < 3') by focusing on the fact that concepts are applicable in a wide range of different situations where they may or may not be instanced, and so range over objects, features, and events.

Notice that, for Frege, concepts are predicative and essentially tied to acts of judgement. I have tried to avoid a strong linguistic thesis by replacing 'predicative' with 'involving a way of thinking applicable to a number of different particulars'. On this reading, different judgements would be related in respect of the element contributed by the common concept. If knowledge or thought comprises a host of such judgements, then it involves the combination of certain elements so as to constitute a range of judgeable contents which are structurally related in virtue of their common elements. Such a view of structure is the nub of Gareth Evans's 'Generality Constraint' (discussed in §1.9) and my own view of concepts.

1.2. Concepts as Predicative and General

Strawson remarks: "the idea of a predicate is correlative with that of a range of distinguishable individuals of which the predicate can be significantly, though not necessarily truly, affirmed" (*Ind.* 99 n.). We could call this the 'generality principle'. It captures the structural role of concepts as generalizable ways of thinking about objects. The internal correlative link emerges from the fact that one ascribes a grasp of a concept by noting that the subject "unifies" a number of different presentations or objects "under one common representation" (Kant). An example makes this clear: If we have a (thinking) subject who can apparently judge that an

---

[10] A. Palmer, *Concept and Object* (London, 1988), 33.
[11] G. Frege, *Collected Papers on Mathematics, Logic and Philosophy*, ed. B. McGuinness (Oxford, 1984).

envelope is yellow but, when asked whether there is anything else in the room that is yellow, cannot identify as being such a sweatshirt, a timetable, or a book, then we can not ascribe to him a grasp of the concept ⟨yellow⟩. When he can correctly pick out instances of yellow, i.e. apply the concept correctly to a number of objects, then we (and he) know what he means by 'yellow' and it is clear that he grasps the concept. Note that this argument is not based on our need to *verify* that he has the concept, but rather on the fact that the possession of certain basic concepts involves the ability to subsume objects under concepts in judgements.[12] Having such an ability is a constitutive feature of grasping the concept in question; it is part of the "grammar" (in Wittgenstein's terms) of 'yellow' (*PI* I. 371). Thus grasping the meaning of (or the rules for the use of) the term 'yellow' commits the thinker to a certain response in an indefinite number of internally related judgements.

Other rules link such judgements to a range of discursive abilities involving related concepts. Thus a concept such as ⟨prime⟩— as in ⟨a prime number⟩—rests almost exclusively on discursive connections. By contrast, discursive aspects are more peripheral to one's grasp of a colour concept than a tendency to go on in the same way with actual samples. Application, we could say, is central in the grammar of 'yellow' and one's going on in this way cannot be justified by an independent formulation; one just recognizes yellow. In this sense it can only be characterized "austerely".[13]

The essential generality of concepts becomes clear if one asks what the subject is thinking when he says 'the envelope is yellow' but cannot make any other judgements about yellow objects. In that case, we could not ascribe (nor could he self-ascribe) the thought ⟨that envelope is yellow⟩ because its content essentially involves the ability to make correct judgements about a series of related thoughts sharing the feature marked by the term 'yellow'.

1.3. Generalizability

The essential generalizability of concepts can be further elucidated by pursuing the analysis of a perceptual concept.

---

[12] Similar points are made by Kant, e.g. *CPR* B171.

[13] M. Platts, *Ways of Meaning* (London, 1979), 254; J. McDowell, 'Virtue and Reason', *Monist*, 62(3), 331–50.

For any thinker to grasp the concept ⟨yellow⟩ she must show a suitable sensitivity to the *colour* of yellow items across a range of situations. The ability to do this enables the subject to respond selectively to just and only that aspect of the situation in virtue of which it counts as instancing the concept ⟨yellow⟩. In order to recognize both that the critical feature is common to a number of situations and that any situation can occasion a range of judgements about such features, the thinker must be capable of flexible control of attention and selectivity of response. Note the active and flexible nature of this ability; it involves more than a differential sensitivity in that it may require that the thinker 'search' for the critical features in what confronts him. And it is not mechanical in that colour classifications do not simply reflect extension; for instance, red hair is quite different in light absorption from red paint or a red rose. Thus, although conceptual abilities are built on natural faculties, they are not wholly produced by them. Thinkers elaborate their natural propensities by adapting to rule-governed patterns of responding governed by criteria for correct use of the relevant concepts. Thus the grasp of a concept is an ability to respond at will according to a rule shaped through multiple applications. It is because such responses are essentially either intersituational- or intrasituational-feature-selective that they have a potentially general use. When a thinker has latched on to an ability of this type we can ascribe (and she can self-ascribe) a grasp of the concept concerned.

In fact four features of thought content emerge from this analysis. The first is the intersubjective nature of content, which is implicit in the need for normative constraints on thought content. These constraints link a subject's self-ascriptions and the general practice in which a grasp of that concept is ascribed on the basis of its manifestation. This is evident when we apply Strawson's 'generality principle' to mental concepts.[14]

To predicate of oneself ⟨a grasp of the concept *x*⟩ is to make a judgement which one ought also to be able to make about other objects. These 'objects' are, of course, other subjects, and therefore the ability to judge ⟨I grasp the concept *x*⟩ is tied to the ability to judge ⟨you grasp the concept *x*⟩, ⟨she grasps the concept *x*⟩, and so on. Thus the link between self-ascription and other-ascription

---

[14] As he does in *Ind.*, ch. 3.

follows from the fact that mental ascriptions are a particular class of generalizable predicative concepts. If one grasps ⟨a grasp of the concept x⟩ as predicative, then one ought to be able to judge whether it is instanced by a range of subjects.

The second implication is that manifestability is an essential feature of the grasp of a concept. It is only because S manifests a grasp of the concept ⟨x⟩ that he can be ascribed it. And the link between self- and other-ascription entails that, even if one need not manifest the grasp of a concept on every occasion one uses it, that grasp is grounded on manifestation (once mastered, exercise of the relevant ability might be covert or concealed).

The third feature links the potential generality of a concept to consciousness. Consciousness is best thought of as the capacity to be sensitive to and interact with the environment in a range of flexible and interest-directed ways.[15] Concept acquisition depends upon a sufficient control of attention and behaviour to allow mastery of shared human techniques. Thus consciousness essentially comprises those capacities on the basis of which concepts can be acquired. The techniques involved are, as I have noted, governed by rules even though a given rule may not be or even be able to be explicitly enunciated.

The fourth feature of this view is its implications for the analysis of the structure of thought. Evans notes: "I should prefer to explain the sense in which thoughts are structured, not in terms of their being composed of several distinct elements, but in terms of their being a complex of the exercise of several distinct conceptual abilities" (VR 101). The exercise of abilities to select aspects of presentations and generalize them at will and then use the results in an action-guiding way constitutes structured thought about experience. It is clear that structure is elucidated by a consideration of what a subject must do to react to a situation as instancing this or that concept. Appreciation of what confronts one involves selective sensitivity and directed attention to various aspects of experience. The aspects picked out have a form determined by links to other experiences which articulate one's conceptual repertoire. To appreciate something as being thus and so is, therefore, to judge that it is both like and unlike other things in certain respects.

---

[15] I have defended this view in 'Consciousness and Brain Function', *Philosophical Psychology*, 1(3) (1988), 327–41.

This gives conscious experience both form and structure and allows the conscious subject to make inferences based on connections in experience. Thus there is an essential link, through the grasp of concepts, between consciousness and discursive reasoning.

1.4. *Worries: Strict Bivalence and Mind-Dependence*

Some thinkers advance an extreme claim about bivalence across the entire range of permissible arguments for any concept. This neglects the fact that there are abnormal situations where either a concept-user is impaired in some way or normal concept-users would have difficulty in making the requisite judgements. But these problems should not influence our analysis of the general features of a conceptual ability which, once set out, can elucidate ascriptions in unusual circumstances. There may well be peripheral or indeterminate cases where we cannot be sure how a competent thinker would exhibit a grasp of the concept concerned and we should not be seduced into a false view by a rigid doctrine covering all (apparently) imaginable circumstances. Concepts or 'functions' may just not work in sufficiently recherché situations. For instance, imagine that an alien landed on earth who is exactly like ET (the extra-terrestrial[16]). A group of children speak and think of this alien as ET. What is the status of their thoughts or beliefs? Are those thoughts vacuous because the indeterminacy about which particular they have in mind makes it difficult to assign plausible truth values to them? If we relax the rigid view of concepts and focus on *use*, the content of the children's thought is made clear.

Notice also that the present view yields a clear sense in which a concept is independent of the mind of any particular thinker. A concept is a normatively constrained function of judgement in and across different experiences. To grasp a concept is to appreciate what it is to respond in this principled way. And this appreciation, *inter alia*, includes the realization that there is a way of going right and wrong. To master a concept is to be able to exercise such an ability with assurance in a sufficient range of cases. Thus a concept

---

[16] H. Noonan, 'Fregean Thoughts', in C. Wright (ed.), *Frege: Tradition and Influence* (Oxford, 1984).

is not only not an object as is a specimen of middle-sized dry goods, nor even a Platonic entity, but it is also not subjective or 'in the mind' in a Cartesian sense. A subject has a concept when a determinate and rule-governed way of responding to items in the world is apt to describe that subject's activity, and a concept applies to a given case when the subject responds in a given set of conditions so as to use the rule-governed technique appropriately. Therefore a concept is identifiable through the activity of thinking subjects but is essentially different in kind from instances of that activity.

1.5. Conscious Subjects and Mere Responders

We can clarify the account by pursuing the distinction between a conscious subject and a mere responder or information processor. The latter reacts in ways that are keyed to certain features. It lacks flexible and structured abilities to pick out one feature and then another or one object instancing a given property and then another. Therefore (1) it does not have concepts which are elements of a structured range of thoughts and (2) it is not conscious.

It does not have concepts because it cannot direct and focus its attention so as to isolate and identify features with multiple instances and a common structural role in related thoughts. A subject who fulfils Evans's Generality Constraint can exercise attentional selectivity so as to pick out instances of a concept by focusing and directing its attention. The mere responder also lacks 'structural generality' with respect to thoughts about a constant object. A thinker can think, for instance, both ⟨this doll is yellow⟩, ⟨that flower is yellow⟩, ⟨the handle is yellow⟩, etc., and also ⟨this doll is yellow, . . . Chinese, . . . old, . . . porcelain, . . . ugly, etc.⟩, according to her interest. These complementary abilities—to discern multiple features of a single object or a constant feature across different situations which may only share some focus of directed human interest—respectively constitute the grasp of structural generality with respect to objects and universals.[17]

The ability to exercise selective and flexible attention in conformity to a rule contributes to the grasp of a concept not only as

[17] I shall return to this in §1.9.

a structured element of thought, but also as an intersubjective entity. A subject makes use of a large and intersecting repertoire of such abilities to think about her experience. Each concept has a role in this structure which becomes richer and more useful as the repertoire expands, e.g. through communication with others. A response to some property is thus only a primitive pre-condition for the concept which is elaborated from it.

What is more, a response which is keyed to a triggering condition (or complex of such) is, in principle, extensionally specifiable. By contrast, judgements do not need extensional triggers. For instance, one uses the concept ⟨red⟩ not only in judging ⟨It is red⟩ but also in ⟨It is not red⟩. Finally any given ascription becomes more secure as the subject's grasp of the interwoven system of concepts becomes more complete so that "Light dawns gradually over the whole" (OC §141). If a child remarks, for instance, 'The ant caused that', then the content of the child's thought is only clear where 'ant' and 'cause' have a role in a range of related thoughts.

The information processor cannot direct its attention in the light of an action-guiding appreciation of the divers possibilities of a situation. If it were a conscious thinker it would discern and exploit these in a flexible way according to patterns of interest. Thoughts show a rich engagement with what is around one and comprise conscious experience in the fully human sense. We can make confident assertions about such experience when we are dealing with conscious human thinkers but, as an organism's patterns of activity tail off towards mere responding, so our assertions (about knowledge, belief, desire, etc.) become more tentative and eventually lose their content. The mere responder merely produces a response when impinged upon by a canonical stimulus and thus we can explain its activity by mechanical information-processing functions and we lack the holistic framework in which to make full-blown ascriptions of content.

To summarize: the abilities which constitute thought are structured and depend on a flexible selectivity of attention and response to the world. The mental activity that results comprises thought with content rather than merely a complex of causal influences which explain the subject's behaviour. The ascription and self-ascription of mental content result from abilities and capacities, congruent between subjects, upon which is built a structure of rule-governed techniques involving agreement in judgements.

1.6. *Following a Rule and Conformity to a Rule*

We are now in a position to address the distinction between following a rule and merely responding in conformity with a rule. A thinker who follows a rule shapes or guides her pattern of responses to what is around her in terms of a conception of there being a difference between going right and going wrong. She therefore holds herself answerable to a prescriptive norm (however inchoate her grasp of its content). She recognizes that her disposition to respond thus and so can be evaluated for its correctness. Thus there is a normative regularity to be aimed at rather than a *de facto* regularity which happens to be true of her behaviour. We could say that she potentially has flexible and interest-directed cognitive access to the norm and sees it as relevant to what she should do.

By contrast, one can conform to a rule quite unwittingly. A subject might, for instance, just have an urge to or be caused to utter the sound 'red' whenever impinged upon by light from a red object. This clearly does not constitute an ability to judge that things are red unless the subject gives us further reason to ascribe to him the intention to shape responses in a certain way. We might ask how the further intention is manifest. It can only be manifest where it is justified to ascribe to the subject concerned an awareness of mistakes as mistakes. Thus he 'tries to get it right', 'wonders if that really does count as red', and evinces a certain hesitancy, e.g. about the application of unfamiliar concepts or of familiar concepts in unusual circumstances.

None of this requires that the subject be able to articulate the rule *per se* but often some form of words will betray what Kant called "the conception of a law": 'Well, you only call it "red" if it is red', or 'I know what I think but is it really a shark?', and so on. To respond to a prescriptive norm requires a certain reflective self-awareness and sufficient self-control to bring behaviour into line with the perceived standard. This, in turn, depends on the ability to make judgements not merely about things but also about one's responses to things. Thus the more structured a set of mental ascriptions which can be made, the clearer the nature of the abilities shown and concepts grasped. And if the subject invokes a rule as reason for acting in a certain way and shows reflective awareness of her own abilities we need have no hesitation in ascribing the concept concerned (indeed, given local holism, we would be justified in ascribing a range of other mental abilities in the relevant area of thought).

1.7. *The Elements of Thought*

The present picture fulfils certain important desiderata for an account of mental content.

The concern for structure has led to an analysis of thought as an interlocking network of rule-governed abilities which pick out common features of the situations in which they are exercised. Hamlyn notes "To have a concept is to have a certain form of understanding; to have a concept of x is to understand or know what it is for something to be an x."[18] There are two aspects to such knowledge: "To have a concept of x we must have not only a formal understanding of what x is . . . but also knowledge of what x is to be applied to." I have argued that both cognitive structure and application are grounded in those practices in which a thinker masters a concept. The rules operative in these practices determine not only the application of concepts, but also the role that the concept plays in thought ("what it is for something to be an x"). Thus we could say that the cognitive role of a concept is given by the way it articulates a range of activities:

The exercise of a given concept in an act of judgment is not in general a definite uniform sort of mental act; it does not even make sense to ask just how many concepts are exercised in a given judgment. Our chess analogy may . . . be of service, in showing why this question is unreasonable. Playing chess involves a number of abilities, which are not only distinguishable but can actually exist separately; for one way of teaching chess would be to play first with the kings and the pawns and then add other pieces successively in later games. It would, however, be absurd to ask just how many of these abilities were exercised in a particular move; although one might perfectly well say that somebody knew the Knight's move, and that this knowledge was or was not exercised in a particular move. Our language about the concepts exercised in a given act of judgment makes sense or does not make sense in much the same way. (Geach, *MA* 15)

<hr>

[18] D. Hamlyn, 'Epistemology and Conceptual Development', in T. Mischel (ed.), *Cognitive Development and Epistemology* (New York, 1971).

In grasping a concept, one becomes competent in a subset of articulated abilities which link situations and combine to shape our activity in the world.

The account is clarified by discussing "canonical links" (Peacocke) and "fundamental ideas" (Evans), which respectively concern general concepts and identifiable particulars.

1.8. Canonical Links

Peacocke's "canonical links" are grounds and commitments associated with a given judgeable content (*TEC* 45). A canonical ground is a condition which justifies accepting that a given content is true. A set of canonical commitments (to think thus and so) then flows from that judgement (*TEC* 19–27). Grasping these links is part of grasping the concept. They are also generalizable so that novel situations can provide grounds for the acceptance of certain contents (with their proper commitments). For instance, if I judge that what is before me is a tree, I commit myself to further judgements (e.g. that it is not about to melt away). It is unclear just which further judgements are commitments as my beliefs may not be closed under implication, but it seems obvious that any subject must grasp certain implications of a given judgement in order to be credited with an understanding of it.

The present account claims that the subject selects from the features (not necessarily perceptual) of any situation those which ground the use of certain concepts in judgements about that situation. His judgements link the situation about which he is thinking with practices in which he has grasped the relevant concepts. In those practices rules for the application of the concept have found some 'bite' on his performances or propensities. The grasp of a concept is not an isolated yes/no ability to respond to stereotyped aspects of a situation in an atomistic way, because the concept-using subject shows a flexible and interest-directed capacity to respond to various aspects of any situation. Thus it may be difficult to say just when a subject first intelligently applies a concept, as difficult perhaps as it is to say when a child first reads what is before her (*PI* I. 157). It is plausible that the development of stable patterns of response according to learnable rules depends on a number of basic judgements about stable and intersubjectively available features of the world. This is because the child and those around her must work toward precision in the techniques being developed.[19]

Conceptual connections between states of affairs are better thought of as "links" than as "grounds" or "commitments" because they may not rest on strict logical entailments. There are usually many links, all defeasible, which, in different combinations and contexts, warrant any judgement.[20] These require a relatively holistic and structured appreciation of a situation (involving the "agreement in judgments" that human beings find most natural) in which the rules governing a given concept do not define necessary and sufficient conditions for use. Canonical links would be made in the core practices where the grasp of a concept is fixed and would involve flexible and generalizable abilities governed by some rule (determining what counts as "going on in the same way") which connects ways of responding both to the environment and to each other. Judgements and their conceptual connections (which, if at all sophisticated, will draw on the terms of a natural language) are both, on this view, essential to the grasp of a concept because thought content is given by rule-governed ways of responding with structural relations to other response patterns *and* application to the world of objects. The structure of thought is revealed by interlocking patterns of response to situations, as Geach indicates by his analogy between mental acts and chess moves; in both there are abilities which can be acquired and used so as to shape a subject's sensitivity and action in a range of related situations.

The present account also suggests why some concepts just 'click', or are, as it were, grasped in a flash of insight. Links to an already existing repertoire can be exploited when a rule or principle of grouping marked by a novel term can 'tap in' to the system in a way that is potentiated by the subject's extant abilities.

We have, however, precluded appeals to such things as Peacocke's "projection class of a given pattern of retinal stimulation" (*TEC* 19) by linking the structure of mental content to public criteria which shape human practices for the use of the terms marking concepts.[21]

---

[19] I will examine this further in Ch. 4.

[20] This would cohere very well with the success of PDP modelling of human cognition (§4.II).

[21] The case of Robinson Junior is discussed in §4.III.

What is more, the close links between directed attention, interest, and human nature imply that the range of objects to which a concept is legitimately applied may not be specifiable by a principled extensional definition. Instances of a concept may be grouped in ways that are only identifiable in human practices.[22] This forces us to look closely at the semantic relation in understanding mental content and I shall return to it in discussing the development of concepts and thought.

1.9. Fundamental Ideas

In a thought, a predicative concept is combined with a conception of an object to yield a judgeable content. Evans's 'Generality Constraint' applies to the latter element:

if a subject can be credited with the thought that a is F, then he must have the conceptual resources for entertaining the thought that a is G, for every property of being G of which he has a conception. This is the condition that I call 'The Generality Constraint'. (VR 104 ff.)[23]

Evans's immediate point is that the structured thought ⟨a is F⟩ can only be understood (or self-ascribed by) a thinker who understands that a number of concepts may be instanced by a.[24] It focuses on the object as (grammatical) subject of a number of judgements and argues that just as a concept like ⟨yellow⟩ requires the subject to recognize a feature as recurring in different presentations so an object must be able to enter into range of thoughts to count as an identifiable particular. That objects should have this basic role and be different from universals in the way they fulfil it is a familiar point.[25]

Evans develops this point by claiming that "fundamental ideas"

[22] I have tended towards this in 'Learning to Perceive', Philosophy and Phenomenological Research, 48 (1988), 601–18, and take it to be one point being made by McDowell.
[23] For the moment this does not take account of Frege's restriction on the range of permissible arguments for a given concept, which is most often discussed in terms of categorical constraints.
[24] Note that "every property G of which he has a conception" is too inclusive because it does not recognize the categorical constraints on those thoughts which can be meaningfully framed. For instance, what does one make of ⟨red is a prime number⟩?
[25] It is defended, for instance, by Strawson in ch. 1 of Ind.

of objects are basic in the structure of thought. The Generality Constraint entails that a thought, such as ⟨a is F⟩, involves two different elements: (1) "an Idea of an object . . . which makes it possible for the subject to think of an object in a series of indefinitely many thoughts in each of which he will be thinking of the object in the same way" (VR 104) and (2) a concept. "Ideas" of objects thus complement concepts. "Idea" (with a capital 'I') denotes the mental ability exercised by a given individual in thinking of an object in a particular way. This ability is tied to the sense of an expression used to pick out the object in that way (VR 104 n.). Therefore, on the present account, an Idea of an object picks out the object as it appears in some conceptual practice (i.e. figures in the rules which govern the use of some expression).

So, what is it to have a conception of an object? Kant attempted to answer this question by framing the general logical features that distinguish objects from properties. He recognized that one needed to give an account of how "the object is viewed as that which prevents our modes of knowledge from being haphazard or arbitrary" (CPR A104) and thus that objects in some sense are the relata of perception as distinct from imagination. But, in accord with his general thesis about the ideality of all the content of thought, he had to ground the determination of objects in a priori laws according to which the subject judged that the representation formed on a given occasion fitted the categorical specification of an object in general rather than that of a universal or "the predicate of a possible judgment" (CPR B94). To do this a representation needed to have dynamic qualities of relative permanence or subsistence rather than transience and thus the ability to enter into causal transactions in which aspects of it would change but it would remain identifiable. He therefore implicitly invokes something like fundamental grounds on which an object can be regarded as the same object in different presentations and representations.

This has some clear echoes in Evans's claim that to think of any given particular one must have some conception of (1) the type of item concerned, and (2) which item of that type one is thinking of. These are linked because identification and reidentification are based on some idea of how it is with that sort of thing: "An Idea of an object is part of a conception of a world of such objects, distinguished from one another in certain fundamental ways" (VR 106). Thus we have "fundamental Ideas":

one has a fundamental Idea of an object if one thinks of it as the possessor of the fundamental ground of difference which in fact it possesses. (Such an Idea constitutes, by definition, distinguishing knowledge of the object, since the object is distinguished from all other objects by this fact. (*VR* 107)

Evans gives one or two examples: "colours are distinguished by their phenomenal properties . . . shapes . . . by their geometrical properties . . . chess positions . . . by the positions of pieces on the board". Recall that to think of a particular item (so that it can figure in a series of related thoughts) a thinker must know not only what constraints govern an Idea of the type of item in question or what counts as being *that kind* of item, but also what singles out just *the one* he has in mind. Notice that both Kant and Evans conceive of the regulative norms governing the knowledge of individuals as secured by features within the cognitive world of the subject.

On the present account, the thinker masters an ability (structurally located within his conceptual system) to recognize items of a given kind through his own encounters with them and knowledge gained from other thinkers about such items. He learns what counts as going on in the same way by drawing on his experience to organize his responses to items of the type in question as structured by the many intersecting practices in which he participates. His attitudes are therefore shaped by the practices in which he has grasped the use of a term.[26] A fundamental Idea of an object or item is thus based in a structured set of abilities to respond to items of that type and involves *tracking* them in the hustle and bustle of life.

These abilities allow me to realize that the tadpole in my goldfish bowl is the same individual through its metamorphosis into a tiny frog, that the chess position I was in yesterday is the same as the one reconstructed from my notebook today, that the fire I left dying on the grate last night is not the same one that greets me when I come home tonight, or that the ice-cream my 4-year-old daughter had yesterday is not the one she is eating today. In each case I draw on those practices where terms serve definite uses. Within the general framework provided by links to such practices, my thoughts tell me about the world and what is going on in it.

---

[26] That use capitalizes on the regularities of the world in which we live and capacities endowed on us by the natural history of human beings.

My ability to track items through situations in which terms are grasped equips me with a grasp of what counts as an item of a given type and also provides experience of how certain types of things behave. Thus our thoughts about particular items exploit: (1) the human ability to keep track of things; and (2) conceptual specifications like ⟨the one I put in the goldfish bowl yesterday⟩, ⟨the one I recorded in my notebook⟩, ⟨the one that she ate in the park⟩, and so on. When we combine our tracking abilities with our capacity for collecting facts about individuals we have encountered, we are enabled to pick out both items of determinate types and determinate particular items.[27] The resultant picture of the furniture of the world is, of course, structured in terms of the myriad articulating links between our practices of rule-governed responding.

At this point I will make some brief remarks about tracking.[28] In order to begin tracking an object the subject must latch on to the particular in question. Two basic ways of doing this would be by the use of a demonstrative expression like 'that dog' or a name like 'Spot'. The former directs the subject's present attention on to a source for further information about that thing. The latter sign— 'Spot'—would serve as a basis for gathering information into bundles on the basis of recognition (Evans, VR 126). Further thoughts about ⟨the dog that I saw⟩ or ⟨Spot⟩ would then require the subject to link information with the thing he has latched on to in grasping the original use of the sign/s. This would depend on some "fundamental perceptual skills" (VR 146) and some cognitively mediated skills underpinning reidentification across situations (for instance, one would expect to re-encounter a rock, particularly a big one, in the same place at different times, but not a dog).

The present view of concepts and the Generality Constraint is, in a sense, prior to that offered by John Campbell. He discusses the structural constraints within thought in terms of "a range of ways of thinking of properties . . . and . . . objects—a repertoire in which the particular concepts exercised are embedded".[29] But then

---

[27] Evans discusses tracking at VR 174 ff. and 195 ff. and information-collecting at 125 ff.

[28] I will address this in more detail in §§4.3 and 8.4.

[29] J. Campbell, 'The Possession of Concepts', Proceedings of the Aristotelian Society, 85 (1984–5), 135–56.

remarks: "It is in virtue of our possession of the idea of a spatial world that we are possessors of concepts".[30] Therefore, thought rests on "recognition-based ideas"[31] and concept-use is grounded in "particular styles of reference"—in fact reference to spatio-temporal particulars—which are "prototypical" for the semantic relations underpinning all thoughts.[32]

I would agree that identifying and reidentifying middle-sized dry goods with a relative permanence in time and space is *a* basic feature of human thought.[33] But an account of the actual abilities involved in predicative concepts and ideas of objects goes beyond the assertion that spatio-temporal reference provides the basis of conceptual thought in that concepts in general and fundamental Ideas in particular are based on rule-governed ways of responding to what a subject encounters, as I have argued.

1.10. Concepts and Language: A Preliminary Glimpse

I have noted that in grasping a concept ⟨x⟩ (e.g. ⟨brick⟩, ⟨anger⟩, or ⟨red⟩), a subject must have some idea of what an x is. In what might be called a 'thought-based' theory, the use of the linguistic term 'x' would be secondary to this.[34] On this view, thoughts are independently contentful and expressed in language. Dummett raises a question about such thought-based theories by asking whether the content of a concept might correspond to the sense of a term which is grasped prior to its use:

Assume for the sake of argument that we can attribute . . . a grasp of the concept, in a non-Fregean sense of "concept"[,] to an individual antecedently to his acquisition of language. When he acquires language, he comes to associate that sense with the word. And now we have to ask what it is to associate the sense with the word? We might think of it as an inner mental connection: when he hears the word that sense comes into his mind. This however is opposed to all that Frege says about senses. A sense is not a mental content, like an idea (*Vorstellung*) or an image: there is no such process as a sense's coming into the mind, and,

---

[30] Ibid. 149.   [31] Ibid. 151.   [32] Ibid. 151–2.

[33] Strawson has very ably made these points in *Ind.* and Campbell has extended and deepened his argument as it relates to the representational world of a given individual. I shall return to these topics in Ch. 8.

[34] J. Campbell, Critical Notice of C. Peacocke, *Sense and Content*, *Philosophical Quarterly*, 36 (143) (Apr. 1986), 278–91.

when we try to conceive of it we fall back on the coming to mind of some representative of the concept, a mental picture or the word itself. Moreover this account runs foul of Frege's attack on psychologism, which is wrong because it makes sense subjective. If this associationist explanation were right, then I should have to take it on trust that you understood me as I intend to be understood, that you associate the same sense with the word as I do. You may, of course, in fact understand the word differently; but since sense is objective, this is something in principle discoverable, whose falsity does not have to be taken on trust. *(IFP* 51–2)

Frege, notoriously, came very close to a Lockean view of thought and language (e.g. *TGF* 59). I have attempted to preserve the public and intersubjective nature of concepts and yet allow that thought might not everywhere be linguistically articulated. A public domain potentially accessible by other thinkers imposes constraints which shape an individual's patterns of responding. That domain is (for most of us) pervaded by shared rules linked to mutually accessible features of the world, and subjects converge in use through participation in practices in which linguistic terms are a prominent but not an invariant feature. The result is that a subject of experience masters ways of responding differentially to things. These ways of responding obey rules shared between co-linguistic thinkers and link any presentation with others past, present, and future. The abilities concerned and the strategies and connections that result constitute the subject's having a representation of the particular or universal concerned. Thus human practices are the basis of concepts, the grasp of which consists in structured abilities. Because human practices are pervaded by signs, thought content is of a kind with and tied to the meaning of expressions (its precise relation to language is yet to be defined).

1.11. *Logical and Psychological*

At this juncture we ought to sketch a contrast between philosophical and psychological accounts of the mind. A philosophical (Frege— "logical") account of thought must reveal the essential features of thought. Thus it should explain the objectivity, normativity, and intentionality of thought and the relation between a thinker and her thoughts. It may offer suggestions about how they could be realized (e.g. according to a logical derivation, or by paradigm matching, feature selection, natural associations, or reference to a checklist). It may even suggest that a certain kind of information-processing mechanism is an enabling condition for a certain conceptual ability, but it could not presume to go any further.

By contrast, a psychological account investigates the empirical mechanisms underlying mental functions. It will therefore answer the question 'How . . .?' by showing what kinds of processes enable one to think. This entails that a psychological investigation could not, for instance, reveal that a thinker really only knew things of type p rather than type q because that involves an account of what counts as knowing p, which is a philosophical task. Therefore, psychology must take account of what it is to think or know that p in order to study the mind (and, vice versa, philosophy should attend to empirical research in developing its account of thought). A philosophical account of what it is to know that p should cohere with facts which cognitive psychology might reveal about the capacities underlying the mental functions concerned.

This has implications for the relationship between genetic and analytic accounts of mental phenomena.

1.12. *Summary*

I have tied concepts to practices in which directed attention and manifest reactions or response types fall under rules. These constitute a structured repertoire of abilities to respond in determinate ways to different situations. This view enables an account of the diverse characterizations of concepts with which I began.

1. Concepts involve ways of grouping objects in that the subject selectively attends and responds to aspects of objects in virtue of which they count as instancing a given concept and groups them on that basis.

2. The aspect of an object which grounds the judgement ⟨this is F⟩ can potentially be the focus of a judgement about any appropriate object. Thus ⟨F⟩ is correlative with a series of judgements as to whether or not certain objects can be placed appropriately in the practices which determine what counts as an F.

3. The principle of grouping or aspect of an object which is denoted by a concept thus has the metaphysical status of a universal rather than a particular.

4. A concept links different situations through judgements which pick out some way in which they may be regarded as the same and is thus based on a function of unity in judgement.

5. The judgements concerned are marked by predicative expressions which may be attached to subject expressions denoting any of a range of objects.

6. The way of responding to an object that is given by a certain concept may or may not be appropriate or in conformity with the rules governing the use of that concept. Thus concepts can be thought of as functions which map objects on to the True by enabling judgements which determine whether the thought (whose content jointly derives from a grasp of the concept and a conception of an object) is true or false.

7. The concept functions in thought when a subject makes judgements about its applicability to a range of objects. In this sense it is incomplete as an element of thought; only in combination with conceptions of objects does it yield truth-assessable thoughts.

8. The link between concepts and truth entails that our interest in various objects is structured and related to a framework of regular and determinate ways of responding governed by rules.

9. Concepts and objects in various combinations yield new possibilities for complex ways of responding to the world which take account of the general features of things and the existence of different particulars. A creature which evinces this kind of compositional structure in its relations to the world can be ascribed thoughts composed of subject and predicative elements.

10. The structural connections between concepts generate secondary (inferential) constraints on content the nature of which may be complex and difficult to unravel. This enables the subject to frame thoughts (which themselves involve new concepts) about the relations between concepts. In this sense concepts are the building blocks of theories.

A thinker masters a concept when a natural pattern of responses becomes principled or rule-governed. For most thinkers, this takes place in an intersubjective network of activity. Thus grasping or possessing a concept is primary in an analysis of concepts. The techniques involved are shaped by rules which constrain (by imposing prescriptive norms upon) a thinker's occurrent inclinations and are recognized by that thinker to do so. The constraints create links between human activity and public items. Therefore, a conceptual ability has a shape determined by something essentially independent of the individual mind in that the rules set a standard to which responses must conform. This entails that the "rules of the understanding" which unify experiences and give form to mental content are, for the individual thinker, mind-transcendent realities; not merely psychological but in essence logical (Frege) or rational (Kant). These rules shape our thoughts.

2

The Subject of Experience

THE present approach to mind is based on the nature of concepts and their role as the building blocks of mental content. On this view, the subject of experience is essentially a concept-user. I will claim that this implies that the mental subject is essentially embodied, that the subject has a significant unity or identity through time, and that first-person content ascriptions cannot be assumed to be evident to a subject without certain conditions being satisfied. These conditions entail that the subject has a special relation to her own thoughts at any time but not on the basis of an ability to make incorrigible reports about private states of affairs.

A concept-user makes sense of his experience by making a series of judgements which represent it as being thus and so. The fact that a thinking subject does this is, in Kant's words, "the supreme principle of the possibility of all intuition . . . in its relation to understanding" (*CPR* B136). Kant thus predicates contentful experience on "the transcendental unity of apperception", a thinking subject who, by the activity of synthesis, introduces order into experience and makes it intelligible (*CPR* B129–65). Kant's view here is subtle and I will pursue only one strand of his argument:[1] "It must be possible for the 'I think' to accompany all my representations; for otherwise something would be represented in me which could not be thought at all, and that is equivalent to saying that the representation would be impossible, or at least would be nothing to me" (*CPR* B131). Kant notes that the contents of thought are "synthesized" or constituted by judgement as meaningful experience when the subject forms representations by using concepts. Therefore Kant does not argue that an object—the self— is present to the subject as an item in experience alongside all the other contents of conscious thought. He contends that for experiences to have mental content which can give rise to discursive

---

[1] His deduction of the necessity for the categories of judgement which order experience is a topic in itself.

thought the subject must make judgements about them. But to make such judgements (and therefore make use of the links between experiences on which they depend) the subject must "unite a manifold of given representations in *one consciousness*" (*CPR* B133). For Kant "synthesis" is the activity of linking and assembling coherent conceptual specifications of one's conscious experience, and he notes that it entails that some thinker is the (unitary, active, concept-using) subject of a series of experiences.[2] Kant remarks that the "analytic unity of apperception is possible only under the presupposition of a certain synthetic unity" and that both require "the *identity of the consciousness in* [i.e. throughout] *these representations*" (*CPR* B133).

The knowledge of the 'I think' is therefore a formal or analytic condition for conceptual thought rather than an introspective impression; it expresses the fact that thought is essentially structured and involves the use of concepts. Thus the subject who makes sense of experience is not only aware of that experience but also can represent himself as being so. Thus "it must be possible for the 'I think' to accompany all my representations" and "The synthetic unity of consciousness is, therefore, an objective condition of all knowledge" (*CPR* B138). And this argument need be wedded neither to Kantian terminology nor to solipsistic assumptions.

All thought, knowledge, and experience involves the exercise of concepts in judgements so as to make sense of what is going on about us. And our study of concepts shows that the structured abilities that form the basis of concept-use involve the engagement with reality that is consciousness. Notice that the subject, as concept-user, has an active role to play in contentful experience. But the concept-using subject is not only conscious of the world, he also acts "according to the conception of laws". Thus the subject is aware of the fact that he is a rule-follower and can exercise reflective self-knowledge about that.

Thus far we can follow Kant but here we part from him. Kant claimed that concepts were based on functions (of unity in judgement) that ranged over representations, but I have argued that they are mastered through participation in object-involving practices where, *inter alia*, the terms of a natural language are used. The

---

[2] I have sketched the link between consciousness and concept-use in Ch. 1 but also defended it at greater length in 'Consciousness and Brain Function', *Philosophical Psychology*, 1(3) (1988), 327–41.

rule-governed techniques that result yield, on reflection, an appreciation of both the applications and the interconnectedness of the concepts involved. To pursue this we need an account of the 'I' of soliloquy and the practice of self-identification which reveals what is implicit in Locke's phrase "the same thinking thing at different times and places".

2.1. The Self as Subject of Thought and Action

Frege remarks "everyone is presented to himself in a special and primitive way, in which he is presented to no-one else" (*LI* 12). In trying to pursue this remark he gets into a familiar tangle:

I have considered myself as the owner of my ideas, but am I not myself an idea? It seems to me as if I were lying in a deck-chair, as if I could see the toes of a pair of waxed boots, the front part of a jacket, in particular the sleeves, two hands, some hairs of a beard, the blurred outline of a nose. Am I myself this entire complex of visual impressions, this aggregate idea? . . . But where then is the owner of these ideas? How do I come to pick out one of these ideas and set it up as the owner of the rest? Why need this chosen idea be the idea I like to call "I"? (*LI* 21)

He does, however, suggest a way of disentangling himself:

A certain idea in my consciousness may be associated with the word "I". But then this is one idea among other ideas, and I am its owner as I am the owner of the other ideas. I have an idea of myself but I am not identical with this idea. What is the content of my consciousness, my idea, should be sharply distinguished from what is an object of my thought. (*LI* 22)

Thus Frege uses the sense–reference distinction to preserve a meaning for 'I' which is not an idea. But this will not work because, on his view, every referent must, on each occasion of being thought, be apprehended according to some sense or other. There is also a phenomenological problem in that Frege's assertion that 'I' denotes an object and that "everyone is presented to himself in a special and primitive way" opposes Hume's claim about our experience:

I never can catch myself at any time without a perception and never can observe anything but the perception. . . . If any one upon serious and unprejudiced reflection, thinks he has a different notion of himself, I must confess I can reason no longer with him. . . . He may perhaps perceive something simple and confirmed which he calls himself; though I am certain there is no such principle in me.[3]

I have suggested, with Kant, that both Hume and Frege are mistaken because they confuse the ⟨I⟩ as (essentially) a subject of experience with the ⟨I⟩ as an object of experience.

Peacocke follows Frege: "the constitutive role of [self] is given by 'the person who has these experiences and thoughts' or 'the person who has these conscious states'" (SC 119). Here "[self]" is a mode of presentation. Peacocke explains:

The position I am endorsing, then, is one according to which (a) . . . the reference rule for "I" fully determines its meaning in English; (b) The first person way of thinking or mode of presentation exists and it is important for understanding "I" that one realize that this word is used to express thoughts containing MPs [modes of presentation] of this type; (c) the reference rule determines what MP is expressed. (SC 138)

Note that in this passage Peacocke links the way of thinking expressed by 'I' to the reference rule for its use. The "idea in my consciousness" or "special and primitive" mode of presentation (MP) expressed by 'I', are both attempts to capture the intuition that ⟨I⟩ is a basic feature of thought in general. Here I side with Hume: I do not seem to be "presented to" in some way on each occasion when I use the term 'I'; for instance, I may be completely caught up in some intellectual problem. Therefore, even if 'I' *is* special and primitive in its meaning, it need not refer to a private MP but rather to a person, *qua* concept-using agent involved in language games and forms of life. This is why there is not an internal Idea indicated by "[self]" which is "the object of my thought" (Frege) when I think about myself.

I shall also argue that Kant is right in that the subject is active in thought, because thought draws on what Evans calls "conceptual abilities" (VR 101) rather than "perceptions" (Hume). Thus ⟨I⟩ is not an MP but a locus of (discursive and conscious) activity. Evans remarks:

the essence of "I" is self-reference . . . "I"-thoughts are thoughts in which a subject of thought and action is thinking about himself—i.e. about a

---

[3] D. Hume, *A Treatise of Human Nature*, ed. E. C. Mossner (Harmondsworth, 1969).

subject of thought and action. It is true that I manifest self-conscious thought, like "here"-thought, in action; but I manifest it, not in knowing which object to act upon but in acting. . . . I have knowledge of myself as someone who has knowledge and who makes judgements, including those judgements I make about myself. (VR 207)

When I think about myself it is as a subject of thought and in acting; I use a principled competence to weave my contact with the world on to the loom formed by those conceptual practices in which I am engaged.[4] In the process of mastering such abilities, I begin to have a use for the term 'I'. 'I' will be attached when judgements are made—'I see the red ball', 'I like Daddy', etc., and when I act—'I am going out to the shop', 'I am looking at the clock', and so on. In each of these avowals I use a term to make manifest which meanings are currently relevant to my behaviour. Thus, in actions and judgements, as a subject I articulate my present concerns with (link them to) an indefinite range of uses and situations. This shows what thought contents currently inform my activity, and provides points of reference for intelligent interaction with me. Wittgenstein remarks:

I only use the terms the expectation, thought, wish etc., that p will be the case, for processes having the multiplicity of expression in p, and thus only if they are articulated. But in that case they are what I call the interpretation of signs.

I only call an articulated process a thought: you could therefore say "only what has articulated expression". (Salivation—no matter how precisely measured—is not what I call expecting.)

Perhaps we have to say that the phrase "interpretation of signs" is misleading and we ought to say "the use of signs". (PR 32)[5]

He suggests that thought is distinguished from other natural activities of human beings by its articulation within a structure of meanings or practices of (rule-governed) use. The subject uses the elements of this structure to articulate her activity as a maker and manifester of judgements. Thus the subject *qua* subject is not an object to be identified in experience but essentially a source of thoughts about and interventions in the world.

---

[4] I shall discuss this further in Ch. 3.
[5] I shall return to interpretation in §6.4.

2.2. *The Reference of 'I'*

I have already espoused Strawson's 'generality principle' and his application of it in the argument that a subject who makes certain judgements regarding self must also be able to make judgements with the same predicative elements about other individuals of like kind.[6] He remarks: "it is a necessary condition of one's ascribing states of consciousness, experiences, to oneself, in the way one does, that one should also ascribe them, or be prepared to ascribe them, to others who are not oneself" (*Ind.* 99). Strawson notes certain constraints on the content of ⟨I⟩ because of its role as the object place-holder in self-referring expressions. First, a particular that can fill this role is an element in the conceptual structure which articulates our thoughts. Thus I, as a subject of mental ascriptions, must satisfy the general conditions that enable items to be the objects of the relevant judgements. These have already been discussed and they suggest that the reference of 'I' (or any denoting term) is a manifest entity:[7]

One can ascribe states of consciousness to oneself only if one can ascribe them to others. One can ascribe them to others only if one can identify other subjects of experience. And one cannot identify others if one can identify them only as subjects of experience, possessors of states of consciousness. (*Ind.* 100)

Strawson allows, for the purpose of argument, a Cartesian view of "states of consciousness" and "experience", but argues that the reference of 'I' is not a private mental entity or centre of pure consciousness contingently attached to a physical 'presence'. Reference rules underpinning the ways of thinking which give the meaning of 'I' must rest on judgements which can be publicly validated because intersubjective, learnable rules are the source of the norms which constrain a given subject's responses. Wittgenstein outlines the use of 'I' as follows:

And it is when I talk about the world that *I* appear on the scene, in the glory of my self if you like. But until I speak or act, I am not to be found; and then it is this human being that you encounter. The only satisfactory representation of the self is, after all, *der Mensch*, the human being.[8]

---

[6] *Ind.*, ch. 3, discussed in §1.2 above.   [7] On this see §1.3 above.
[8] L. Wittgenstein, *Remarks on the Philosophy of Psychology* (Oxford, 1980), i. 281.

Strawson remarks:

So, then, the word "I" never refers to this, the pure subject. But this does not mean . . . that "I" in some cases does not refer at all. It refers; because I am a person among others; and the predicates which would, *per impossibile*, belong to the pure subject if it could be referred to, belong properly to the person to which "I" does refer. (*Ind.* 103)

Support for these arguments emerges from the fact that thought has a conceptual structure. Mental ascriptions have the form $\langle a$ is $F\rangle$ such that 'I' is one candidate to occupy the place held by 'a'. But the predicative elements of these ascriptions figure not only in self-ascriptions but also in other-ascriptions: 'I scream, you scream, we all scream for ice-cream' and 'I am in pain, you are in pain, so not only is someone in pain but at least two people are'. These examples remind us that the predicates of self- and other-ascriptions are univocal.

Evans, as we have seen, links this structural feature of thoughts, including those involving mental ascriptions, to "fundamental ideas" (a conception of an object such that any thinker in possession of it knows that it is to make predications to an object of that type):

our thinking about ourselves conforms to the Generality Constraint. And this means that one's idea of oneself must . . . comprise . . . a knowledge of what it would be for an identity of the form $\langle I = \alpha t\rangle$ to be true, where αt is a fundamental identification of a person: an identification of a person which—unlike one's "I" identification—is of a kind which could be available to someone else. (*VR* 209)

Thus we might agree with Strawson and Wittgenstein and accept that the fundamental idea for $\langle I\rangle$ is $\langle person\rangle$ not $\langle Cartesian\ self\rangle$. If the "fundamental identification of a person" is a feature of any thought about self or others as instances of the concept $\langle person\rangle$, then it underpins mental ascriptions. Evans links this feature to a cognitive map and thus to spatio-temporal identification: "to know what it is for $\langle \alpha t = I\rangle$ to be true for arbitrary αt, is to know what is involved in locating oneself in a spatio-temporal map of the world" (*VR* 211). But this does not yet tell us why particulars of *our* type are subjects of experience.

The understanding of mental predicates is tied to our experience of identifiable and reidentifiable persons.[9] A fundamental idea of

[9] See my 'Reasoning about Persons' and D. Wiggins, 'The Person as Object of Science, Subject of Experience and Locus of Value', n. 23, both in A. R. Peacocke and G. R. Gillett (eds.), *Persons and Personality* (Oxford, 1987).

any type of thing, such as a person, is based in the language games where we encounter and individuate particulars of that type and learn the use of the appropriate sortal term.[10] 'Person' is, of course, used in interactions where one learns what people are like and collects information about them over time.[11] Therefore this term has an especially rich meaning and pervasive role in thinking about one's own life and experience. To know that I am a person is to know that I fit, in a reciprocating way, into those forms of life where interpersonal discourse occurs. But to know *that* is to know far more than how to locate myself in a spatio-temporal framework; it locates me in a social and interpersonal context where I am a node of personal activity and relationships.[12] To understand the "fundamental idea" of a person is therefore not only to *know* something but to *be* something. In this mode of being I am referred to by an individuating term, my name, which picks me out as a particular. My identity and activity as a subject of experience is nurtured in this milieu and I learn to ascribe and self-ascribe using mental concepts by participating in the practices of judgement to be found there.

Therefore the 'I' who is a subject of conceptual thought is not only the "subject of these conscious states", but also an objectively identifiable and engaged member of a set of conceptual practices, or, as Strawson puts it, "a person among others" (*Ind.* 103).

2.3. The 'I' of Soliloquy

How do I understand the 'I' of soliloquy, the vanishing point of subjectivity and centre of my experience who, it seems, could be identified by another name or even inhabit another body?[13] It is clear that I can know certain things about 'I' that do not depend on any adequate conception and are "immune to error through misidentification" (*SC* 108) (e.g. ⟨I am angry⟩). But does this mean that 'I' inhabit and can transcend that objective self who is engaged in the outside world and that I am immediately presented to myself?

A person performs actions and makes judgements and her

---

[10] §4.I discusses language development.
[11] Wiggins, 'The Person as Object of Science'.
[12] H. R. Harré, *Personal Being* (Oxford, 1984).
[13] T. Nagel, *The View from Nowhere* (Oxford, 1986), 54 ff.

knowledge of these doings is not the same as knowledge about the objects (and other persons) she encounters. But this does not mean that 'intendings', 'believings', or 'judgings' are events in an inner realm which she contemplates in a special way because she is 'in there' and has 'immediate access' to them. It merely shows that the person doing any of these things is differently placed from the person observing them being done by another, just as a person bruised or insulted is differently placed from either the assailant or an observer of the insult. But the difference is not merely perspectival. To intend, act, or judge is to do something, to exercise an ability; for Kant, the thinker is active or "spontaneous" in mental life.[14]

As well as these features there is a further aspect to the uniqueness of first-person knowledge. The agent not only exercises the mental abilities in play, but also has a particularly close and detailed knowledge of the cumulative content of his thought. Perceptions that things are thus and so, interpretations of remarks by other individuals, or trains of thought may not be manifest but may be important in a subject's reasoning. One can, *inter alia*, conceal thoughts from others (with varying degrees of success and possibly only in a limited way). The holistic interaction of experiential history and context in which one's mental acts occur can, therefore, never be accessible *in toto* to another person. The subject not only has a different perspective on his own experience but also stands to it as creator rather than observer and can take account of his motives and its longitudinal context in assessing it.

I have a different place in the world from that occupied by any other living thing and chart a different course through the experiences of life (one informed and indeed formed in part by practices in which I have participated). Thus to say 'I am *F*' is not to report a mental state from an inner vantage point (one could neither make sense of such reports nor learn to make sense by them), but to say 'This person here, a co-participant with you (albeit with my own mental history), is thus and so'. This is a unique statement-type and if I were to go wrong sufficiently often in such statements then my conceptual competence (grounded in such avowed judgements) would be suspect and with it the entire contents of

---

[14] This use of "spontaneous" does not explicitly include a crucial feature for Kant, who held that the agent is a terminus of rational (non-causal) explanation.

my thought. Thus there is something immediate or basic in 'I' thoughts.

2.4. Self-Ascription

How does it come about that one makes judgements about one's own mental life if not by observing and describing one's inner states and events? The present discussion of concepts, rules, and judgements argues that it must be public criteria, the actions and reactions of identifiable individuals, that ground our judgements in general and thus mental ascriptions in particular: "An inner process stands in need of outward criteria" (*PI* I. 580). On this account, self-ascription is best understood by considering how one learns to make judgements and perform actions and how these abilities, in turn, entail a grasp of self-reflexive judgements. This leads to a distinctive approach to mental holism, the concept of a person, and reactive attitudes.[15]

Making judgements involves responding to the world according to rule-governed practices of use. Thus it involves mimicking the responses of others, latching on to the use that they make of certain terms, and using these discoveries in one's own activity. In doing this the subject recognizes that norms are brought to bear upon her responses and judgements are made about them. We judge whether her responses are apt, intelligent, meaningful, and so on. But seeing one's own activity in this way, as it were 'profiled' against rules and practices in which other thinkers act and also make judgements, involves taking attitudes to one's own attitudes. Thus self-reflexive judgements are intertwined with the general business of grasping concepts. Similarly, to perform an action of a certain type is to use conceptions to form and guide one's behaviour by 'shaping up' one's activity according to the rules and practices ("customs" and "institutions", *PI* I. 199) that determine the conceptions in question.

This is easily illustrated. When a thinker finds herself in the woods near Windsor and remarks 'I can see the round tower through the trees', she expresses the judgement that a certain bit of the world falls under a certain conceptual specification. Or,

---

[15] P. F. Strawson, *Freedom and Resentment and Other Essays* (London, 1974).

similarly, 'I have a pain' expresses the fact that the (generalizable) predicate 'pain' is warranted as applicable to her present experience. She is responding to the criteria for the judgement ⟨a is in pain⟩ as instanced by herself. She may well go on to make other judgements involving the grammar of pain as constituted in language games involving human injury, distress, suffering, pity, consolation, concern, and so on. By using interpersonal techniques of discourse available within these practices she can convey an accurate, even tell-tale, specification of her pain to anyone trained to correlate such specifications with bodily conditions and pathological processes. Again when a person says 'I intend to go to Aunt Jemima's', she is indicating how her present activity is articulated with her activity at other times. If sincere she will structure what she is doing by the conceptual rules which govern the intelligent use of the terms comprising her expression. In each case the acting manifest human subject declares how her behaviour is to be mapped on to a conceptual structure and expresses judgements about that behaviour. Thus self-ascriptions are not just reports of states within the person, but represent the use of terms to order and direct the attention and activity of social and rational beings.

2.5. The Conscious Subject

I shall briefly rehearse the view of consciousness that emerges from the present account.[16]

The grasp of concepts depends on rule-governed techniques for gathering information from the environment. To be conscious of something is to be able to use these flexible techniques to assemble information *and* make judgements about that thing. This depends on the subject directing attention on this or that aspect of a situation according to current interest and intention. The more such material is widely engaged with one's conceptual repertoire, the more it is unequivocally conscious. Compare, for instance, A making a reflexive adjustment of posture with B detecting that someone is observing him. Imagine that, in fact, the discomfort which caused A to adjust his posture was due, in part, to his being watched. Nevertheless, the content of A's experience (and therefore A's

---

[16] I have set it out in some detail in 'Consciousness and Brain Function', and in 'Consciousness, the Brain and What Matters', *Bioethics*, 4 (1990), 181–98.

knowledge) is quite different from that of B. A could not 'tell' (note the revealing ambiguity) what was influencing his behaviour, nor reason about it, nor elucidate it further. For B these are all possible; he can scrutinize his observer and try to unravel her actions. This puts the two subjects in vastly different epistemic circumstances.

Because the potential content able to be gathered around a given experience is open-ended for a conscious subject, it is very difficult to give a succinct précis of what-it-is-like-to-be-an-x (where x refers to a conscious subject of a given type). In particular, the many ways in which the content of an experience can be explored by a human subject (as evident in poetry and music) make it impossible to say what is distinctive about human conscious appreciation. Consciousness, on this account, becomes a matter of degree with more complex creatures having a richer set of sensitivities and response-types to explore their experiences. What is more, the close link between consciousness and conceptual abilities implies that consciousness has a definite function in that it enables an indefinite and flexible set of links to be forged between a given experience and the experiential history of the organism.

Self-consciousness can then be analysed as the ability to make judgements about the ways in which one is thinking of this and that and to scrutinize one's own performance as an agent. Both of these facets of self-consciousness are closely linked to the fact that information can be engaged with a diverse repertoire of concepts according to current intentions. The idea of exploring one's mental life by the use of cognitive skills also suggests a fruitful account of irrationality.[17] Unconscious mental life, on this reading, involves content which cannot be explored in the light of the norms for judgement and inference that govern our normally clear apprehension of mental content.[18]

2.6. A Metaethical Aside

In order to suggest one direction in which this chapter might lead, I shall offer a metaethical conjecture. Our reactions to those things

[17] G. R. Gillett, 'Multiple Personality and Irrationality', *Philosophical Psychology*, 4(1) (1991), 103–18.
[18] This is close to the account given by J. Church in 'Reasonable Irrationality', *Mind*, 96 (1987), 354–66.

that impinge on us are basic in our conceptual system. But some of the features of the world to which we respond *matter* to us. What matters to us is linked to a range of concepts like ⟨pleasure⟩, ⟨pain⟩, ⟨hurt⟩, ⟨distress⟩, ⟨joy⟩, ⟨care⟩, ⟨love⟩, and so on. These concepts are, of course, shared with others just as are those that are more 'neutral' or 'descriptive'. I have argued that self-ascription and other-ascription are essentially linked. If this is so when the concepts concern what matters to us, then there is a natural and implicit link between my appreciation of what matters to me, what moves me, or what I think should happen to me, and my appreciation of how it is with others with whom I share the relevant concepts. It seems, therefore, that there is a very natural basis for moral concern which, when it is nurtured, links self and others.

Such an understanding of moral sensitivity and reasoning would not require a dissolution of the belief in the reference of 'I' (or the importance of personal identity) to provide a conceptual basis for and even foster altruism (*pace* Parfit). It would rather suggest that concern and appreciation for others could go hand in hand with self-understanding, self-awareness, and maturity. Indeed it suggests that the command "Love thy neighbour" has a natural place in the thought of a subject of experience as user of concepts rather than requiring a 'no-self' view of human personality (thus it properly involves "as thyself").

2.7. *Summary*

I shall summarize the present view (and hint at its relevance for ethics) by comparing and contrasting it with that of Gareth Evans:

1. "Our self-conscious thoughts about ourselves are irreducible to any other mode of thought . . . Both 'I'-thoughts and 'here'-thoughts are ways in which the subject's capacity to locate himself in the objective spatial order is exploited" (*VR* 256). I have argued that 'I' thoughts do not rest solely upon the ability to locate oneself in the objective spatial order, but also involve the fact that any given subject both makes responses and experiences the responses of others to them. These inform him about himself and his actions and shape his future judgements. He must therefore see himself as located not only in space and time but in the interactions which

govern his use of concepts. The latter is primitive as it enables the subject to take normative attitudes to his own conceptual judgements, and thus, *inter alia*, refine and master the recognitional and demonstrative abilities upon which spatio-temporal identification is built.

A pertinent empirical fact is that a person with dementia retains a sense of self and the ability to make simple verbal and conceptual judgements longer than other cognitive abilities and well after spatio-temporal orientation is lost. This would be expected on the present account in that self-identification and self-awareness go hand in hand with making judgements. In fact, in any judgement ⟨that is red⟩, ⟨this is a cat⟩, etc. the subject actively responds to the world and thereby, in Kant's terms, reaffirms the 'I think' (a purely formal reflection of his nature as a concept-user). One would therefore expect that complex modes of judgement requiring the ability to locate oneself in space and time would deteriorate before the fundamental ability to make basic judgements (such as those using concepts like ⟨red⟩, ⟨sweet⟩, ⟨come⟩, and ⟨hurt⟩).

2. "Our thoughts about ourselves are about objects—elements of reality" (*VR* 256). I have agreed with this claim but argued that it is not secured by systematic spatio-temporal judgements (which, after all, might relate to a structured notional world) but rather by the fact that each of us participates in language-use as an objectively identifiable particular. The basis of the claim that mental predicates attach to identifiable or manifest items emerges from Strawson's generality principle. We apply mental predicates (like all other predicates) to various particulars to which they might meaningfully be applied. These particulars are manifest so that the predicates are univocal in first-, second-, and third-person uses and can make 'functional' links between them.[19] Thus mental predicates necessarily apply to manifest subjects, of whom we can have knowledge. Evans remarks: "All the peculiarities we have noticed about 'I'-thoughts are consistent with, and indeed, at points encourage, the idea that there is a living human being which these thoughts concern" (*VR* 256). I would claim that persons—living, interacting (or at least acting) human beings—by engaging in shared practices, give 'I' thoughts a structured conceptual role and therefore content.

[19] i.e. links which function in the conceptual and inferential structure of thought.

3. "The Ideas we have of ourselves, like almost all Ideas we have, rest upon certain empirical presuppositions, and are simply inappropriate to certain describable situations in which these presuppositions are false" (*VR* 257). I have argued this in detail elsewhere.[20] The basis of the argument is that our techniques of predication form a holistic set of practices in which we come to understand and interact with other human beings—creatures like ourselves. This carries certain implications about the nature of beings who can serve as subjects of mental ascriptions. It implies, most obviously, that they must be creatures who are like us in a sufficient number of ways for us to make sense of what they do. Only thus can our judgements about them be warranted in similar situations to the corresponding judgements about ourselves: ⟨I am in pain/hungry/tired/etc.⟩ is contentful and comprehensible but ⟨that sea anemone is . . .?⟩ Evans doubts that we could have the same mental capacities if the spatio-temporal and physical constraints upon our relations to objects were all disordered, and Campbell goes on to claim that a simple mechanics is fundamental in epistemology. I argue that these claims rest on the conditions required to enable a creature to participate in activity where mental ascriptions are grounded. Thus the fact that we are creatures of a certain type who are equipped to engage in rule-governed activity underwrites our conceptual system. We just cannot imagine what it would be like were a significant part of this framework for mental ascriptions to go awry.

4. "Our thoughts about ourselves are in no way hospitable to Cartesianism. Our customary use of 'I' simply spans the gap between the mental and the physical, and is no more intimately connected with one aspect of our self-conception than the other.[21] The argument that this must be so hardly bears repeating. The holism in mental ascriptions and the myriad connections between many of those ascriptions and states of need, perceptual sensitivity, physical–motor capabilities, entail that mental and physical attributes are closely tied to each other. At this point we can also recall the remarks on the privacy of ⟨I⟩.

Each of us charts a course through the practices, interactions, and experiences which go to build up his conceptual world. As he does so each of us makes judgements which he is uniquely

---

[20] Gillett, 'Reasoning about Persons'.   [21] Ibid.

placed to make. Once he has mastered the rules which govern such judgements he has the option of conducting his reasoning about and conceptual exploration of the world with a minimum of manifestations. Thus two logical gaps open up: one between the totality of our thoughts (and thus the detailed context of any particular thought) and what others can detect on the basis of manifestations, and the other between one's own way of thinking about things and the truth. The potentially covert nature of our thoughts allows one both to keep oneself to oneself and to 'drift' from adherence to generally warranted beliefs about the world (*ITI* 168 ff.). The fact that a thinker can outstrip the need for openness in his thought life (and do so quite quickly) allows him to develop both a unique conception of the world and a privileged epistemic status with respect to that conception. Because nobody else quite knows the 'ins and outs' of my thinking from my perspective, nobody else knows *me* in just the way that I do.

We can now profitably consider the nature of mental ascriptions, their special epistemological status, and the way in which they explain behaviour.

3

Mental Explanation and the Content of Thought

I HAVE argued that the content of mental ascriptions is essentially tied to rules and shaped in interpersonal contexts of activity. A subject who makes use of rule-governed techniques of responding to the world is ascribed the grasp of certain concepts. These techniques are marked by signs. For instance, if, in responding to a mug, she uses the term 'mug' to say what she is doing and her use is appropriate and shows the correct links to other areas of discourse, she could self-ascribe a grasp of the concept ⟨mug⟩. The links concerned do not, however, form a set of necessary and sufficient conditions for ascription because such things as the fact that mugs are human artefacts might be part of a full grasp of the concept but may not be known by a child who merely knows how to apply 'mug'. Nevertheless, a grasp of the application of a sign and sufficient of the connections to individuate the concept ⟨mug⟩ is essential to ascription (and therefore self-ascription) of propositional attitudes (PAs) involving this concept. These normative constraints, entail, on the present account, that there is a link between understanding and manifestation on the basis of which I have characterized the subject as an identifiable entity engaged in interpersonal activity. This, I will argue, suggests a non-causal view of mental explanation.

The prevailing view is that mental explanations are causal and explain the behaviour of human beings by reference to antecedent states and events. It is understandable that methodological solipsism (which ties mental ascriptions and their content to states in the thinker) is an influential strategy in causal theories of mental explanation. It holds that events and states which occur in the agent are the causes of actions and that the cognitive role of an element determines its function in action explanation. On this reading, cognitive role is analytically dissociated from links to external objects and the components of an action explanation are analysable in terms of what goes on 'in' the agent. This is in tension with the present analysis because I have argued that content ascriptions essentially involve the world in which the subject's engagement with objects is shaped by practices and rules.

Davidson's account of mental explanation is causal but more subtle than most and quite unsympathetic to solipsism. It is based on the essential relation between thought and language evident in the conceptual or propositional content of both. He notes the a priori constraints inherent in the holism of mental explanation which entail that one cannot assign a list of thoughts to a person without regard to the inferential connections between them. On this view, the occurrence of any given element in a mental explanation constrains what others can be included. These constraints are broadly rational and help us *make sense* of the thoughts and actions of others.

But Davidson leaves a loophole for the solipsist. If mental explanations identify the causes of behaviour (which are contentful states and events within the agent), then thoughts have causal roles in virtue of their content. Thus Peacocke links Davidson's theory with the solipsist thesis that thoughts are, in some sense, structured states in the mind or brain of subjects (*HE*; *SC*).

A challenge to all theories of action is to account for the 'because' in explanations like 'He jumped out the window because he thought his mother was a devil' in such a way as to respect the essential nature of mental content. In doing this one gives a principled account of which among the many reasons and thoughts of a given person actually do provide an explanation of his behaviour in a given situation. This requirement often defeats theories which deny that mental ascriptions denote causal states and events forming the antecedents of actions.

3.1. Explanation

There are several types of psychological explanation:

1. One type gives an empirical explanation of the thinker's cognitive capacities and the information-processing capacities of his brain. It tells us what brain functions might realize certain mental abilities. If mental terms denoted states causally antecedent to behaviour, then such states could be identified with these brain states (even if 'bridging laws' or 'mapping functions' were not possible). This would allow a belief or any other mental ascription

to be linked to "a (physical) state which stands in a constitutive relation to the believing".[1] But the neural or information-processing levels may still not, of course, provide 'how it is' stories with any explanatory power.

2. One might wish to explain *what it is* for a thinker to grasp a given thought at a given time. Such an explanation elucidates mental ascriptions and is normative in that it spells out what counts as an incidence of a given ascription. In doing so it must explain two related things: first, a thinker can go right or wrong in his mental acts, and second, there are a priori rational constraints on the explanatory role of a given thought. These constraints reflect the structure of mental content and are evident in the fact that content ascriptions are sensitive to other mental ascriptions and to the context of the subject. I have argued that they are explained by the rules governing the use of concepts which link concepts both to one another and to conditions of manifestation.

3. We might wish to explain why a thinker thinks certain thoughts in a certain situation. We could do this in one of two ways:

(a) by an extensional account of the conditions correlated with certain psychological phenomena;

(b) by an intentional account which ascribes some particular pattern of thought relating thinker to context.

The strengths and weaknesses of the former account lie in its extensional specification of the relevant variables. It can produce statistical or probabilistic formulations of causal connections but often fails to disclose what is significant or meaningful to the subject (which depends upon directed attention, current purposes, and so on).[2] Its (lawlike) regularities therefore do not yield a fine-grained understanding of the reasoning and motives of particular individuals in particular contexts. Because the thoughts of the individual subject are important in explaining behaviour, such psychological laws are tentative and defeasible by factors which may be relevant to one person but not another. They are therefore of limited use in our general dealings with human beings.

We can contrast such 'laws' with a contextually sensitive account which explains in detail the behaviour of a given individual.

---

[1] M. Morris, 'Causes of Behaviour', *Philosophical Quarterly*, 36 (1986), 123–44.
[2] H. R. Harré and P. Winch have both discussed these problems in some detail.

Such an account is not necessarily limited to properties of the individual subject (unless one adopts the thesis that actions are caused by things within the agent). On the present account, mental explanations may use terms which relate individuals to non-individualistic norms: "The non-individualistic character of our mentalistic notions suggests that they are fitted to purposes other than (or in addition to) individualistic explanation . . . [which] include describing, explaining, and assessing people and their historically and socially characterised activity against a background of objective norms—norms of truth, rationality, right."[3] These norms, which the subject represents to himself and which explain the structure and content of thought, prima facie distinguish mental ascriptions from purely physical–causal descriptions but do not necessarily exclude mental explanation from the general rubric of causality; it could be a type of singular causal explanation. This thesis is widely accepted on the basis of Davidson's work.

Davidson argues that the a priori rationality of mental explanation "has no echo" in the contingent causal relations between physically construed entities.[4] Thus he holds that mental explanations are irreducible to physical explanations in that the lack of psychophysical bridging laws entails that patterns of mental explanation defy analysis in terms of physical schemata (even if mental events are token-identical to physical events). But along with this irreducibility thesis he holds that (PAs and) mental events are the *causes* of human behaviour and thus that mental explanations are causal.

Peacocke goes further and argues that it is only because the connections concerned *are* causal in nature that they provide interesting explanations of behaviour. He considers that the mental terms (which explain behaviour according to a priori and holistic principles) are useful because they denote the operative causes of human action by appearing in *differential explanations* of actions.

The idea of differential explanation is developed from Price's attempt to specify how a perceived object figures in the causal antecedents of a "percept".[5] It captures what interests us in mental explanations because adequate mental explanations must make

[3] T. Burge, 'Other Bodies', in *TO* 118.
[4] D. Davidson, 'Mental Events', in *EAE* 222–3.
[5] H. H. Price, *Perception* (London, 1932).

sense of the behaviour of the agent in the 'right' way, and pick out just those mental terms which both *can*, according to a priori principles of rationality, and *do* explain the particular actions being considered. Many beliefs, inclinations, motives, habits, skills, and so on contribute to the mental life of an agent, but one needs a principled way to identify a particular combination of PAs from the range that could conceivably make sense of the behaviour concerned. Peacocke claims that certain PAs are the right ones because they identify the states and events which have an operative causal role in a given situation (even though strict causal laws cannot be formulated in terms of PAs). But if there is a causal connection, then, according to this neo-Humean account, there are causal laws applying to some description of the entities being picked out. It is these laws (which operate between the physical states realizing the mental entities denoted by the terms in the explanation) that underwrite action explanations and rule out deviant causal chains (*EAE* 208; *HE* 36).

Peacocke has two arguments for grounding mental explanation in causal relations between physical states and events:

1. He claims that the a priori principles of mental schemata themselves stand in need of explanation. Why *should* these constraints apply to mental explanation and what *is* their basis? If the basis of the explanatory constraints is causal, then it is lawlike and therefore not solely determined by the anomalous norms that govern mental ascriptions.

2. Human behaviour is "physically embedded" in that there are causal interactions between mentally described events and states and physical events and states. 'Mental events' are thus part of a realm of physical interactions in which causal laws operate which are closed under explanation. But if mental events do fall, in virtue of their causal efficacy, under laws which make no mention of the mental, then under some description they must be subject to those laws. Thus it is plausible that holistic mental explanations rest upon lawlike causal connections between the physical realizations of the mental events and states in question. In fact, it is more than plausible because there are no other candidates for the source of that explanatory force that attaches to mental explanations. This, in conjunction with the claim that physical states are not type-identical to but merely token realizations of mental

ascriptions, implies that mental events are irreducible to physical events but *supervenient* upon them and allows one to defend what Davidson calls "the autonomy of the mental" (*EAE* 214).

3.2. Causality and Mental Explanation

Anomalous monism embeds an account of the causal basis of mental explanation, but there are reasons to doubt that mental explanations are causal in nature.

Davidson claims that PAs are identified according to a holistic system of mental ascriptions which interpret the activity of a person in conformity to an a priori norm of rationality and that mental ascriptions actually denote states and events which are antecedent to and distinct from the actions that they cause. Although these states causally explain actions we cannot describe them in mental terms so as to exhibit their lawlike nature. Therefore the theory turns on the twin claims that mental ascriptions denote internal states and that mental explanations are causal. But both of these claims can be called into doubt.

Michael Morris urges that certain (Humean) conditions are essential for a causal explanation:

causal explanation . . . satisfies two conditions, which I shall call the "Non-*a priori* requirement" (NAP) and the "Independent existence requirement" (IE). Consider an explanation of the form: *p* because *q*. . . . such an explanation is causally explanatory if the replacements for "*p*" and "*q*" meet these conditions:

(NAP)   It is not possible to know *a priori* that *p* on the basis of knowing that *q*, or vice versa;

(IE)   the replacements for "*p*" and "*q*" are true in virtue of facts about states or events *e* and *c*, respectively such that: *c* does not depend for its existence upon the existence of *e*.[6]

He explains these conditions as follows:

they seem to isolate just that class of explanations which, if we are making distinctions, it is natural to isolate as causal. (NAP) rules out those explanations which can be called semantical, conceptual, logical or mathematical. And (IE) rules out explanations which connect something *c* with something *e*, in such a way that the connection is not *a priori*

------

[6] Morris, 'Causes of Behaviour', 123–4.

knowable, but in which *c* is held to constitute, or partially constitute
... *e*. In addition (IE) provides a characterisation of causal priority; it
thus supplies a want which should seem pressing if we are sceptical about
the possibility of temporal relations to do the job.[7]

This last claim is unclear in that the sense of "depend for its
existence" needs spelling out. Consider:

(1*a*) The table top is 3 feet off the ground because the legs are
3 feet long.

(1*b*) The legs are 3 feet long because the table top is 3 feet off
the ground.

(2*a*) The window's breaking was caused by the brick passing
through it (or, if you like, the brick releasing quantum *q*
of energy at *P*, the plane of the window).

Let us denote the states and events as follows:

(1*e*) The table top is 3 feet above the ground.

(1*c*) The legs are 3 feet long.

(2*e*) The window breaking.

(2*c*) The brick passing through it (or releasing *q* at *P*).

In each case the causal priority seems clear but the existence-
dependence condition is ambiguous. 1*e* depends on 1*c*, but one
could argue that were it not that 1*e* had been decided by the
carpenter before the legs were made, then 1*c* would not have been
the case. 2*e* is dependent on 2*c*, but 2*c* also depends on 2*e* because,
if the window had not broken, then the brick would not have
passed through nor have released *q* (*q* would have been retained
as kinetic energy in some reflected direction). Thus Morris's conditions will not give us what we want without some specification
of the mode or manner of existence-dependence sufficient to exclude the carpenter and suchlike. He could invoke laws of nature,
but these, of course, rest on causal connections (or something so
closely related that it makes IE viciously circular as an analysis of
causal priority). I shall return to causality in due course.[8]

Morris goes on to ask whether beliefs or desires are metaphysically, and not just logically or descriptively, independent of
actions by asking whether they are immanent or transcendent causes
of actions. He notes that having a belief does not necessarily entail

---

[7] Ibid. 126.   [8] See §4.4 below.

that one behave in any specific way but also that a mental ascription totally insulated from manifestations is suspect, although he rather hastily skates over the implications of this point.[9] The present account argues that manifestation is the basis of mental ascriptions and thus makes a strong case for an essential link between other-ascription and self-ascription.

Morris next asks whether a belief could be identified with a physical or functional state and uses the analogy between mental ascriptions and ascriptions of value. He claims that any reductive explanation or appeal to the physical–causal properties of mental ascriptions is ill grounded because a physical description carries no a priori guarantee that it will answer to the criteria for mental ascription (a variation of Davidson's point about the norm of rationality and interpretation) and thus there is no internal relation between the sortal features of physically specified kinds and those of mental kinds:

What makes it bad to defer in the ethical case is that what counts as consistent or improved ascription is determined by features internal to morality, which no naturalised method can be guaranteed to capture. Just the same feature appears in the case of ascription of beliefs. For in ascribing a belief to a subject, we commit ourselves to a view about the rationality of the reactions we thereby explain; precisely by attempting to verify the existence of a believing without verifying the existence of the reactions it causes, the physical level method of verification debars from consideration the very factors that determine what counts as consistency and improvement in the ascription of beliefs.[10]

Morris concludes that mental descriptions necessarily have some manifest basis and yet cannot be identified with a pattern of manifestations: "believings are Immanent causes with respect to reactions generally, but Transcendent with respect to almost every interesting sub-category of reactions. Let us call this the Diverse Independence view (DI-view)."[11]

He distinguishes between different mental ascriptions on the basis of their links to reactions and other-ascriptions, arguing that we must be cautious about the spatio-temporal properties of 'mental states'. "A believing cannot exist, on the DI-view, unless it causes some reaction; and . . . reactions must occur in space and time. But there is no need to give a time to a believing except in

---

[9] Ibid. 135–6.　　[10] Ibid. 138.　　[11] Ibid. 140.

a way that is parasitic upon the times of the reactions it causes."[12] He argues that mental ascriptions do not denote causal antecedent states which explain behaviour in the way that physical causes explain their effects: "we should be wary of the reifying style of much talk about the mind; . . . it at least encourages a conception of psychological states as independent of their effects in just the way which the DI-view denies that they are".[13]

Morris finally points us toward topics addressed in the present study: "even if the DI-view is right, this is only a beginning: we still need some account of the necessity of psychological explanation, of the epistemology of belief ascription, and of conceptual content".[14]

I have argued that thoughts and their content rest on judgements which obey constraints of rationality and norms operative in public discourse. Judgements rely on manifest criteria, or the reactions and responses to which Morris adverts. And it is precisely because the responses of a subject do not show any surveyable causal relations to environmental conditions that we need to find out which meaningful signs a person is operating with. Thus there is further reason to claim that thoughts and the attitudes to which they contribute are inappropriately construed as internal causal states lawfully tied to antecedent events.

3.3. Kant, Causality, and Reason

Kant provided an elegant defence of the view that PAs or "rational determinations" are not causal states and that the terms in which we think of them are incompatible with the view that they obey physical–causal laws:

on Kant's view, the paradigmatic case of rational action is a case in which: first, I form a concept of some event, object, or state of affairs which I choose to bring into being; and second, I do something which I believe will actualize that which my concept represents. In short, I act so as to realize my end. When I thus act, I am moved by my thoughts. But I am moved by my thoughts *qua* representations having cognitive significance, not by my thoughts *qua* mental events having temporal location and, hence, phenomenal causes and effects.[15]

[12] Ibid. 141.   [13] Ibid. 142.   [14] Ibid. 143–4.
[15] R. P. Wolff, *The Autonomy of Reason* (New York, 1973), 111.

If thoughts influence action in virtue of their representational content and the concepts which give rise to that content resist a causal analysis, then we need a non-causal account of the way that mental ascriptions explain actions (and we should question Wolff's unqualified use of "move").

Thoughts and their content reflect the way that a subject uses terms with meaning to structure his activity. This is not captured by an account in terms of spatio-temporal states which causally interact with other states. The brain functions by a kaleidoscopic and seamless web of state or event transitions in principle explicable by causal laws, but thoughts, and thus whatever mental ascriptions denote, are not part of this story. Strawson's discussion of causality sharpens the contrast:

I am suggesting, then, that we should regard mechanical transactions as fundamental in our notion of causality in general. . . . It is not then to be wondered at that such transactions supply a basic model when the theoretical search for causes is on; that we look for causal mechanisms; that, even when it is most clearly metaphorical, the language of mechanism pervades the language of cause in general, as in the phrases "causal connection", "causal links" and "causal chain".[16]

Where mechanical links connect states and events into a coherent story we are on solid ground with a causal explanation. But when we look for states and events of this type corresponding to mental terms we find a metaphysical mismatch. Not only does Morris undermine the independent existence of mental causes and effects, but also the analogy with moral judgement shows us that physical states and the laws which constrain them do not answer to norms in the right way to secure, as a matter of principle, the constitutive features of mental explanation. What is more, physical states are not dependent on the rationally directed judgements of thinking subjects. (It is just as well for neuroscience that they are not; if physical states were dependent upon the rational determinations of subjects, then neuroscience would have difficulties with causal relations far outstripping any found in quantum physics. We are not yet, and one hopes never will be, in a situation where neurones and neurone assemblies make decisions or act intentionally according

[16] P. F. Strawson, 'Causation and Explanation', in B. Vermazen and M. B. Hintikka (eds.), *Essays on Davidson* (Oxford, 1985), 124.

to their charm, quirkiness, or other aspects of their non-existent personalities.)

But rejecting a causal view of "the pattern of explanation" evident in psychological explanations is, as Morris concedes, "only a beginning: we still need some account of the necessity of psychological explanation". Louise Anthony remarks: "What is needed is some account of how a reason can be efficacious" and "we also need to know how it is that reasons can have causal efficacy in virtue of their reasonableness".[17] To meet this challenge and yet demur from the demand for a causal account, I will pursue the analogy with moral judgements.

3.4. Rational Determinations and the Origin of Action

A plausible claim is that an action is a set of physical events caused by a bodily movement. Of course, not just any bodily movement will do, and therefore we need criteria for deciding which ones count as actions. We could claim that an action is a bodily movement caused by an intention or a trying and then go in one of two directions. We could say *either* that an intention or trying is itself an internal state that needs to be caused in the right kind of way by the agent, which leads direct to the homunculus fallacy and an infinite regress, *or* that a bodily movement is caused by patterns of nerve impulses of some type and that a specification of the relevant type defines the class of actions. We note that muscles can be paralysed or peripheral nerves blocked and yet in some sense one still does the trying; so we conclude that the essence of action must be fairly proximal. We then potter about in the holistic flow of brain activity to try and isolate something that might do as the essence of an action. Such a search will probably lead us to a pattern of impulses from the premotor area of the cerebral cortex. But this explanatory node in brain activity has no distinctive status in its own terms; so why identify *it* as the essence of action?

The attempt to push the antecedents of action inside the organism seems to end with an intentional homunculus which produces 'tryings', or in losing sight of action altogether. There are also limits going the other way. Many of the knock-on effects of a given action cannot be regarded as essential to it or to the intention of the agent. If I pull a piece of string because it is hanging irritatingly in front of my eyes and thereby blow up No. 10 Downing Street, I am hardly guilty of treason. Somehow a line must be drawn which tells us when the obligations of a given mental explanation have been discharged.

It would simplify analysis if we could at least begin with a favoured class of bodily movements (we might, after Danto,[18] call them "basic actions"). If there is a class of movements such that they are what I do when I act and there is nothing else I do to make those movements, then at the core of every action would be a bodily movement (which is what I actually do) apt to be explained by appeal to states of the individual. But there are difficulties with this view. First, many actions involve entirely disparate sets of bodily movements, all of which qualify as a single action-type. I can sign my name in pencil, ink, crayon, paint, or with a chisel in stone, and in each case I aim at producing a signature of a certain form and not at producing the highly diverse patterns of bodily movements which achieve that result (even if there are motor distinctions in these cases, it would need to be proven that they were significant for psychological explanation). The unity that links together what I do in all these ways is a certain conception and not the movements which are performed. Action explanation must preserve the role of that conception.

Second, many actions can neither be described nor intended in terms of the body movements which comprise them: tying shoelaces is a salient example, but saying a word, looking to see what something is, searching for something, or mimicking a facial expression would serve equally well. One cannot do these things if one tries to perform certain bodily movements. The only way to do the action is to get the right conception in mind. But it is nonsensical to say that I intend to do that of which I can form no conception, so the actions cannot be identified with the bodily movements they involve. I intend to *operate on the world* in a certain way and that is what I do.

The core of any action is the conception which is guiding the agent's activity and thus "a man is the agent of an act if what he

---

[18] A. Danto, 'Basic Actions', *American Philosophical Quarterly*, 2 (1965), 141–8.

does can be described under an aspect that makes it intentional
. . . action does require that what the agent does is intentional
under some description, and this in turn requires, I think, that
what the agent does is known to him under some description"
(*EAE* 46). The examples mentioned make it clear that the description is often world-involving. This is, of course, a pleasing result
in the context of the present account because it is convergent with
the discussion of mental content. It also leads us directly back to
Kant: "in our judgments in regard to the causality of free actions,
we can get as far as the intelligible cause but not beyond it" (*CPR*
B585). He explains "the intelligible cause" or "the causality of
freedom" (the power of agency) as follows: "By freedom . . . I
understand the power of beginning a state spontaneously" (*CPR*
B561); it is "A causality which can therefore begin a series of
events entirely of itself" (*CPR* B562).

He contends that, in order to explain an action *qua* action we
are led to the rational determinations or reasons of the agent.
Thus action explanation puts the reasoning subject in the driving
seat and essentially focuses on his judgements ("inner determinations") as the source of his behaviour.

3.5. The Nature of Mental Explanation

When we hit upon the right explanation in terms of the actual
reasons which explain an agent's behaviour there is an *evident*
connection between the ascriptions we make and the agent's acting as he did. It is not a mechanical connection because he must
freely hold those reasons and their force is normative rather than
physical or deterministic. The efficacy of mental states must
therefore both accommodate the normative (and therefore non-
mechanical) property of representations or conceptions and show
their connection to an action or intention.

Davidson notes that one reason to think that an action explanation is a type of causal explanation is the word 'because' as in
'He did *x* because he believed she was a vampire'. But this is well
recognized to fall far short of motivating a causal view as there
are obviously non-causal uses of 'because'; for example, 'But
the product must be even because one of the factors is even', 'He
cannot have done it because it was done by a large man', or 'It

must be the school bell because it is now 3 p.m.' Thus we must look further for our causal conviction about the 'because' of mental explanation.

Hume saddled us with the idea that a subject must be moved to act on the model of causally conditioned changes in inanimate substances. Kant pointed out his mistake by focusing on the special nature of thought and action. Just as, in thought, judgements are made according to the (normatively constrained) applicability of concepts rather than according to mere causal conditions, so, in action, the subject's physical activity is formed and directed by his conceptions of the world and, of course, conceptions are constructed out of concepts. Thus if concept-use proceeds without compulsion and is responsive to the claim of reason, it imparts this same feature to action. I have argued above that the understanding or the ability to use concepts is governed by prescriptive rather than descriptive or purely dispositional norms. Therefore, both theoretical and practical reason involve 'oughts' and not just dispositions to be moved thus and so. This creates a special status for mental ascriptions.

Mental ascriptions, like moral judgements, have properties unlike those of physical states. In a very real way, epistemic and orectic ascriptions are constituted by the subject's making up his mind.[19] Unlike physical states, which exist to be discovered or disclosed by reading their nature off from mind-independent evidence, mental attributes come into being (can be truly avowed) when the subject makes up his mind. In the case of belief, one does not merely react, but rather "has to answer a normative question, to form a belief on the evidences of truth, as one takes them to be".[20] Thus whenever I form a thought, belief, intention, or desire I could say to myself 'I feel inclined thus and so but is that how it should be?' If I feel uncertain where I really stand then it will not be because I cannot get at certain facts about states within me, but that, in the light of the relevant norms, I have not yet made the relevant decisions.

If therefore someone were to say to him, in this situation of uncertainty, "You must want x" and "You must admire y", he would normally take

[19] S. Hampshire, 'Some Difficulties in Knowing', in T. Honderich and M. Burnyeat (eds.), *Philosophy As It Is* (Harmondsworth, 1978).
[20] Ibid. 294.

this "must" as prescriptive, as an imperative of rationality or even of morality—perhaps as meaning "You have compelling reasons for wanting x and admiring y". There would be an implied allusion to some standard of correctness—for example "You must, on pain of being inconsistent" or "You must, on pain of being utterly misguided in your desires and admirations". The "must" would not naturally be taken as "It must be the case that you do in fact want x and admire y".[21]

The connection with morality is now obvious (and deeply satisfying to a neo-Kantian). In mental ascriptions and self-ascriptions, as in moral judgements, there are implicit prescriptive norms to which the subject's inclinations must be sensitive. Because his recognition of such a norm is part of mental self-ascription, we find reason or "spontaneity" (Kant)—the ability to act thus and so for reasons rather than as a result of antecedent conditions—at the centre of thought life. When he acts, the subject structures his activity in accordance with rational determinations. This contrasts with Hume's view in which occurrent states or passions move the subject to act and reason merely refines the strategies for effective action.

At this point we can make a useful comparison of the present view with Blackburn's account of PAs. Blackburn remarks: "The content of a belief is not an item in space and time to which a subject is related. It is an abstraction from facts we want to know about the organisation and awareness of the subject."[22] He goes on to identify propositions which enter into PAs as "abstracta", with the PAs themselves as states of the person who has them. This allows him to claim that "neurophysiological truth shows us how internal states cause and explain behaviour", but also that propositions are not entities in the head.[23] "The proposition is literally an abstractum from the psychological similarities of all those whose mental lives are organised with that proposition as a focus."[24] I have also argued that mental ascriptions—and PAs— are not states, but have a more subtle ontological role. I have suggested that, with Kant, we should see the rational determinations of the subject as unlike causal entities and metaphysically unsuited to fall into causal explanations because they are not spatio-temporal

[21] Ibid. 297–8.
[22] S. Blackburn, 'Finding Psychology', *Philosophical Quarterly*, 36(143) (1986), 116.
[23] Ibid. 114.   [24] Ibid. 116.

in nature. The terms in a psychological explanation necessitate behaviour because they pick out the conceptions which guide or articulate the agent's activity. When one identifies the right conceptions one can discern the points at which the agent's action answers to his experience. Picking out the conceptions with which he is working allows one, in part, to predict and understand how and why his behaviour answers to his context, including his internal context. One can also reason with him, admonish him, engage in moral discourse, and form "reactive attitudes"[25] on the basis of how he "makes up his mind". This is exactly the kind of explanation that we want because it shows why the influences on action do not have a mechanical effect but depend on the agent's judgement.

The present account centrally turns on the points at which an action is sensitive to meaningful experience. Adam Morton suggests that we take only "rational considerations" to which an action is sensitive as part of its explanation.[26] I have already set out the reasons why rational considerations invoke rules defined in an interpersonal milieu. Thus we can endorse Burge's remark that mental ascriptions are essentially non-individualistic, normative, and intersubjective.[27]

In fact we converge with Melden's view of action. He brings out the normative element by comparing an action with a move in chess (c.f. Wittgenstein):

To attempt to understand a move in a game of chess in terms of bodily and psychological processes occurring at the time the agent makes his move is to leave out what is essential to the move—the fact that what transpires in the way of such occurrent processes is a case of following the rules.[28]

Briefly I am maintaining that just as in the case of the concept of a chess move, so in the case of the concept of any action, the context of practices in which rules are obeyed, criteria employed, policies are observed— a way of thinking and doing—is essential to the understanding of the difference between . . . bodily movements and actions. Just as this way

[25] Strawson coins this phrase in *Freedom and Resentment and Other Essays* (London, 1974).

[26] A, Morton, 'Because he Thought that he had Insulted him', *Journal of Philosophy*, 72 (1975), 5–15.

[27] Burge, 'Other Bodies'.

[28] A. I. Melden, 'Action', in D. F. Gustafson (ed.), *Essays in Philosophical Psychology* (London, 1964).

of thinking and doing marks in the one case a chess player, so it marks in the other a responsible agent, one who has acquired a complex of practices, among others the practice of observing moral rules and principles. The concepts "action" and "moral agent" or "person" are thus correlative.[29]

Melden highlights the links between guiding conceptions, actions, and the concepts, rules, and practices which invest our behaviour with significance.

There is a further analogy with a daub of paint in a picture. Just as it would be futile to try and unlock the reason why the paint was there by looking closely at its physical properties, it is futile to try and elucidate the essence of an action by looking closely at it as a bodily movement. To understand the role of the daub of paint is to see it as part of the picture; this shows why it is a particular colour, shape, and so on. To understand an action, one locates it in the articulated intentional life of the agent and comes to appreciate its motivation and meaning.

A person grasps and follows rules which allow him to think about his world or conceive of it in articulated ways. Thus he need no longer merely react to immediate conditions but can guide and control his activity. Such structured activity sensitive to the conceptual content in experience is intentional, and to explain an action is to latch on to the rule-governed techniques an agent is using to deal with his environment at a given time. This understanding allows one to get inside, as it were, his present "ways of thinking and doing" and to appreciate the necessity of his acts.

This view is clarified by comparing it with current causal theories of mental content and explanation.

3.6. A Causal View of Content and Explanation

Davidson, as we have seen, bases content ascriptions in verbal and non-verbal behaviour and argues that such ascriptions token-identify states which explain the relevant behaviour. Peacocke pursues this approach and argues that the content of experiences or mental states derives ultimately from perception and thus from the "sensational and representational properties" of "perceptual experiences". I have already presented arguments against the inherently

---

[29] Ibid. 73.

Cartesian view of content implicit in his theory but will here focus on details which elucidate the nature of mental explanation.

On Peacocke's view, a thoughtful agent differs from an automaton in terms of the states causing its behaviour. But the prima-facie problem for action explanation in terms of such states is the object-directedness of intentions and actions. In addressing this problem, Peacocke makes a thorough attempt to flesh out a causal theory of content.

Objects must be perceived and then represented as being thus and so in order to be acted upon:

> The representational content of a perceptual experience has to be given by a proposition or a set of propositions, which specifies the way the experience represents the world to be ... we can draw a distinction between sensational and representational properties of experience. Representational properties will be properties the experience has in virtue of its representational content; while sensational properties will be properties an experience has in virtue of some aspect—other than its representational content—of what it is like to have that experience. (SC 5)

Perceptual experiences, on this view, are inner states in the mind of a thinker and bear an unmistakable resemblance to sense data:[30] "the more plausible of the claims the sense-datum theorists made can be translated into ... talk about sensational properties" (SC 52).

Peacocke then addresses the problem of distinguishing a being with "contentful mental states" from a mere stimulus–response information processor. He suggests that we should ascribe the "tightest", or most austere, set of concepts required to account for the behaviour of a given individual over time and only ascribe conceptual structure where the subject shows the requisite sensitivity or, we might say, articulation of behaviour (SC 78). One would not, for instance, suggest that a dog expected his master home 'next Tuesday' as one could not establish that it grasped that concept.

Peacocke first considers the relations of organisms to things around them. He examines spatial concepts and argues that these can only be ascribed where the subject has a "perspectival sensitivity" to "places and perceptual objects in his immediate environment" (SC 57). He argues that this sensitivity to changes of

---

[30] It might be noted by some that there is also a strong resemblance between "sensational properties" and Humean "impressions".

perspective should be of general applicability, rather than being so limited that it could be explained by invoking a set of stimulus–response patterns or reactive dispositions. He remarks: "It is harmless to summarize the claim that an organism displays perspectival sensitivity or has spatial attitudes by saying that it has a mental map of its environment" (*SC* 76).[31] He later links this to *demonstrative content* so as to give an account of singular thought in terms of the mental states of the concept-user.

He next isolates a set of "observational concepts" (e.g. ⟨O⟩) which depend only upon experiences (e.g. as of O) and are not defeasible on other grounds. ⟨Square⟩ has such an observational form because it can be taken to involve no more than the way that square things look to normal people;[32] ⟨tomato⟩ does not, because the judgement ⟨that *A* is a tomato⟩ depends on *A* "being of the same underlying kind as". The distinction between observational and non-observational concepts is important because Peacocke considers that observational concepts are basic to conceptions of a spatial world. Given that a subject has such concepts, we must still (1) explain how perceptible objects enter conceptual thought and (2) explain the fact that there may be different ways of thinking of an object (so that identity statements are informative). Peacocke secures both by a conjunction of claims:

1. A judgement of a certain content has canonical links to certain evidence or grounds and also commitments to further judgements which follow from it (*TEC*).[33] I have noted that these are analysed in terms of mental states of the thinker.

2. Objects can be thought about solely in terms of the perceptual relation one has to them, e.g. as ⟨that *F*-instantiating object over there⟩.[34]

3. The *mode of presentation* of an object is a function of the current "perceptual states" of the thinker.

---

[31] Compare this with Evans's "cognitive map".

[32] Which is a deceptively simple way of putting things, as any AI experimenter will tell you; there is no surveyably simple specification of this condition.

[33] This supersedes the theory that "canonical evidence" for a certain thought provides prima-facie justification for the judgement concerned, e.g. 'that *p*'.

[34] Peacocke does not pursue this, but it is extremely important as it implies that no single or unitary function is involved in a concept like <baboon> but rather growing familiarity with its place in the structure of rules and their applications which constitute a conceptual system.

This means that a given object can cause a judgement ⟨Fa⟩ by its "perceptual relations" to the "experiential states" of the thinker concerned. Thus the object can be variously identified in different acts of judgement on "canonical grounds" constituted by occurrent "perceptual states".

These three claims entail a view of:

1. the Russellian 'principle of acquaintance', and
2. the individuation of objects by contentful states.

1. I am acquainted with any object x which is the cause of perceptual states or experiences as of x. The causal relations between me and the object are themselves evident in the demonstrative elements of content. These elements reflect the way we locate the object in egocentric space by means of a flexible set of spatial abilities. States with demonstrative content are, Peacocke claims, central in action explanation: "no set of attitudes gives a satisfactory propositional attitude explanation of a person's acting on a given object unless the content of those attitudes includes a demonstrative MP [mode of presentation] of that object" (SC 158). Thus items figuring in action explanation do so because of their causal role in dispositional and representational states of the subject.

2. Perceptual states (caused by objects in combination with perceptual and perspectival sensitivities) constitute the content which explains the role of an object in action. Thus an object, *qua* object in the world, need not figure in thought and mental explanation because its role is filled by a set of mental states.

Peacocke therefore analyses thought content of all types in terms of causal states with content (which explain the behaviour of a given individual). These states figure in PA explanations in virtue of the role of the underlying brain states in causal and computational or neurophysiological sequences linking sensory transactions to overt behaviour (SC 210). The brain states reflect the structured contents of the neo-Fregean thoughts they realize. Thus mental content and the "because" of mental explanation are both secured by orderly sequences of brain states and events which realize mental states. Mental content is therefore a function of inner states of an individual thinker and is causal in nature in virtue of its supervenience upon brain activity.

3.7. *Comparisons and Contrasts*

There are several points of contrast between the present view and the causal view sketched above: First, I have argued that mental ascriptions only make sense within a wider context than the internal states of an individual agent, indeed that they are grounded in the way that the (human or other) thinker's activity maps on to rules and regularities found in human (or other) discourse. Second, an analysis of action explanation should exhibit the essentially conceptual nature of an action, which it cannot do if it is confined to inner states. Third, the structure and function of occurrent states of the brain themselves stand in need of some explanation if they reflect articulated thought content. Fourth, mental content, the crux of mental explanation, is not causal in nature.

These four worries tell against the notion that mental ascriptions denote elements in causal explanations of behaviour and the claim that mental ascriptions denote states whose causal properties are to be understood at another level.

3.7.1. *Content Revisited*

We specify the content of our thoughts by reference to the things in the world around us: clocks, colours, shapes, faces, buildings, the actions of others, etc. Thus mental content, prima facie, draws heavily on the furniture of a public world. But 'inner entities' seem inescapable in that surely some explanatory role is played by the brain and its cognitive processes. However, content involves concepts and concept-use is normative in a way that makes it hard to tie thought solely to inner states.

In using a concept, a thinker does not merely respond but can represent to himself the fact that a norm governs that response and is independent of it. Therefore, quite apart from what a thinker is causally inclined to do in a given situation, there are *both* criteria by which his performance can be assessed *and* an (informal) assessment process which shapes that content. These criteria and what counts as meeting them determine the content of any given thought (or "inner process") and are based in public practices and the rules which operate there (and are therefore "outer" (*PI* 1. 580)).

For the present purpose, suppose that there were an inner state, conscious or causal, which regularly preceded a given thought. The content of that thought would still depend upon the criteria which fix its role. These give that thought form and content by having shaped the mental activity which constitutes it. If, with Frege, we reject the idea that content (which is linked to truth) depends upon the inner or conscious states of the subject, then it could not be a function of antecedent states but is better related to the rules which shape the activity of the thinker.

Indeed Sartre notes that brain events or "psychic processes" only have content in virtue of their role in the activity of an intact human being: "When the unity of cerebral functions is shattered, phenomena are produced which simultaneously present a relative autonomy and which at the same time can be manifested only on the ground of the disintegration of a totality."[35] My thought has certain content in virtue of its links to a public use; this is not adequately explained by invoking inner causes necessary (or even sufficient) for it to occur. Therefore, and essentially, content is specified in terms of what is outer so that "inner experience in general is dependent upon outer experience in general" (Kant).

I have noted that Peacocke's view of modes of presentation carries with it misleading perceptual connotations. The present account stresses the active role of the thinker in framing his thoughts and in information-gathering by the use of techniques he has mastered.[36] In fact a subject, in discourse with others or purposeful interaction with his environment, responds to various features in ways that are articulated by the practices in which he participates. These patterns of activity provide "outward criteria" and make sense of what he is doing in terms of "objective norms—norms of truth, rationality, right" based in practices of representation. Syntactically structured neurophysiological processes (or mental or inner entities conceived with them in mind) cannot hope to capture this. That is why we must insist that behaviour, including utterances, be understood within the rich and varied pattern of human interests, activity, and interactions in which a thinker is involved, *and* that only as it is shaped by the rules that govern conceptual content does it constitute intentional action.[37]

[35] J.-P. Sartre, *Being and Nothingness*, tr. H. E. Barnes (London, 1958), 623.
[36] Cf. J. Z. Young, *Philosophy and the Brain* (Oxford, 1987), 128 ff.
[37] In this sense the individual is mapped on to more general norms (see Blackburn, 'Finding Psychology'; Burge, 'Other Bodies').

3.7.2. *Then, What Is Important about the Brain?*

Imagine a neurophysiological process Np' which results from a capricious electrical discharge in one of my temporal lobes (as in an automatism due to temporal lobe epilepsy). Let us say that it causes a hallucination of meeting my Aunt Agnes at the church fête. My hallucination has just *this* content because the information role normally served by the brain processes aberrantly stimulated is determined in the hurly-burly of everyday experience where I have met and learned to recognize Aunt Agnes.[38] Interactions and experiences have structured those brain processes in such a way as they fulfil a particular informational or causal function.[39] Their role in my aberrant thought draws on what I would normally be thinking and doing when events like them happened in my brain. Thus my thoughts as a result of these brain events must be understood in terms of my normal experience as a thinker who has grasped certain concepts (in public practices of use). Only because processes sufficiently like those underlying my hallucination are normally active when I am engaging in certain activities are they associated with content. (Note that this is recognized by a sane thinker as being abnormal content probably because the total situation and configuration of processes is different from that in the normal case.) But what accounts for the "normal" processes and their function?

The brain is an information processor. Its functions are structured causal processes which take shape in childhood and remain, to a certain extent, plastic throughout adult life. These processes work with information available within limits set by our sensory capacities and their technological extensions. Within these limits the brain (by evolving patterns of causally articulated function which depend upon the meanings appreciated by the thinker concerned) allows one to take note of one's environment in terms whose significance is determined by the actions, projects, and interests of oneself and others.[40] In a human thinker, for instance, the processes in the superior temporal gyrus of the dominant

---

[38] NB 'recognize', not describe.

[39] G. R. Gillett, 'Perception and Neuroscience', *British Journal of Philosophy of Science*, 40 (1989), 83–103.

[40] On this see my 'Concepts, Structures and Meanings', *Inquiry*, 30 (1987), 101–12.

hemisphere which allow phoneme detection and the parsing of words into phonemes differ in their functional structure between individuals from different linguistic groups.[41] Thus the exact effects of incoming patterns on brain function are constrained in part by genetically determined structure but critically shaped in the course of experience. What is more, when neuroscientists attempt to unravel brain function they relate identifiable patterns of neural activity to reported experiences of the individual (*qua* thinking subject). Thus meaning structures not only the way the brain functions but our understanding of that function. We could say that brain function is both determined by meaning and unlocked by meaning. Only thus do we discover the important regularities in the physiological events we study. Therefore, communication ineliminably provides the elements of mental explanation because it determines the structure of conceptual systems.

In addition to these facts about the functional 'shape' of the brain, a subject actively shapes his perceptions, which must therefore be understood to be a function of persons *qua* rational, active, conscious agents. "The environment can act on the subject only to the exact extent that he comprehends it; that is, transforms it into a situation."[42] In this the concept-using subject uses meanings (which are essentially detachable from antecedent conditions) to illuminate and guide his activity. Thus mental content reflects his experience as a person in relation to others and the world. The brain is merely that part of him which enables him to have reason and reflection and think about himself, the world in which he lives, and his own place in it, but study of the brain does not, and cannot, reveal *what it is* to be a thinking creature because the elucidation of thought and action does not depend on processes in the skull or causal relations between them.

3.7.3. Causality and Differential Explanation

I have already attempted to lay the ghost of causal voluntarism in terms of 'acts of the will', 'tryings', and so on construed as intentional events immediately preceding an action. I have argued that an action is individuated by the conception which structures the

---

[41] A. R. Luria, *The Working Brain* (Harmondsworth, 1973).
[42] Sartre, *Being and Nothingness*, 572.

activity of the agent and that a conception, *qua* mental content, is neither causal in nature nor analysable in terms of inner physical states. It remains to account for the differential explanation of actions by mental ascriptions.

Peacocke suggests that the a priori structure of mental explanation entails that we need a means of selecting the correct empirical candidate among competing explanations for a given piece of behaviour. He argues that because all the candidates fulfil the normative constraints on mental function, a causal mechanism (imperfectly described and understood) must underwrite differential explanation. It is true that a pattern of behaviour could be made sense of in a number of ways and that we need some basis on which to discern the particular way that it should be explained on a given occasion. But surely the actual reasons that a person had for doing what he did emerge as one interacts with the individual in question and thus in the context of the norms and regularities of interpersonal discourse, which, as I have argued, is the essential milieu of action explanation.

Imagine that a schizophrenic patient becomes able to say:

I could not cope with the pushing and pulling inside; I sort of wanted to say things but I couldn't. It was as if my mother was there and she shut me up ... as she always used to when I asked those questions as a child. ... She was the red witch you see ... she was the one who was behind the plot to strangle me. ... At least that's the way that it seemed to me, caught up in it all.

Having heard this, one can begin to deal with him; his system of delusions about his mother become useful and informative in understanding his behaviour and thoughts. Prior to such articulation these are merely senseless phenomena, presumed to be caused by states inside him. But this presumption, absent any engagement in a framework of public discourse, is of no help in untangling his psyche.[43] We need an explanation which allows interpersonal communication, reflective thought, and some hope of a return to self-determination on the part of the patient, not just one which gives a causal history for his behaviour. We therefore need mental or meaningful explanations and we make extensive use of them in both everyday and psychiatric settings. They are complex, sensitive

---

[43] I have discussed this in 'Neuropsychology and Meaning in Psychiatry', *Journal of Medicine and Philosophy*, 15 (1990), 21–39.

to context, particular to the agent and his biography, embedded in interpersonal relationships, and display a rational structure. Mental ascriptions and explanations illuminate the relation between the agent concerned and his world in such a way as to make sense of his actions. And it is not at all clear that such explanations can be depersonalized in the way that natural causal explanations must be.

It is constitutive of rational explanation that the reasons (1) involve "norms for persons to follow" (Peacocke) and (2) are adopted or rejected by a rational agent so that they do not have an impersonal vector of influence.[44] If the force of such explanations rests on the assent of the agent concerned, then they are not causal or mechanical as are the causal relations in physical sciences. The fact that the thoughts of a disturbed person become more ordered as he begins to return to normal is only naïvely taken to reflect changes perspicuously explained in terms of the relations between causal sequences in his brain. The essential change is that at a certain time his behaviour is not merely caused to occur by states in his brain but begins to make sense, and that reflects a change in his interactions with others and the world.

Peacocke suggests that differential explanation must involve the antecedents of a given action, and he argues, after Davidson, that their explanatory force is secured by, although it cannot be spelt out in terms of, lawlike relations, i.e. causal connections between structural–functional brain processes (*HE* 67–8). In order to make rational explanations fit the pattern of causal sequences he dismisses Adam Morton's account of differential explanation, which, as I have noted, is in some ways close to my own. This account holds that differential explanation reveals the points at which the thinker's behaviour is sensitive to experience and thus implies that, if a thinker is not influenced by a given content, it has no valid role in the explanation. Peacocke's justification for dismissing this suggestion focuses on Morton's concern that rational sensitivity to facts should operate right up to the last moment before an action is performed. It is couched in terms of a putative description of an action as a set of neuro-muscular events and their temporal properties. He claims that this "last moment" escapes us and that we actually need a specification of a chain of states in which each

[44] A. J. P. Kenny, *Will, Freedom and Power* (Oxford, 1971).

stage is causally effective and necessary for the action to occur. He believes that in this chain of states "The essential initiating event takes place in the cortex" (*HE* 89). Leaving aside his simplistic caricaturing of the neural activity involved in human action, it should now be evident that the objection fails on other grounds.

Action explanations, as I have already argued, express a relation between the thinker and the world as he conceives of it. They are informative and detailed in so far as they give his reasons for acting and no further. An item is legitimately included only if a 'pro-attitude' is focused on it.[45] Therefore, many of the information-processing states in Peacocke's account do not qualify although they indeed underpin the crucial relations between actions, thought, and the world. The differential explanation of action as *action* is intentional, and thus in terms of projects, things, and people around me, and it distinguishes actions as a class from other, non-mental phenomena such as reflexes, involuntary changes of posture, automatisms, and the like. Neural events cannot serve as criteria for this distinction. Automatisms, for example, involve complex performances, often in some apparent relation to persons or events in the immediate vicinity of the subject, which look rather like intentional actions but are not sensitive to reason, subject to reflective modification, or explicable by the agent as other than an affliction which he suffers. They are caused by complex and articulated functional processes in the brain triggered by aberrant electrical activity, but they are not actions because they are insensitive to rational considerations; the present account secures this conclusion. It is because the differential explanation of an automatism involves brain processes but not reasons for action that it is excluded from the range of human actions (note that the bodily movements involved are no help).

I have noted that the brain takes on a functional 'shape' as we mature, perceive, relate to others, act, acquire a language, imbibe a culture, consider religious claims, and so on because its structure and function, even at the neurophysiological level, is profoundly influenced by such experiences. The differential explanation of this shape and its functional properties is found in the experience of participation in conceptual activities. Peacocke claims that physical realizations and causal patterns provide the causal underpinning

---

[45] 'Actions, Reasons and Causes', in *EAE*.

for mental explanation. Given the nature of human beings, the brain and its capacity for information-processing is essential to mental life, but what the brain actually does is dependent on the conceptual structure of the person whose brain it is. There is, therefore, an undischarged explanatory debt in resting mental explanation on brain function.

If we seek to explain the character and role of a given thought and what it is for a thinker to act on that thought, then we must look to the patterns of information sensitivity that the thinker uses in acting as she does. These are elucidated by a study of the rule-governed practices in which she participates and are pervaded by the essential features of those practices. Asking neurophysiological questions about the brain as an information processor is a matter for empirical science and just gets the cart before the horse. The essential nature of information as it figures in the explanation of human action remains a matter for philosophy of mind.[46]

3.8. Conclusion

In what sense can we explain an action? A plausible view is that we are identifying the causal antecedents of behaviour. I have argued that this cannot be the right view. Talk of thought and action concerns the rational control, by a thinker, of his own activity, and thereby explains how it reveals his mental life. A mental explanation appeals to the ways that an agent reasons and thus it concerns the rules which articulate his activity. Human agents are able to reason because their brains function in causally regular ways, but the nature of their reasoning, and thus the structure and content of mental explanation, only emerge when we consider them as rational and social beings. Mental explanation tells us which concepts are being used to shape an action. Concepts involve rule-governed links between a subject's behaviour and the world and thus determine the way that an action is sensitive to that world. The same concepts make possible linguistic interaction with him.

This account sees an action explanation as concerning what an agent thinks about things rather than as a description of a causal

---

[46] *Contra* Churchland's claims in *Neurophilosophy* (Cambridge, Mass., 1986).

chain. The ascriptions involved and the ways they fit together appeal to a far richer conception of persons and their relations than that found in such an impoverished model. Of course, the organization and function of the higher centres of the brain may well eventually be described without the extensive appeal to representation that is currently made, but that description, as Davidson has remarked, involves a change of subject.

4

Cognitive Development and Cognitive Systems

THE arguments of the first three chapters are strengthened and clarified by an account of the way in which thought matures and is realized in brain structure under the demands of 'logic' that is "asserting, thinking, judging [and] inferring".[1] Thought matures during cognitive development, a process that has traditionally been seen as the emergence of individual 'internal' or Cartesian mental functions. I will suggest that this is an inadequate view and that in cognitive development thinkers internalize an essentially public and social set of techniques which organize and make tractable the features of the environment that have been found relevant by their social group.[2]

Thought is realized, on any broadly Aristotelian view, in brain function. Again we have tended towards a methodological solipsism about brain function in which a kind of physicalized Cartesianism has attempted to analyse thought and its content by attending to causally structured processes in the head. I will argue, on the basis of current work in cognitive neuroscience, that attempts to reduce cognition and mental content to causal transactions are misinformed and misdirected. The present account suggests that the brain itself—the source and focus of physicalist inspiration— realizes operations shaped in an interpersonal milieu and unable to be understood without reference to that context.

I. COGNITIVE DEVELOPMENT

4.1. *A Shift in the Development Paradigm*

The present account has implications for both the development of concept mastery and the realization of that mastery in a physical

---

[1] G. Frege, 'Thoughts', in *Collected Papers on Mathematics, Logic and Philosophy*, ed. B. McGuinness (Oxford, 1984), 351.
[2] This view is similar to that of John Morss ('The Public World of Childhood', *Journal for the Theory of Social Behaviour*, 18 (1988), 323–44).

system. One would expect a number of points of contact between an adequate analysis of thought and current theory in developmental psychology and cognitive neuroscience. In fact these convergences clarify the relation between signs and stimuli and the difference between prescriptive and descriptive norms.

I will develop the view that the human subject develops not merely as an input-driven accumulator of dispositions, but as an active organizer of experience who uses certain (rule-governed) techniques. This implies that what Frege calls "logic" (which concerns what counts as going right or wrong in certain judgements) has a formative role not only in the conceptual system of a thinker, but also in the cerebral information-processing network that realizes that system. In the final section of this chapter, I sketch an account of the thought of a solitary thinker.

Until recently Piaget's theories about the cognitive structures that shape human thought have been dominant in psychology and education. That is no longer so. The following survey of Vygotsky's thought summarizes some corrective strands in contemporary developmental psychology:

Vygotsky's insight is that the relation between thought and speech is an internal relation. By the metaphor of "internality" Vygotsky seems to have in mind the logical dependence of the two relata: that we do not understand what it is to exercise one independently of what it is to exercise the other. The criteria by which we individuate the two faculties are inextricably interwoven. That is, we cannot identify something as an expression of (developed) thought without appeal to considerations about the way in which that thought is made manifest to others, is expressed in behaviour and conversely, we cannot identify linguistic expressions independently of considerations about that which they express, without seeing them as a manifestation of thought.[3]

I will pursue both the link between content and manifestation and the implications of development for our understanding of the possession of concepts.

Hamlyn contends that "to have a concept is not an all-or-none affair; there are degrees of understanding and degrees in the complexity of what is understood".[4] If this is true then the full

    [3] D. Bakhurst, 'Thought, Speech and the Genesis of Meaning', Studies in Soviet Thought, 31 (1986), 189–209.
    [4] D. W. Hamlyn, 'Epistemology and Conceptual Development', in T. Mischel (ed.), Cognitive Development and Epistemology (New York, 1971), 10.

meaning of what a speaker says may outstrip her own understanding of it and the richness implicit within certain content may not be grasped fully by the thinker. Both possibilities undermine the thesis that formal or categorical structures with bivalent truth-functional properties realized in the minds or cognitive mechanisms of thinkers are the basis of concepts and representation.

4.2. *The Natural Basis of Thought*

A child's natural tendencies to react to the world in certain ways are modified by shared rules to form conceptual abilities. In this process certain responses for which the child is naturally equipped are refined into determinate ways of responding, each firmly located in the conceptual structure with which the child is in contact. I have argued that the abilities concerned require directed attention and the generalization of patterns of response.[5] The human interactions in which these patterns of responding are shaped impart both precision to the thought of the individual and agreement (in judgements) between that individual and others. Hamlyn remarks: "from the earliest days when interchange of smiles, for example, is possible, communication is built into the web of behaviour that takes place in the context of personal relations between child and mother". In such interchanges the child naturally exhibits reactions which are, to a certain extent, congruent with those of mature concept-users. Children notice, *inter alia*, bright lights, loud noises, human faces, and possibly middle-sized dry goods (whether stationary or moving) as salient items in the environment and are therefore naturally equipped to latch on to the practices of adults. They learn to detect the things that adults detect so as to develop their communication and interaction with adults.[6] Thus the innate potential of the child and the resources offered by his social milieu conjointly provide conceptual form which can be used to shape his activity and experience:

A person is a social being from childhood and the knowledge that he has to acquire is equally socially determined in an important sense. For

---

[5] §§1.2–5 above.
[6] Many of the first moves in these practices will be over-interpreted by adults, who will make ascriptions of content which the child has not yet grasped.

knowledge presupposes criteria of truth, and those presuppose the agreement in judgments of which Wittgenstein spoke. Hence learning on the part of an individual is as much as anything his initiation into a framework over which there is wide agreement, even if there is plenty of room for individual deviation from the norm. For this to be possible there has to be and is a background of common interests, attitudes, feelings, and . . . cognitive apparatus. There must be, to use Wittgenstein's phrase, agreement in forms of life. By "cognitive apparatus" I mean everything that makes possible a common and shared sensibility and ways of thinking—physiological make-up, sense organs etc.[7]

The social milieu with its prescriptive norms for behaviour creates an interpersonal domain of shared meaning in which the child finds a repertoire of concepts and in response to which she refines and structures her mental life. This milieu is both the setting (*de facto* or as a matter of genesis) for cognitive development and its basis (a priori or as a matter of essence).

4.3. Early Cognitive Development

Piaget's theories concentrate on the way that individual children approach problems in controlled settings. He discusses "concepts" and "operations" based in "structures" which explain the child's behaviour and constitute the mind. He thinks of these structures as complexes of cognitive operations which provide action schemes to deal with new situations.[8] He notes that cognitive development occurs within a context involving emotional, social, and biological factors, but this receives no emphasis in his analysis.[9]

It is both interesting and informative to identify the strategies which children use to solve problems, but calling them "structures" or "operations" should not be taken to imply that they comprise a set of causal transactions occurring in an internal cognitive milieu. This can deflect us from a more perspicuous understanding of the nature of thought and concepts. In fact, "operations" and "structures" refer to patterns evident in the

[7] D. W. Hamlyn, 'Human Learning', in R. S. Peters (ed.), *The Philosophy of Education* (Oxford, 1973), 188–9.

[8] Hamlyn, 'Epistemology and Conceptual Development', 13.

[9] J. Piaget and B. Inhelder, *The Psychology of the Child*, tr. H. Weaver (London, 1969), 128.

techniques and linguistic exchanges that are observed. We cannot equate these with functional states in an 'inner' realm because we are merely describing the interactions between a task, an experimenter, and the children he is studying. However, to urge this 'thin' or 'weak' reading of the data leaves us with a burden of explanation.

Piaget identifies the first phase of childhood activity as a *sensorimotor* stage (from 6 to 18 months), which involves a dynamic relationship between the child and things in her environment based on sensorimotor patterns of neural connection. He argues that a young child lacks a concept of a continuing object at this stage on the grounds that she will often not attempt to recover a toy that has moved from her view.[10] He concludes that, for the child, there is no (persistent but obscured) object to be sought, but rather a succession of impressions. This Humean thesis suggests that our knowledge of objects is a construct out of more simple and transient percepts.

However, other explanations for the child's lack of object retrieval are demanded by the fact that in many situations children of this age *do* act as if objects persist and can be reidentified, the most consistently recognized being other people.[11] It is of course quite plausible that the child does not understand how various things behave and thus lacks an adequate repertoire of fundamental ideas for the things it meets (some of which manifestly do not persist through time). Rocks, flames, towers made of blocks, pictures on the television, and ice-creams indicate how inappropriate a single object concept would be for thought in general. In fact we spend our lives extending the range of our knowledge of the identity and persistence conditions for things we meet (adult atomic physicists have the problem *a fortiori*). We could say that in this phase the child learns to track items in the environment in two related ways. First, it learns the sensorimotor and attentional skills needed to maintain an information link with a perceived item.[12] The child also learns to track an item as an individual of a certain type by making use of information from other thinkers that links various presentations of that item. These two elements of conceptual

[10] J. Piaget, *Psychology and Epistemology*, tr. P. A. Wells (Harmondsworth, 1972), 11.

[11] M. Donaldson, *Children's Minds* (London, 1978), 26-7.

[12] This notion comes from Gareth Evans, *VR* 107 ff.

'tracking' develop in tandem and give rise to the ability (central in our conceptual system) to individuate things of this or that type. As the child manipulates objects he perceives the effects of his actions on them and on this basis can begin to formulate thoughts about how things behave. But in this enterprise he is not alone as he is exposed to the language and practices of adults, which he can imitate and use in his own activity.

Piaget believes that the child is living in a subjective world and claims that activity in the sensorimotor phase is directed to wish-fulfilment. He calls the child's language-use at this stage "autistic" and "egocentric" (in a cognitive rather than a moral sense). But this seems to be a mistake even in early development when perception and action are just beginning to emerge:

There is abundant evidence that even at this early stage the child's cognitive development is a social process. . . . evidence from films of more than 100 exchanges between mothers and their infants of two or three months of age forces us to conclude that a complex form of mutual understanding develops even at this age . . . this kind of early interpersonal responsiveness is the source from which the whole of human intelligence springs.[13]

A child first exhibits natural and spontaneous activity, and then, by selective attention to and manipulation of what is around him (directed by linguistic exchanges), he refines and extends that activity. Thus his interactions with the environment are shaped by the appreciation that he can develop successful ways of responding according to rules which greatly expand his access to and action in the environment. It is clear that workable and repeatable ways of responding have great advantages over haphazard and hopeful one-off attempts. Note that in the process of mastering such techniques he learns that his environment is accessible both to himself and to other thinking beings with whom he has to do (recall the essential truth-relatedness of thought).

4.4. Play, Problems, and Symbols

Play reveals a great deal about a child's thought.[14] The early stage of *functional play*, in which the child does things just for the sake

---

[13] Donaldson, *Children's Minds*, 29.
[14] C. Buhler, *From Birth to Maturity: The Child and his Family* (London, 1935).

of doing them, is important in developing basic techniques of sensorimotor control and also prepares the way for symbolic or imaginative play.

In *symbolic play* objects stand for other things because significant roles are conferred upon them as the child uses words to structure his activity. Piaget, as we have noted, considers that in this period the child's speech is egocentric, arising out of the autistic or wish-related use of language and without an important social function. He sees such speech as no more than an expression of the child's cognitive activity and unrelated to the presence of, or communication with, others. Vygotsky has forced a reconsideration of this view by showing that there is an essential social dimension to "egocentric speech". His evidence suggests that the child uses resources acquired from interaction with others to tackle his problems and that his verbalizations are dependent on the understanding that others can appreciate what he is doing and saying. Vygotsky has shown that if this presupposition is negated the child stops speaking.[15]

Structure, organization, repeatability of response, are all aided by *marks* or *terms* which signpost or flag the ways of responding that are being developed. Thus 'tower' might mark a situation where three or four blocks stand on one another; 'give' would have a role in the techniques to be used for obtaining something one wants. Such symbols bring the world of others into the centre of the child's life through the structured medium of language. The child is not just a wish-fulfilling, drive-satisfying, internal-state-regulating organism who builds for himself a picture of the world based on his (essentially private) cognitive states. Through normative social contact he appropriates symbols and applies them to his experience. This is how 'logic' (in its broadest sense) shapes the mind. The child is, in fact, extremely sensitive to the intentions and human interests which confer meaning upon utterances and uses the cues they provide to pattern his behaviour. This runs counter to Piaget's suggestion (based notably on the 'three mountains' experiment) that children of 4 years or so cannot see the world from perspectives of others and thus could not see it as a shared world. If the experiments are modified so as to maximize

[15] L. Vygotsky, *Thought and Language*, tr. E. Hanfmann and G. Vakar (first pub. 1929; Cambridge, Mass., 1962), 133.

the contribution of interpersonal understanding these claims evaporate.[16] Donaldson concludes:

> The point is that the motives and intentions of the characters are entirely comprehensible, even to a child of three. The task requires the child to act in ways which are in line with very basic human purposes and interactions (escape and pursuit)—it makes human sense. Thus it is not at all hard to convey to the child what he is supposed to do; he apprehends it instantly. It then turns out that neither is it hard for him to do it. In other words in this context, he shows none of the difficulty in "decentring" which Piaget ascribes to him.[17]

One might wonder whether escape and pursuit are so basic in human activity, but these facts, along with the role of speech in play and the use of language in problem-solving, make it look as if the infant makes sense of her experience and thought life in essentially interpersonal ways. Here we find a convergence between developmental psychology and a claim derived from Wittgenstein, namely that mental life is not a stream of inner events or 'conscious experiences' but is a matter of using terms (whose meaning is established by use) as signs to articulate one's feelings, inclinations, reasons, and actions.

The argument to date suggests that in thought we structure our activity by drawing on the practices around us. On this view, cognitive development is a progressive articulation of a child's activity by those rules that shape the practices in which she participates.[18] The terms used mark and thereby relate the events, objects, and features and responses of other people in those situations where the child finds herself. Thus concepts are abstractions from abilities developed within this milieu. Some concepts mark objects, e.g. ⟨bed⟩, ⟨book⟩, and ⟨block⟩, and others do not, e.g. ⟨away⟩, ⟨big⟩, ⟨colour⟩, ⟨negation⟩, and ⟨good⟩. As the child develops the articulated abilities indicated by these marks they enhance her activity in a shared world and enable this activity to become more explicit and purposive. This process intertwines her life and thought with the lives of others.

---

[16] In the modified form the child hid a doll so as to take account of the viewpoint of a policeman doll.

[17] Donaldson, *Children's Minds*, 24.

[18] Some things that happen are captured by ascriptions (including mental ascriptions) to self and others.

4.5. The Active Nature of Cognitive Development

Notice that the picture which is emerging is that of an active cognitive subject accumulating and organizing techniques which enable him to extract and use information from the world. The child begins to represent the world by taking the action patterns he has evolved and the symbols (marking conceptual abilities) which mark them and distilling a conceptual understanding of what goes on around him. Sometimes he makes the wrong sorts of inferences about how things work because he puts concepts together wrongly in seeking to extend his range of competence with them. Piaget takes this to indicate the lack of certain cognitive functions such as identity, reversibility, and conservation, but we should recall that any learning process involves making mistakes. The child, in fact, needs to make certain mistakes because that is how the rules governing concept-use are tested and their range of applicability determined. In this way the child begins to relate regularities in what happens to regularities in concept-use. (It is, of course, likely that in learning about rule-governed patterns of activity, many of which are closely related to one another, there would be some definable and relatively frequent types of mistake made by most children.)

Once the child is confident about the relations between concepts and situations, there is room for creativity. Just as in his play he puts simple components together to make something complex, so in thought he puts concepts together in new ways. Imitative games (functional play, like pretending to go to the shops, putting dolls to bed, digging the garden, etc.), in which adult activity is just copied, are superseded when novel situations are imagined and explored. This allows the child to elaborate the structure of his thought and explore the potential of the conceptual system into which he is being initiated by moving from fact to counterfactual and then back again and noting matches and mismatches. (Notice that such trains of thought require mental abilities which are not tied to the immediate context.)

Piaget explains this growing expertise in terms of the maturation of various logico-mathematical "structures" which regulate thought. He claims that each structure involves a number of functions which operate on sensory input to provide data for action and adaptation. For instance, the input might be visual and the function might subsume an apparent change (in raw percepts) under a rule or general covering principle such as 'conservation' (e.g. of mass or number). But the epistemology implicit in this picture is suspect as the child is using shared symbols rather than developing a world picture from internal states. On the present view, the normative constraints which tie thought to the world of things do not operate on private events but adapt the use of marks or signs to what is happening in the environment. And here we can recall Wittgenstein's contention that ⟨same⟩ and related concepts need to be learnt: "The use of the word 'rule' and the use of the word 'same' are interwoven" (*PI* I. 225). It is not enough to state that two things (even mental states) are the same: one must also give the rule under which they count as being the same. No array is just *given* as being the same as another in some respect: we assimilate them when we judge that they fall under some concept. Such judgements allow a presentation to be thought of in a range of specifiable ways. Thus, in cognitive development, the child accumulates abilities to use a system of rules to make sense of or structure his activity in the world.

For Frege, each concept involves a determinate function which maps a term on to items in the world, and he and Piaget both regard mental life as a colloquy of operations going on in the subject. But I have argued that the way in which a concept or function maps mental activity on to the world is a result of the rules and practices in which the subject participates. Rules govern what counts as 'the same' and thereby shape the "functions of judgment" (Kant), which structure the content of thought. Thus concepts are not determined by inner states and cognitive processes, but by rules which shape the child's responses.[19] These normative regularities explain the truth-related nature of thought and the world-related nature of action, both of which are central in a philosophical study of the mind. Therefore we can agree with Piaget that the child does require a certain maturity in her information-processing to grasp concepts, but insist that the structure of the conceptual system depends on the rules that shape it by determining what counts as an instance of any given concept.

---

[19] The brain, in fact, changes its information-processing structure as a result of experience, which is pervaded by the rules and practices to which the individual is exposed.

A child's grasp of concepts develops as she embraces more and more of the prescriptive norms constitutive of that system of thought in which she is maturing. To grasp a concept is to link one's own activity to rules embedded in a linguistic and social structure which transcends a subject's own mental states. This implies that to elucidate the nature of concepts and the content of thought, we must appeal to the life, language, and activities of a human community, however small.[20]

4.6. Concepts and Causality

These facts reinforce the present view of the relationship between normativity and causality:

the relationship which comes to exist between concept and object in perception is not a causal relationship at all. A concept is not the sort of thing which can have a causal relation with an object . . . to have a concept of x is to know what it is for something to be an x. Correspondingly the growth of knowledge is not itself a causal matter (however much it may depend on causal factors of a physiological kind, i.e. on bodily conditions).[21]

An object can cause all kinds of effects, but it patently cannot cause it to be the case that it *counts* as being of this or that type. Therefore rules and the subject's ability to follow them, rather than causal impingements, are central in conceptual content, and Kantian distinctions between rational and causal transactions can begin to bite. If a concept is an ability to make judgements which obey certain rules and this is what one must develop in learning to think, then a model in which concepts are processes caused by environmental stimulation is not adequate. In grasping concepts the child learns to make and communicate reflective judgements about experience. This is not just a matter of twitching the same way as others, but rather involves an appreciation that there is a right way to react and requires the child to have an intention to conform to it (i.e. according to the conception of a law, however automatic obeying that becomes). In fact, when a child applies concepts in the presence of others it seems that he implicitly invites

[20] It is an open question whether an infantile Robinson could have a rich and fully conceptual thought life (see §4.III).
[21] Hamlyn, 'Human Learning', 209.

normative responses directed upon his reactions.[22] This process refines his patterns of response and potentiates the articulation and direction of future behaviour. Once certain of his own mastery of any rule, the child can dispense with the check provided by others although it always forms a background to his own activity (and thus, in many subtle and insistent ways, 'keeps him on the rails'). For human beings, the acquisition of concepts, and through them discursive, inferential, and hypothetical thought generally, occurs within a context of communication and interaction (even though we cannot rule out in advance the possibility of an individual's judgements being shaped by some other type of mind-independent, or, better, occurrent-disposition-independent, constraints upon his inclinations).[23]

Thus we can share Piaget's basic insight that the child is an individual who acts and explores his world on the basis of biological propensities. But the child develops thought through interactions with others. By means of the language he shares with them he learns to use rule-governed resources (with more and more skill) to deal with the world. For this reason, concepts cannot be understood solely in terms of the "structures" and "operations" within the mind, but rather involve public rules which a child learns to follow.

4.7. Concepts, Detachment, and Imagination

The present account is relevant to imagination because it explains in part the rich projectibility of human thought.

In mastering a concept, a human child acquires the ability to suspend her immediate inclination to react to something. This allows her to construct a response in which her conceptual abilities displace or transform her natural reactions to what confronts her. She tries various strategies, as it were, and selects a way of responding from resources provided within the conceptual system. Rarely, in real life, does one need to do this, but the possibility of so doing is implicit within experiencing things as being thus and so. Concepts, in effect, provide the subject with a potential detachment from an immediate response to context and with a consequent flexibility of thought and action. This results in a range of diverse possibilities of conception and intention.

---

[22] This is implicit in Vygotsky's finding that activity-related speech has a 'social' function.   [23] See §4.III.

This also explains several features of human thought. First, it enables the subject to discover ramifying and recurring themes in experience and make comparisons which illuminate various aspects of any presentation. This is evident when we compare the reactions of an aesthete and a philistine to the same work of art, or indeed those of a tourist and a sailor as they observe a skyscape.

Second, concept mastery implicitly brings multiple perspectives to bear on the subject's experience because others impart the rules governing understanding and meaning in situations which they view from their own diverse perspectives. Thus, in applying a concept, one does not see the item in question as $\langle x$ for me$\rangle$, but as an x which is publicly accessible. To see it thus implies both communicability of the subject's responses and convergence in the ways that co-linguistic thinkers make sense of the world.

Third, because a concept draws on links to items not present and perspectives not one's own, there is an essential detachability of human thought from immanent conditions. A human being can use her conceptual system to create conceptions which illuminate a present situation but also to create conceptions which fit neither the present nor indeed any perceived situation. A person can imagine things, often fantastic things, and elaborate her thoughts beyond the daily round for any purpose she chooses. She may do this just for the fun of it, or perhaps to see familiar things in a new way, or even to cast light on her life so as to integrate it according to a novel, perhaps inchoate, conception. All of these possibilities are closely related to features which are essential to the mastery of concepts, namely the ability to detach from one's present experience and see it in terms of a powerful and structured repertoire of meanings. Where such abilities are manifest in an individual it is no wonder that she is ascribed a quality of experience quite unlike that of creatures which have no grasp of concepts. To the former, one could say, belongs the kingdom of fantasy (perhaps even the kingdom of heaven).

4.8. Summary

On the present view, a child conceives of himself as a person among other persons who stimulate and react to his own activity. He refines his own thought by using terms he shares with other people and so learns to see the world in the enriched way that concepts make available. Conceptual thought draws on natural human capacities and activities and transforms them by the rules operative in a realm of public rule-governed practices and shared meaning.

II. COGNITIVE SYSTEMS

The view that children structure their cognitive activity by making use of the signs that figure in the practices of those around them and internalizing the rules that govern the use of those signs is consistent with current work in cognitive science.

The brain is a highly selective information processor; it is constantly weighing inputs according to their relevance to ongoing activity and goal-state specifications influenced by emotional and motivational systems. My brief survey of cognitive development has favoured the view that the activity of adults and interactions with adults plays a major role in priming the selective structures that deal with the information available to a developing human being. It is also evident that the shape that the system adopts during development forms the basis of adult thought. But when taken together with the earlier discussion of rules and concepts this implies that thought is not related in any simple way to the environment, but rather is structured in terms of the techniques of directed attention and control of responses that are imparted by those thinkers with whom the subject habitually interacts.

If this is so, an understanding of the causal entities in the world and a detailed understanding of the entities in the brain may well not fit together without an appreciation of how the brain is attuned to certain things in the world by the activity of human beings. The concept of "attunement" is derived from the work of J. J. Gibson, who claimed that perceptual learning is a process whereby the brain forms processing networks or structures which are attuned to significant features of the environment. These make joint use of the causal impact of the environment on the organism and the feedback from effects caused on the environment by the prior activity of the organism. This is a radical departure from the view that the organism is a spectator who attempts to construct a theoretical or detached conception of reality.[24]

---

[24] The notion of attunement I learnt from Ulrich Neisser, who had distilled it from the writings of Gibson and developed it into a dynamic view of perception and cognition which takes account of the interactions between organism and context. See e.g. Neisser's *Cognition and Reality* (San Francisco, Calif., 1976).

4.9. *Representations as Information in a Processing Network*

In many developed organisms which make use of information-processing networks, simple stimulus–response (S–R) links are insufficient to explain behaviour. In such organisms we must posit a representation of the world which can be used in a variety of ways to guide behaviour in different situations. This means that there are, in one sense, structures in cognition which selectively process complex stimulus configurations that figure in behavioural control by tracking or being attuned to actual items in the world. It is not always necessary to posit these where organisms interact with objects. For instance, the information that there is a moving black object subtending 5° on the retina and moving across the retinal field might trigger fly-catching responses in the frog. If so, one could say that there is a representation of the fly in the frog's brain which tells the frog to respond by tongue extrusion, snapping, or whatever; but this description is much too rich. What we should say, strictly speaking, is that the stimulus configuration described triggers a motor pathway in the frog's brain (which perhaps also requires potentiation by food deprivation—monitored by glucostats or something similar) and causes the tongue response that catches the fly (the cerebellum of the frog would actually do the targeting to ensure a hit). We can get by without invoking a representation of the fly if a surveyable set of S–R linkages will explain the behaviour.

In higher animals which exhibit marked flexibility of response to the same stimulus configuration, we can only explain behaviour by invoking representations of objects. For instance, consider a monkey who, for the first time, uses a stick to retrieve a banana outside his cage and beyond his reach. We cannot write this off as a simple S–R association because crucial elements in the cognitive process—namely the stick, the distance of the banana from the cage, and the use of the stick as a tool—must be combined to produce the behaviour. And where objects and their relations must be invoked to explain behaviour we cannot avoid appealing to mental representations as part of the story.

Our appeal to representations provides an explanatory framework that outstrips networks of S–R links because the representation of the object is only there to supply what is lacking in the S–R model. We get flexibility of response at the expense of surveyable mechanistic connections between antecedents and results. A representation-based (therefore flexible) response to an aspect of the environment influences the configuration of an organism's behaviour on a variety of occasions and is, *ex hypothesi*, diversely connected to patterns of information-use. What is more, such representations have, in human beings, certain functional features:

1. they are flexible in their effects and embedded in or meshed with the activity of the organism;
2. they may not be reducible to simple features;
3. they are potentially communicable; and
4. they are robust in the face of input variations.

The first feature reasserts the link between representations and flexibility of response. It also reflects the fact that "Perception is an active process of gathering information in order to do something."[25] The second tells against the idea that all perception is built from a set of canonical or basic elements which have their own informational roles. The third feature links representations to shared practices and the signs which are characteristic of them. The fourth feature, like the second, creates problems for systems which assemble atomic informational elements into formal specifications of higher-order stimuli. In fact, human cognition seems to deal with informational items according to ramifying and multi-dimensional sets of likenesses to other stimulus configurations.

These features are well accommodated by a promising new approach to human information-processing.

4.10. Information Networks

Recent advances in artificial intelligence have focused on information-processing networks.[26] Human subjects often use multiple simultaneous constraints to optimize performance on cognitive tasks:

Intuitively, these tasks seem to require mechanisms in which each aspect of the information in the situation can act on other aspects, simultaneously influencing other aspects and being influenced by them. . . . Parallel

---

[25] J. Z. Young, *Philosophy and the Brain* (Oxford, 1987).
[26] I have discussed this more fully in 'Representations and Cognitive Science', *Inquiry*, 32 (1989), 261–76.

Distributed Processing (PDP) models . . . assume that information processing takes place through the interactions of a large number of simple
processing elements called units, each sending excitatory and inhibitory
signals to other units.[27]

A succinct outline of such systems is as follows:

There are eight major aspects of a parallel distributed processing model:

* A set of processing units
* A state of activation
* An output function for each unit
* A pattern of connectivity among units
* A propagation rule for propagating patterns of [activity] through the
  network . . .
* An activation rule for combining the units impinging on a unit with
  the current state of that unit to produce a new level of activation for
  the unit
* A learning rule whereby patterns of connectivity are modified by
  experience
* An environment within which the system must operate.[28]

PDP models therefore have a number of important attractions:

1. They have a physiological flavour:

The brain consists of a large number of highly interconnected elements
which apparently send very simple excitatory and inhibitory messages to
each other and update their excitations on the basis of those simple
messages.[29]

2. They are true to the time-scale of human cognition:

biological hardware is just too sluggish for sequential models . . . to provide a plausible account, at least of the microstructure of human thought.
And the time limitation only gets worse, not better, when sequential
mechanisms try to take large numbers of constraints into account. . . . Yet
people get faster, not slower, when they are able to exploit additional
constraints.[30]

3. They explain perceptual completion:

a model describing the role of familiarity in perception based on excitatory
and inhibitory interactions among units . . . provide[s] a very close account of the results of a large number of experiments.[31]

[27] D. E. Rumelhart and J. L. McClelland, *Parallel Distributed Processing: Explorations in the Microstructure of Cognition*, i (Cambridge, Mass., 1986), 10.
  [28] Ibid. 46.   [29] Ibid. 10.   [30] Ibid. 12.   [31] Ibid. 20.

Both PDP and human cognition complete corrupted, degraded, or novel patterns in terms of more familiar ones. This is clearly linked to the fact that cognition operates in an environment in which it is attuned to significant items which may be presented in a variety of ways.

4. Human memory has a high level of flexible and optimizing content addressability which is difficult to simulate in formal search and indexing schemes:

> But suppose that we imagine that each memory is represented by a unit which has mutually excitatory interactions with units standing for each of its properties. Then, whenever any property of the memory became active, the memory would tend to be activated. . . . Though it would not be immune to errors, it would not be devastated by an error in the probe if the remaining properties specified the correct memory.[32]

This feature explains a number of properties of human cognition. Degraded information can access cognitive systems via the strategy of default assignments whereby an array will be dealt with as if it satisfies a certain specification provided that it is close enough to doing so. These systems also make spontaneous generalizations by linking information similar to or resembling that activated by a canonical input. Such facts argue against cognitive structures defined formally in terms of configurations of necessary and sufficient conditions.

Two features correlate particularly well with findings in neuroscience. First, the PDP system has modifiable strengths of informational connection between units, and, second, it can use parallel clues to disambiguate patterns in various ways. The first recalls what we know about synaptic connections in neuronal assemblies. The second implies that, as well as salient or common patterns of stimuli becoming effective as inputs, certain patterns may be picked out from multiply ambiguous arrays by using collateral input which can either inhibit or enhance the impact of the input pattern. This is reminiscent of human learning, where, as I have noted, a child is sensitively attuned to the responses of conspecifics in his attempts to make sense of the world. The environment consists of arrays which confusingly share many features rather than neatly falling into definite patterns. In the midst of this "computationally

---

[32] Ibid. 26.

explosive" ambiguity, "cues" or "correlated teaching inputs' allow the system to make discriminations which would otherwise elude it.[33]

I have stressed the role of conspecifics in imparting rule-governed responses to the developing thinker. The rules teaching us what counts as instancing a certain concept are intersubjective in that they are shared by those who grasp the concept and they are conveyed in human interactions. In order for a subject to learn to use concepts, these rules must shape the conceptual system of that subject. We shall return to this point in due course, but the role of correlated teaching inputs recalls Wittgenstein's remark: "Here the physiological is a symbol of the logical" (*PI* 210e). PDP thus represents a hopeful model for the nature of human cognition and meshes well with facts about brain function.

4.11. *The Shape of Brain Processing Networks*

How does the brain take on its mature processing shape? The neurones in the brain may be imbued with all their connections from birth (as in a PDP system the nodes and connections may be hardwired). But synaptic connections change their properties as a result of experience so that some connections become more and some less effective. The changes allow for selectivity of attention and response tuned to the multiple interacting constraints determining patterns significant in the informational history of the system. Thus the neuronal networks transmit information in ways that reflect both innate propensities and experience and weight the inputs so that incoming information can be used to direct the overall activity of the individual optimally in the light of adaptive learning.

A subject encounters many different permutations and combinations of simple receptor-specific stimuli (e.g. red light falling on a spot on the retina, a light touch on the skin, an aliquot of chemical interacting with the nasal mucosa, or a sound frequency and intensity triggering a cochlear receptor). In order to group and associate these stimuli in ways that reflect significant patterns of co-presentation, the system must select those which are significant.

[33] Ibid. 184 ff.

The selection could be by a retroactive effect from events reflecting need or drive satisfaction, but probably also depends on the complex and pervasive role of other subjects in human learning. The capacities of PDP systems, and the fact that human infants are attuned to the environment by the responses of others who share that environment, suggest that human neural processing takes on its shape by using collateral information furnished by the activity of those others. The infant, we could say, develops classifications and differential responses to stimuli on the basis of the responses of other human beings around it.

4.12. Representations and Information

To summarize: The brain is a system which controls the activity of the organism in the light of information arriving through the sensory systems and sorted by a network of structured processing assemblies. These have informational 'shape' according to motivational effects and the activity of conspecifics which direct the attention and reactions of the individual.[34] Flexibility of information-use depends on representations of the items concerned.

We need to be clear what does and does not follow from this. First, the representation has an *explanatory* role in the causal structure controlling the activity of the organism. It is a 'node' which makes cognitive explanations surveyable and thus can be expected to figure in any model of the cognitive system of the organism as a focus upon which feature detectors will converge and from which effects on other fragments of the system can usefully be traced. Second, the nature of the effect on behaviour is *causal* (even if multiple interactive constraints introduce such indeterminacy of causal role that the effects of activation of the posited explanatory node are not surveyable in a mechanistic way). The result of a processing activity is *evoked* and not inferential or evaluative. Therefore terms like 'groundedness' and 'justification' have no role as the analysis is in terms of causal power or efficacy in producing activation in other parts of the system.

By contrast, a *conceptual* representation obeys certain rules. A

---

[34] I have discussed this in 'Perception and Neuroscience', *British Journal of Philosophy of Science*, 40 (1989), 83–103.

conceptual representation must be based on what *counts* as instancing the concept in question. This is, of course, a prescriptively normative requirement and cannot be reduced to a question about what output the system is disposed to produce under certain input conditions. The output and the dispositions producing it must be compared to what it *should* produce (which is essentially a different matter) to make sense of the normative notions like accuracy or veridicality that many cognitive scientists neglect.

4.13. Normativity and Intentionality

A processing account reveals what the organism is inclined to do and explains its performance in a range of trials but tells us neither what conception that performance answers to nor what rules govern it. These rules, based, as I have noted, in interpersonal practices, show how a certain form of representation or sign can introduce a structure into one's activity. The actual output of the system must exhibit that structure for the rule to be ascribed so that the individual *counts* as forming the representation in question.

The other feature which is important in conceptual activity is the active nature of the mind in thought and judgement.[35] A rule not only constitutes a standard to which the performance does conform, but also sets a standard to which the subject intends to conform whether he is gathering information or using it to guide his activity. The subject assembles and manipulates information according to recognized normative constraints. This contrasts with information detectors, such as cameras, and mere responders. The rules which determine mental content or thoughts have a more complex nature in that to grasp a concept a subject responds consistently to certain inputs, but also represents to himself the fact that there is a way of going right or wrong in that response.

The child masters concepts when she recognizes that there is a rule to be satisfied, intends to do so, and can produce the requisite performance. (Perhaps children are tentative in the manifestation of conceptual and linguistic abilities because, unlike the spontaneous and ungoverned activity which just comes spilling out of them, conceptual activity has criteria of success or failure as part

---

[35] Outlined in Ch. 1.

of its nature.) This construal finds considerable support from neuroscience.

The cerebral cortex is the most complex and elaborate processing array in the human brain. It exerts the higher control that transforms a range of primitive behaviours into the complex conceptual behaviour of an adult, as shown, for example, in language-use. Because the cortical processing systems which detect significant stimulus patterns and then track them weave objects into action in a myriad different ways, we speak of the brain representing the world. But if the 'upstream' parts of cerebral systems are destroyed, disconnected or dysfunctioning 'release phenomena' occur: primitive response tendencies are released and exhibited regardless of their suitability to current activity. This happens, for instance, in fluent dysphasia, where the patient talks a great deal but with almost no relation to his current situation. Here the controlling functions which peg linguistic output to context and rule-governed responses to conditions are plainly unhinged. A further revealing set of phenomena is found in frontal lobe syndrome, where patterns of behaviour are exhibited which do not conform to social norms or demonstrate normal human sensitivity to context and interpersonal relations. These findings illustrate the fact that the 'higher' centres regulate and direct more primitive patterns of activity and reactivity.

This meshes with idea that conceptual development involves an extensive repertoire of rules which govern responses and impose constraints upon them in the light of experience. It also supports the contention that action involves the refinement and direction of activity by one's conceptual system (and thus that the view of action as primarily pushed or moved from within is mistaken).

The intentionality (in both senses) of mental states is illuminated by the fact that brain activity is essentially attuned to objects, features of the world, and the practices where control systems have taken shape. Thus intentionality (as object-directedness) is seen in the fact that the processing system, as I have noted, takes shape as a result of the way that intersubjectively identified items are picked out or 'presented' to it. Intentionality (as reason-governed activity) reflects the widespread articulation of brain excitation patterns through systems monitoring ongoing stimulation (related to perception), regulating inner homeostatic and drive states (related to needs, desires, pro-attitudes), setting reactive tone (related to emotion, mood), drawing on past experience (related to memory), and enabling the use of information detached from present occurrent stimulation (related to imagination, expectation, counterfactual reasoning, and conjecture). Both readings show the conceptual system exploiting and modifying natural propensities made available within brain function. Reflection upon aspects of one's mental life (whether natural or abstract), directed attention, and guidance of behaviour add up to being rational and fully conscious of what is in and around one. This activity depends on the processing capacities of the cortex.[36] Therefore the explanation of human behaviour goes beyond the antecedent states causing bodily movements and appeals to the structure of rules and practices that has moulded the system evincing that activity.

4.14. Epistemology and Cognitive Science

Epistemology and philosophy of mind use the notion of representation quite differently from cognitive science and are only misleadingly conflated with it. Representation in epistemology relates to interpersonal activity, culture, and meaning, and depends on a myriad of interwoven practices in which terms are used by thinkers to articulate their activity. But the cognitive scientist's use of 'representation' is linked to the causal properties of processing networks and states of excitation in information systems which, necessarily, concern only one organism and what it does in certain conditions. Such a study has no conception of how the individual *should* react nor of the nature of this 'should'. Thus, even if cognitive neuroscience is the only way to understand the mechanisms involved in thinking, discourse about human mental activity is not about goings-on in an inner realm of causal representational states.

III. ROBINSON JUNIOR

The strong link which has been forged between language and thought calls for one or two remarks about a junior Robinson Crusoe (and these are extendable in part to animal thought).

[36] On this see my 'Consciousness and Brain Function', *Philosophical Psychology*, 1(3) (1988), 327–41.

The implausible conclusion to be avoided is that Robinson Junior (Rj) cannot think until he talks, and therefore, before Friday comes along, does not form representational thoughts. Rj clearly can develop rules which govern his own responses so as to yield a set of techniques learnable by any other suitably equipped interlocutor. The structure and thus the generalizability of his conceptual scheme may, however, be quite impoverished because he is deprived of interpersonal perspectives and commentary on his own acts and encounters. Given the holism in human thought, it is implausible to suggest that he has the same concepts as us because, although his responses may be similar to ours over a certain range of cases, they lack the detailed structure given by language. In the cases of Rj, the pre-linguistic child, and, more remotely, animals, we can say that they have thoughts and make inferences in virtue of the fact that their activity is similar to that comprising the practices on which our conceptual structure is built. But our concepts are developed in an intersubjective milieu:

> The development of human knowledge may be represented as an en-largement of experience, an enlargement of the individual's intellectual environment. (The part played in this by social factors is obvious.) The things which are the individual's immediate and original concern are particular and concrete. As experience is widened and enlarged, as too it becomes more interpersonal, so it must inevitably become more general and abstract.[37]

The perspectives of other thinkers confer both richness and objectivity on an individual's experience. This is essential to general and abstract thought and also to the evaluation of one's current experience against some wider conception. The role for general and abstract thought in many of our sortal concepts (and thus our fundamental ideas of certain objects) therefore has profound implications for the characterization of Rj's thought content. Because he lacks the detailed enunciation of content provided by language, we cannot justify a full range and content of mental ascriptions in the case of Rj, the pre-linguistic child, or an a-linguistic creature.

[37] Hamlyn, 'Human Learning', 211.

5

Representations

REPRESENTATIONS represent things other than themselves and are therefore intentional in the sense of being *of* this or that. Because mental representations have content which is related to belief, intention, thought, and action, they are also intentional in the sense of being purposive.[1] An understanding of both readings of 'intentional' emerges from the present account of concepts. This has linked thought content to public practices where rules articulate the activity of thinkers. It allows us to explore the fact that a thinker not only represents things to others, but also represents things to herself and uses those representations to organize her activity.

5.1. Representations and Normativity

Human thoughts have contents which can be spelt out in propositional form and (*inter alia*) represent the things we encounter. 'Contents' such as ⟨this house is red⟩ rest on the thinker's grasp of concepts such as ⟨house⟩ and ⟨red⟩. An analysis of thought should therefore reveal how the contents of our thoughts can rest on properties of the thinker and yet be about things in the world. These (worldly) things could not, in any literal sense, be 'in the head', but thinking is, in some cases, private and, for instance, can go on while one is pretending to be asleep. Indeed, thoughts seem to be prime examples of things that go on 'inside' one. Therefore the contents of thoughts would seem to be on the proximal side of a thinker's engagement with the public world, and it is both natural and plausible to say that our concepts get organized into *mental representations* of things in the world.

---

[1] J. Haldane ('Naturalism and the Problem of Intentionality', *Inquiry*, 32 (1989), 305–22) refers to these two senses as "intensionality" and "intentionality" respectively.

Thoughts (like concepts and the meanings of linguistic expressions) have normative aspects. For instance, the thought ⟨that frog is green⟩ is based on the grasp of the concepts ⟨frog⟩ and ⟨green⟩, and I should only think ⟨that frog is green⟩ if the frog I am demonstratively identifying *is* green. I have already discussed the rules which govern concepts, individuate thoughts, link them to objects, and determine how they ought to function in reasoning. Because rules govern both reasoning and observations, both can go right or wrong. Thus there is something wrong with ⟨that cat is black, therefore it is an artefact⟩ absent supporting premises. With thoughts like ⟨green ideas sleep furiously⟩ or ⟨surd elephants sublime in twenty-three⟩ one can say neither what would make them true nor how they would figure in a train of reasoning, and thus they are comprehensively defective and lack content.

The dual dependence on inferential structure and application to the world can be further illustrated if we imagine interviewing a patient with a certain kind of brain damage:

INTERVIEWER. Can you see the green block?
PATIENT. Yes, the red one, I can see it.
I. No, the block, the green one.
P. Oh, the block.
I. Yes. What colour is it?
P. Red.
I. No, it isn't: it is green.
P. Oh, you mean green; yes, that's it.
I. What is?
P. Well, just as you said, the red ball is green.

We cannot get hold of the thought of this patient. And he is no better off himself because thoughts can neither be ascribed nor self-ascribed in the face of such incoherence. But thought ascriptions also fail if canons relating terms to the world are not respected. Thus there is something wrong with 'Pass me that yellow book, please' if there is only one book on the table and it is blue. Or consider 'Oh look, there is Notre Dame. I love its imaginative oriental feel'. Now, has this person seen Sacre Cœur and confused the name, or has he really seen Notre Dame and confused the description? Until we discover just which rules relating thoughts to the world and each other he is misusing we do not know what he thinks.

5.2. Representations and Intentionality

People represent things in all kinds of ways. But before we examine the use of 'representation' in the analysis of thought we ought to be clear about the more straightforward uses. For instance, I might set up and manipulate two matchboxes so as to represent what happened in a car crash either for interpersonal or intrapersonal uses. (I can convey to you what happened in a car accident by using matchboxes or I could use them to sort it out for my own information.) To do this the matchboxes would have to be linked to the cars in some way, probably by words such as 'Let this matchbox be the Porsche'. The need for a link points to a general feature of representation and gives us one reading of their *intentionality*.[2] Searle remarks: "mental states are directed at, or about, or refer to, or are of objects and states of affairs in the world other than themselves".[3] But Searle's comment has let far too much into the picture all at once. It has suggested that there are "mental states" which, in some sense, have a separate existence from the things they represent. I have resisted this view. We must therefore retreat to some weaker claim like 'Thinking is about things other than the acts which constitute that thinking' or 'Acts of thought cannot fully be captured by descriptions confined to the activity comprising them'. This further strengthens the claim that "narrow" or "inward-looking" views of the content of thought are, at the very least, problematic (*TEC* 52).

First, thoughts are often about something out in the world and thus their specifications transcend what is 'inside' the thinker. This applies to perception (which requires an account relating sense experience to objects in the real world) and also to action (where an adequate analysis must tell us how intentions are defined in terms of operations on external objects and trains of events). Here Locke, Berkeley, and Hume, and the modern methodological solipsist, are all in a similar position. They accept that our thoughts comprise 'proximal states' and on that basis try to provide the subject with an understanding of 'external' objects, states, and events. On this view, operations upon proximal states must give a thinker both what he needs to build a workable picture of the

---

[2] On another reading, the intentionality of content focuses on reasoning and purposive activity.   [3] J. Searle, *Minds, Brains and Science* (London, 1984), 16.

external world and grounds on which to assess the objectivity of any given part of that picture.

Second, an adequate understanding of thought should acknowledge that the contents of experience obey constraints independently of the subject's tendency to respond. I have argued that one's own inclination to respond thus and so answers to a standard of right judgement. This normative feature secures a definite role for any element of thought in inference, understanding, and action. In fact, any mental ascription, even when the subject does not describe or report on a state of affairs, can be assessed for whether it *counts* as, say, ⟨the intention to *y*⟩ or ⟨the desire for *z*⟩ and thus has normative properties. But if there is a standard against which the subject's response or disposition to respond is assessed, then 'states' of the subject which dispose him to act thus and so are not the whole story.

Third, *de re* thoughts (which concern a given particular essentially and the content of which cannot be specified without appeal to that particular) present a challenge to methodological solipsism (and universalist theories of content in general). Some argue that such thoughts are of crucial importance for our orientation in the world and even that they are basic in the representational structure of thought.[4] A weaker but still considerable claim is that they are essential for any conception of an objective order of things. In any event, the nature of *de re* thought should be part of a theory of content, and, prima facie, a range of proximal states with descriptive or universal contents would not accommodate them.[5]

We can pursue Searle's reading of intentionality by returning to the relation between thought and language.

5.3. The Form of Thoughts

Thoughts can be expressed in language some if not all of the time. If the essentials of a well-formed thought can be captured by some expression or expressions in the natural language of the thinker,

---

[4] John Campbell argues that the individuation of content is crucially linked to singular thought (demonstrative or recognitional) and that our concept of a world as distinct from our perceptions of it rests on such a foundation. He thus develops Kant's claim that inner representation in general depends on the outer. The general approach follows Strawson's attempt to disclose the basic features of the conceptual system which characterizes human knowledge.

[5] The arguments against methodological solipsism are in Chs. 1 and 7.

then it is clear that such thoughts must be able to be grasped by more than one thinker.[6] Frege also claims that there is a sense in which a thought has an invariant relation to truth in a way that the conscious states of a given thinker never can. This claim rests on three other claims: (1) a central and important range of thoughts must somehow aim at truth; (2) it is not possible to develop an adequate theory of truth which can vary according to who apprehends it; and (3) thinkers can communicate their thoughts to one another without being hampered by systematic ambiguity of content. For the moment I shall accept all of these claims.

But also a thought and its elements must be things that a thinker can make use of. A thinker is able to attend to a thought, understand, express, assent to, or question it, request that it be realized, and so on. These possibilities should be part of our account of thought and have led Fodor to a theory of representation which contrasts sharply with that in the present study.

5.4. Fodor's Theory

Frege's claim that a thought is linked to and expressed in natural language but logically distinct from the cognitive act in which it is grasped has inspired, *inter alia*, the view that mental representations are "symbols in the 'language of thought' ".[7] Fodor posits that there are, within the brain of any given thinker, structured entities, each of which is causally related to the world in some way so as to secure its referential role and structurally related to other entities so as to realize the function of the corresponding element of thought. The causal role of any representation is given by its propositional syntax or the structure and relations of constituent "symbol tokens" that make it up:

You connect the causal properties of a symbol with its semantic properties via its syntax. The syntax of a symbol is one of its second-order physical properties. To a first approximation, we can think of its syntactic structure as an abstract feature of its (geometric or acoustic) shape. Because . . . syntax reduces to shape, and because the shape of a symbol is a potential

---

[6] I shall take this case—a well-formed thought expressed in a natural language— as a paradigm to provide us with an analysis which can then be modified in the light of the possibility of non-linguistic thought.

[7] J. Fodor, 'Fodor's Guide to Mental Representation', *Mind*, 94 (1985), 76–100.

determinant of its causal role, it is fairly easy . . . to imagine symbol tokens interacting causally in virtue of their syntactic structures. The syntax of a symbol might determine the causes and effects of its tokenings in much the way that the geometry of a key determines which locks it will open.[8]

Intersubjectivity of thought content is secured as follows:

1. thought elements are causally related to items outside the brain; and
2. representations are elements of a language of thought shared by competent co-linguistic thinkers.

Thinking a thought, on this view, involves being in a relation to a (complex, structured) token of mental language (which, perhaps through perceptual experience, has become causally linked to the world). This token has a causal role in transactions between psychological states on the basis of its syntactical structure. Fodor argues that the generative abilities ("productivity and constituency") of language-users show that we need to take account of the structure of thought, and therefore that there must be token representations comprising the senses of subsentential expressions: "The collection of states of mind is productive: for example, the thoughts that one actually entertains in the course of a mental life comprise a relatively unsystematic subset drawn from a larger variety of thoughts that one could have entertained had an occasion for them arisen."[9] The role of mental representations as constitutive relata in propositional attitudes (PAs) is derived from a conception of the way that the mind must work: "There must be mental symbols because, in a nutshell, only symbols have syntax, and our best available theory of mental processes—indeed the only available theory of mental processes that isn't known to be false— needs the picture of the mind as a syntax-driven machine."[10] (Note that this "only available theory" of the mind—as a syntax-driven machine—assumes that mental ascriptions denote the operations of a biological computer using formal symbols. But this assumption, and thus the conception of mind which it supports, is questionable.[11])

---

[8] Ibid. 93.   [9] Ibid. 89.

[10] Ibid. 94. Recall, in passing, that this contention is under serious threat from developments in cognitive neuroscience discussed in the preceding chapter.

[11] This is suggested in §4.II but argued at length in my 'Representations and Cognitive Science', *Inquiry*, 32 (1989), 261–76.

5.5. Semantics

Fodor's account has consistently struggled with semantics:

to summarize: the syntactic theory of mental operations promises a reductive account of the intelligence of thought. We can now imagine—though, to be sure, only dimly and in a glass darkly—a psychology which exhibits quite complex cognitive processes as being constructed from elementary manipulations of symbols. . . . But a theory of intelligence of thought does not, in and of itself, constitute a theory of intentionality. . . . of the semanticity of mental representations we have, as things now stand, no adequate account.[12]

Here one must observe that intelligence seems fairly vacuous if it is not *about* anything. And if content does pervade structure, the "semanticity" and syntax or structure of thought may be analytically inseparable.[13] Indeed, this is suggested by several cognitive psychologists who stress the need for "ecological validity" in cognitive science.[14] Allport remarks (in a piece revealingly entitled 'Patterns and Actions: Cognitive Mechanisms Are Content Specific'): "overwhelming evidence has accumulated for the existence of specialised neurones responding selectively to particular (quite often abstract) invariant properties of the sensory input as a major design feature of the central nervous system of man and other animals".[15] He argues for the idea that cognitive structures are specific to their semantic content and that this determines their function within the system. Neisser, in *Cognition and Reality*, remarks that many cognitive structures are best thought of as "embedded schemata that interact with their environment".[16] Therefore philosophical worries about an analytic dualism of syntax and semantics in mental content are in tune with contemporary cognitive psychology.

Fodor has recently attempted to fill this lacuna with a causal theory of content which predicates causal links on the covariance of the semantic value of a term with the things which instance

---

[12] Fodor, 'Fodor's Guide to Mental Representation', 98–9; he has subsequently helped himself to the causal relations suggested (*Psychosemantics* (Cambridge, Mass.: MIT Press, 1987)).

[13] Chs. 3 and 5 and my 'Tacit Semantics' (*Philosophical Investigations*, 11 (1988), 1–12) argue that this is so and claim that the categories which form part of our intuitive understanding of grammatical structure are semantically based.

[14] G. Claxton, *Cognitive Psychology: New Directions* (London: Routledge & Kegan Paul, 1980), ch. 1.   [15] In Claxton (ed.), *Cognitive Psychology*, 28.

[16] U. Neisser, *Cognition and Reality* (San Francisco, Calif., 1976), 24.

whatever it is that that term denotes: "what makes 'star' mean *star* is *that* the two are connected not *how* the two are connected".[17] He attempts to secure semantics by causal relations relativized to the normal, reliable referent of a given term, but does not quite explain how the selective definition of the referential relation to just the right conditions is secured. One can only say that this is a remarkably weak claim on which to base a theory of content and that we await some account of the causal relation that connects 'star' with stars in the world in the right kind of way to yield the content implicit in the concept ⟨star⟩. In view of the arguments already offered, we could go further and say "the cognitive relation, being one of reference mediated by conceptual (and phenomenological) content is clearly non-extensional".[18]

· There is, however, another worry about Fodor's theory in that the idea of a relation between a subject and a token of "mentalese" is confused.[19] Persons have various relationships—they relate, intentionally, to the objects about which they think and they relate to other thinkers via language, systems of communication, and everyday exchanges. In each there is a clearly identifiable relation and one relatum is an identifiable and conscious agent. But the posited relation between a thinker and a token of propositional content within his own informational system ushers a metaphor on to the stage and allows it to run amok. It is, in fact, wholly misconceived. A subject can interact with distinct relata in the intentional ways suggested above and in other ways: he can manipulate them, they can be specified independently of him, and they can be the objects of his attention (and often the attention of others). Where such conditions hold, we know what it is for a thinker to be related to something. However, with functional entities in the head (à la Fodor) none of these conditions do hold. Because the entity is part of the thinker, he cannot be said to manipulate it, attend to it, or grasp it. All that can be said is that this entity, however it is individuated (perhaps as a disjunctively or mereologically specified set of events), has causal relations to the physical events at the periphery of a thinker's body and the physical

[17] Fodor, *Psychosemantics*, 126.
[18] Haldane, 'Naturalism and the Problem of Intentionality', 309.
[19] I shall leave the innateness hypothesis, the problem of development of conceptual competence, and the 'sentence-crunching' model of cognition largely untouched although they represent further weaknesses.

events elsewhere in his brain (taxonomized so as to fit the theory). But, although something of a causally regular (and possibly structured[20]) nature must go on as part of a subject's brain activity when she is thinking, there is no place within that description for the features of mental representations that we are trying to analyse. In fact, we have an unholy epistemic matrimony between two insights here (even between belief and brute, physical 'anti-belief'). One insight is that thought involves relations between a thinker and intentional objects and the other that processes in the brain, by regularities in their activity, enable one to think. The resulting model has people fiddling about with things in their brains (not just in neurosurgical operating theatres but in public places in broad daylight).

Therefore Fodor does not give us an account of representations which reveals how thoughts have normative features, involve intentional relations, and can be about things in the world. I believe that his failure can be attributed to the deeper problems with causal theories of content which I have discussed above.[21]

5.6. Footprints, Photographs, and Information

One persuasive argument for the causal theory is the footprint analogy. In one sense a footprint or a fossil contains information about affairs other than its present state and structure in virtue of its causal origin (SC 7). A photograph could be said to represent its subject for the same reason (HE). There is a clear and tempting thought here, in that if the creation of a structured state in a plastic causal medium (such as wet sand or a photographic film) could produce operations with the same properties as our thoughts about the world, then a bridge would be made between causality and rationality via (representational) content. Representational theories of mind (such as Fodor's) claim that causal transactions produce states in a system with intentional properties and thus the states and inner events concerned have representational content. According to this theory, content is to be elucidated in two ways: first, by relating the states to external events, and second, by

---

[20] But we should recall the caveats raised by connectionism for any realist construal of mental states as brain states.   [21] See esp. Chs. 1 and 4.

spelling out the structural relations between the states themselves. In fact, accounts of this type need not identify mental states with actual syntactically structured causal entities in the brain. A concept or an element of thought could be a function from a structured state on to items in the world which does not depend on linguistic syntax.[22] But all such theories must claim that a mental representation is a state resulting from causal transactions in the thinker. There is, however, more to mental representation than the creation of such states.

5.7. Thin and Thick Information

I have argued that an explanation of the conceptual form of experience falls into two parts:

1. a specification of what is involved in the mastery of a concept; and
2. an empirical understanding of how the capacities for thought might be realized in a biological organism.

My contention has been that the analysis of thought and its content essentially implicates the concept-using subject, who judges that what confronts him counts as being thus and so. I have argued that this is not just a matter of a conditional disposition to respond in a certain way but involves prescriptive norms, and that any account which neglects that fact must be regarded as deficient.

The normative aspects of thought content lead us to make a distinction between 'thin' and 'thick' information. The thin reading allows a formal, nomological–deductive or causal analysis of content. Thin information is present in many structured processes and is used in systems and information-processing theory: for example, retinal excitation patterns might be traced through the brain according to causal transitions they produce (although this fiendish task would involve a great deal of simplification). It is clear that there is no warrant for the use of terms like 'judge', 'grasp', 'understand', 'be aware of', or 'have an attitude to' in relation to thin information because the analysis is solely in terms of causal transactions between spatio-temporally specifiable states

---

[22] See e.g. G. Evans, 'Semantic Theory and Tacit Knowledge', in S. H. Holtzmann and C. M. Leich (eds.), *Wittgenstein: To Follow a Rule* (London, 1981); *SC* 214.

and events and has no place for normative features linked to judgement.[23]

By contrast, thick information is conceptual and is therefore essentially tied to reasons, inferences, understanding, perceiving, knowledge, belief, and meaning.[24] Because it has "a place in the logical space of reasons" it is at home in epistemology and intentional explanations. A reductive account of the possession of thick information would only implicate thin information and the non-intentional (perhaps causal or physical) concepts proper to it.

However, notice that the footprint and the photograph both contain thin information until a thinker takes them to be of something and derives thick information or knowledge about that something. The thinker must have some warrant for this judgement in terms of his reasons for believing that they contain the thick information concerned. Even if he does not understand the transaction in which the impression was made, he must be able to defend his judgement as well grounded (in this or 'nearby' worlds). Therefore thick information engages with "reflexivity . . . the possibility of belief, assessment, revision and other features associated with rational thought".[25]

Part of the intuitive appeal of the empiricist representational theory of mind (ERT) is due to the fact that certain things do contain information which is causally explained. For instance, the visual properties of a photograph closely resemble the world as we see it (which is, of course, different from the way that it is seen by a bat or any creature for whom movement and contextual cues play a necessary role in figure versus ground differentiation). To a human the photograph obviously represents a certain array, and apparently does so because it is caused in a certain way. What is less obvious but still true is that it only represents something as a result of being *taken* to show this or that. When a photo overtly demands a judgement as to whether it is veridical or misleading—in, say, a case of blackmail—the acts of judgement surface and betray their essential role. And this is equally true of the footprint. For instance, Robinson Crusoe might think:

[23] This also shows in the problems attendant on causal theories of knowledge (see O. Gjelsvik, 'Dretske on Knowledge and Content', *Synthese* (in press); §4.2 above).

[24] John McDowell, Lectures on the Subject and the World, Oxford, Trinity Term, 1986.

[25] Haldane, 'Naturalism and the Problem of Intentionality', 309.

1. that mark is a human footprint on wet sand (note the conceptual judgement involved);
2. a human being must have stepped there since last high tide;
3. there may be another human being on this island.

Thus a footprint or photograph does not convey thick or epistemic information just in virtue of its structure or causal relations; it does so only to a thinker who can derive thick information from what he sees in front of him (a crab, for instance, may not be as alarmed as Crusoe). Therefore both analogies have an undischarged analytic debt to judgement and give only spurious support to reductive accounts of mental content.

5.8. 'In the Head'

How do the manifest objects we think about figure in an understanding of what goes on 'in the head'?

If a child is using mathematical equations or words to work something out or express something then it is obvious that he is manipulating signs. But if he is doing the sums in his head or thinking his way through a verbal puzzle then there are no obvious or concrete signs that he manipulates, so whatever is going on is 'in his head'. In fact, even in the overt case, the mental properties which give the signs their life or meaning seem to outstrip those signs:

It seems that there are certain definite mental processes bound up with the working of language, processes through which alone language can function. I mean the processes of understanding and meaning. The signs of our language seem dead without these mental processes; and it might seem that the only function of the signs is to induce such processes, and that these are the things we ought really to be interested in. (*BBB* 3)

But, if Wittgenstein is right, how is it that *signs*:

1. have intentional and normative features;
2. figure in the contents of mental acts;[26]
3. mark the conceptual structure of mental contents;
4. allow the content of mental acts to be manifest?

---

[26] If there are such 'acts', given the semantic and categorial difficulties involved: G. P. Baker and P. M. S. Hacker, *Meaning and Understanding* (Oxford, 1983), 323 ff.

To answer this we must be clear about what should be said about thought being 'in the head'.

Recall that we need not describe the processes subserving thought (which are within the domain of cognitive science and neural theory). But we must explain how creatures in whom these processes occur can perform intentional acts with a definite meaning and thereby represent things in ways which are adequate or inadequate, accurate or mistaken. We could do that by linking overt signs (with rules governing the role of each) to covert activity controlling behaviour.

Consider a silly example (close to the beliefs of psychological behaviourists at one time). A person learns to read and write numbers and do written calculations. She then begins to write smaller and smaller until the numbers are illegible, but still does the calculations and reports her answers. Eventually she dispenses with writing altogether. Must a philosophical explanation invoke some new kind of entity or determinant at any stage in this process? At every stage the activity obeys the same rules and thus requires mental operations of the same types. Thus it is structured by the rules governing the use of signs even though there are no obvious signs being used. There may well be a cognitive story to be told about how regularities in human performance enable established conceptual operations to be used to deal with new instances, but, for the present purpose, we can just accept that human beings are creatures who can follow rules (due to certain psychobiological facts). To elucidate their performances we must understand the rules and the shape they give to human activity, both overt and covert. Therefore the essential nature of thought is revealed by rules which give human activity its form and not by the processes which enable one to follow them. This returns us to the relation between language and thought.

5.9. Language and Thought

The representational nature of thought could be secondary to or independent of an understanding of language.[27] Peacocke argues

[27] J. Campbell, Critical Notice of C. Peacocke, *Sense and Content*, *Philosophical Quarterly*, 36(143) (Apr. 1986), 278–91.

that thought content is logically independent of language. First, he suggests that there are:

modes of presentation which are not fully captured by linguistic expressions. Second, there are words in the natural language, most particularly proper names and natural kind terms, for which there is no way of thinking such that in order to understand the word one must think of its referent (object or kind) in that particular way. Third, in classifying attitudes to given contents we often need an apparatus which discriminates more finely than that which is straightforwardly made available by the natural language . . . Fourth, even when we take sentences which do fully express particular contents, the contents expressed are sliced too finely to capture the level at which we want to characterise general features of their role in propositional attitude psychology. (TEC 102)

(Note the prima-facie tension between the last two of these arguments.) There are counters to each point:

First, ascriptions of content which the thinker can neither express nor understand in language are problematic.[28] Of course, expressions may not always individuate a certain content solely in virtue of their (dictionary) meaning (e.g. ⟨that colour⟩ or ⟨that thing⟩). But thoughts which cannot be specified in linguistic terms are heavily embedded in practices of language-use and their content becomes clear within those practices. Thus, even if a term cannot be found which expresses or defines the content that the thinker has in mind, locating that content in linguistic practices reveals its meaning. The lack of an exact linguistic specification does not undermine the essential link between thought content, language, and language-related practices. An analysis of mental content should reveal this natural connection to linguistic meaning and understanding.

Second, one can think of, say, London or tigers in many different ways. That a term may not fully specify the content it expresses does not show that the content concerned outstrips a broader range of descriptive (and 'reactive') terms that can express exactly what one thinks, say, of London. But two further things need to be said: (1) any given experience of London has a richness which may not, in fact, be rendered in explicit linguistic form (some will be better at this than others—poets, for instance); (2) no linguistic composition ever adds up to being in London—there

---

[28] 'Thought and Talk', in ITI.

is an undeniable difference between London in the flesh and reading a vivid, even poetic and evocative, description of it (just as
being told you have been punched in the nose does not produce
blood, even if it is true), because a thinker who soaks up the
sights, sounds, smells, and atmosphere of London is differently
placed from one who has a mere description of it: his thoughts
have different (and open-ended) contents.

Third, a subject can distinguish colours for which he has no
concept-term. But one can both learn to detect and, in principle,
communicate about such qualities so that an account of representation based on language should be able to embrace them. In fact
a broader analysis of content in terms of rule-governed practices
in general rather than just linguistic practices defuses the objection.
But our response to the world in such cases is always refined and
defined by the "stage setting" (*PI* I. 257) that language provides.

The fourth objection just seems wrong. It is common to most
accounts of propositional attitudes (PAs) that they are linked to
reasons and therefore have discursive and inferential properties in
virtue of their propositional semantics and syntax. Thus language
is eminently suitable to "characterise general features of their role
in propositional attitude psychology" (though not without an
adequate account of cognitive role or 'sense'). In any event, the
richly discursive properties available through the use of language
articulate our PAs, and, notoriously, shades and nuances of meaning
which betray what people really think are detected by close and
perceptive attention to their use of words.[29]

There are also, however, problems for a strong linguistic thesis.
First, propositional attitude (PA) psychology can be used to explain
some of the behaviour of non-linguistic thinkers such as animals
and small children. Therefore any account of thought which makes
a strong appeal to language and linguistic meaning must specify
how and why PA psychology can be applied in this way. I have
argued that content is revealed by rules governing the activity
(including linguistic activity) of thinkers. This allows us to exploit
recognizable similarities between the behaviour of non-linguistic
animals and that of human beings in making PA ascriptions but
respect our intuitions and reservations about such ascriptions, e.g.
in moral judgements.

[29] This was, of course, a major thrust of 'ordinary language philosophy'.

A second problem is that it is intuitively plausible that a child must know what a term is to be taken to denote if it is to grasp the criteria for projectible use. But if a child must have some idea of what an x is in order to learn a term for x, then it would seem that the idea pre-dates the understanding of the term. I have suggested that x is an item or feature of the world presented in human practices and that the term used for x both marks and 'crystallizes' the techniques of responding which pick it out.[30]

On the other hand, there are problems which ought to give pause to a 'primacy of thought' theorist. First, as Dummett observes, "the philosophy of thought, conceived of as independent of and anterior to the philosophy of language . . . will have to explain in what the properties of being true and being false, possessed by the bodiless denizens of the realm of sense consist" (*IFP* 42). This problem is related to the normative aspects of thought content and thus to the determinacy and individuation of content. It is particularly acute for a truth-based theory of thought. The theory must explain how the individual can have both a disposition to think that x applies to this or that and a recognition that this thought answers to a norm governing what (objectively) counts as an x. It could try to do this in terms of the spatio-temporal order: "the thought-theorist will take grasp of objective truth to be given not by grasp of a public language but by the conception of oneself as in a spatial world".[31] The problem is that truth then reduces to truth in a representational world. Prima facie this runs counter to Frege's concern for objectivity. An alternative appeal to coherence in thought (1) fails to specify where the thinker gets a grasp of true coherence as distinct from apparent coherence, and (2) cannot in itself secure an intersubjective and individual-transcendent conception of truth. Neither defect is avoided by appeal to things such as "projection classes of all patterns of retinal stimulation".[32] I have appealed to the rules which govern the judgements underpinning our concepts and our use of linguistic terms. Thus thought is tied to language to the extent that the rules in question focus on its use.

---

[30] I have noted that these also rest on a child's natural propensities to latch on to this or that congruently with other human beings.

[31] Campbell, Critical Notice of *Sense and Content*, 279.

[32] See e.g. Frege's discussions on pp. 20–1 of *TEC* for an apparently solipsistic view.

Second, any theory must account for the structure of thought. Thoughts are structured by concepts, and the structure of a propositional thought is mirrored in the sentence which expresses it.[33] By and large, the more explicit the thought, the more expressible it is, so there is a strong case for the claim that thought structure is essentially tied to the propositional structure of natural language (in some non-Fodorian way). Peacocke argues that structure derives from "canonical links" ("grounds" and "commitments") which tie judgement about a certain content to the thinker's experience. He remarks: "Judgment aims at the truth of the content judged. So, in learning what is necessarily involved in judging a given content we can learn something about the nature of that content itself" (*TEC* 46–7). This implies that patterns of canonical acceptance conditions (relative to perceptual experience or other content) give a theorist "what he needs for a good answer in his substantive theory of content. An adequate account of thoughts according to which they are individuated by reference to canonical acceptance conditions will already entail that thoughts are essentially structured" (*TEC* 114). His claim is that the patterns of perceptual impingements are cross-linked in such ways that the relations between "observational contents" are as structured and interrelated as experience itself. If the observational case is basic for thought, then this will give an "independent" and "anterior" theory of thought:[34] "The thought's structure and constituents are intrinsic to it . . . it is impossible for someone to be judging that very content, and not to be judging something with the given structure and constituents" (*SC* 114). Peacocke declares for an "outward-looking theory" in which thought contents are analysed in terms of "relations to external objects and their properties" (*TEC* 54) and yet also for an account of the acceptance conditions of thoughts as a function of their relations to mental states (*TEC* 63–4). This creates problems.

The notions of 'grasp' and 'judgement' have normative properties which I have linked to language, language-associated activities, and communication. Dummett remarks:

[33] For the moment I will defer the claim that the meaning and thus the thought expressed may not be simply read off from the structure of a sentence and may involve deep grammar, categories, and the like.

[34] The claim about the basic role of the observational case is developed by Peacocke in *SC*.

A grasp of a concept may be manifested in different ways and one such manifestation adequate in itself to ground an attribution to someone of the grasp of the concept, is the use of the word which, in the language to which it belongs, expresses that concept. Hence an account of language will, by itself, be an account of thought. (*IFP* 52)

I have argued that the grasp of a concept rests on the constraints imposed by rules for the use of terms. The resulting abilities provide the thinker with the elements of mental representation. On this reading a thinker represents things to himself by using and exploiting the techniques which structure his activity and relate it to things around him. The detachability of these techniques from extensional conditions and their independence from causal antecedents entails that concepts can be manipulated so as to provide spontaneously generated, hypothetical, and imaginative content to reasoning in addition to that which derives from perception. It is important to notice that thought rests on rules which are independent of the thinker's inclination to achieve consistency of response. Thus representation, both to oneself and to others, depends on what is public and on the shared norms which persons follow to regulate and articulate their activity. Because concepts are, in this sense, independent of a thinker's inclinations and under constraints that moderate his dispositions, we find that intersubjective norms pervade the individuation and structure of thought content. This view links self-ascription and other-ascription and is clearly an "outward-looking theory" which holds that thought trades in signs developed in a public milieu, so that, as Wittgenstein remarks, "We may say that thinking is essentially the activity of operating with signs" (*BBB* 6).

5.10. Summary

Intentionality, normativity, and structure are essential to thought. Thoughts are about things other than themselves, are governed by rules, and have inferential structure. I have rejected the strong linguistic thesis represented by Fodor's language of thought theory because of its reliance on a 'sentence-crunching' model of thought, its separation between syntax and semantics, its causal analysis of the semantic relation, and its confused idea of the relation between thinkers and representations. *Contra* a causal account of representations, I have agreed with Kant that concept-use involves judgement and with Wittgenstein that such judgements obey rules for the use of terms which one learns to obey in shared practices. I have suggested that thought content is tied to the grasp of concepts and thereby to a natural language. The crucial link is via rules and regularities in human activity (which are conveniently marked by using linguistic signs). I have argued that Peacocke's attempt to tie the structure and intentionality of thought to 'perceptual links' both fails and belies his disclaimer about "inward-looking views" because, in focusing on mental states, it does not explain the normative properties of representation.

Over the next three chapters I will spell out the implications of the present view for the philosophy of language.

6

Linguistic Meaning

THE relationship between meaning, rules, and human thought lies at the heart of the present study. I have rejected the strong thesis that thought is the activity of operating with covert propositional items, but accept that there is an essential link between thought and linguistic meaning. Because thoughts, *inter alia*, give meaning to and are expressed in our speech acts, the present approach implies that an account of meaning should reveal what it is that determines the representational properties of an expression and also show how the meaning of complex expressions is systematically and "generatively" given by their structure and linguistic components.[1]

6.1. Sense

I will begin with Frege's notion of "sense" as the manner or mode of presentation, or "way of thinking" (Evans), involved in a subject's apprehension of an object. Dummett remarks:

an account of the sense of an expression is . . . a partial account of what a speaker knows when he understands that expression. . . . in regarding sense as determining reference . . . the contribution of extra-linguistic reality is thereby taken into account . . . a capable speaker must know more than the reference of a complex expression; he must at least know how its reference is determined in accordance with its composition out of its component words.[2]

When a language-user grasps the meaning of an expression, he knows what is being talked about and can respond according to what is said to him. This requires more than a knowledge of

---

[1] Meaning is "generative" (Fodor) in that an indefinitely large range of expressions may be generated from a finite base of component terms whose meanings allow those novel expressions to be understood by a competent language-user.

[2] 'Frege's Distinction between Sense and Reference', in *TOE*.

which objects or features of the world are denoted by an expression. What more it involves emerges from two related features of meaning: one is the determination of the meaning of an expression by rules governing what to do with it, and the other is the structure that links the meanings of different expressions.

To specify how the sense of an expression grasped by both speaker and hearer is determined is to explain why there is a right and wrong way of responding to a given expression (a normative feature of linguistic meaning). An adequate account should also explain the connections between meaning and the behaviour of language-users, in that behaviour is guided by the way an individual thinks about an object and not just the extensional properties of that object.

I have noted a tension in Frege's account. He links sense to the mental life of a given thinker but also to truth so that it is communicable and objective. Sense thus has an essential connection to events, objects, and features that are independent of consciousness. But while Frege recognized that an analysis of sense should exhibit its independence from individual "states of consciousness", his essentially Cartesian understanding of mind did not allow him to resolve the tension apparent between this and the fact that meaning is central in psychological explanation (*VR* 17):

The grasp of a thought presupposes someone who grasps it, who thinks. He is the owner of the thinking, not of the thought. Although the thought does not belong with the contents of the thinker's consciousness, there must be something in his consciousness that is aimed at the thought. But this should not be confused with the thought itself. . . . A thought belongs neither to my inner world as an idea nor yet to the external world, the world of things perceptible by the senses.[3]

If the sense of any expression has a determinate meaning, is essentially related to truth, and must be grasped in a particular way, then, as Frege remarks, the thinker cannot proceed by "creation but in the discovery of true thoughts". Something as fundamental to human enquiry as meaning cannot be such that "it depends on men's varying states of consciousness", and a thought must remain invariant although different minds grasp it. Only such invariance in the sense of an expression or thought in all its occurrences can secure a determinate connection between it and the world. Thus,

---

[3] G. Frege, 'Thoughts', in *LI*.

even though the mental lives of co-linguistic thinkers differ, they must implicitly appreciate the invariance of meaning in order to communicate and to have a conception of truth. I have already cast doubt on the attempt to explain this essential feature of meaning by relating senses to the world via causal connections.

The present account links sense (and thus the content of communicable thoughts) to something independent of the mental life of the individual thinker without invoking causal connections between the subject and his environment.

6.2. Normativity and Communication

The meaning of an expression is determined by rules. Once the subject knows how the expression *should* direct his interactions with the world, he understands its meaning. But notice that this requires intentional terms such as 'belief' and 'understanding' to appear in the analysis of meaning and truth:

> It is indeed a harmless and salutary thing to say that to know the meaning of a sentence is to know under what conditions one who utters it says something true. But if we wish for a philosophical elucidation of the concept of meaning then the dictum represents not the end but the beginning of our task. . . . when we come to try to explain in general what it is to say something true, to express a true proposition, reference to belief or to assertion (and thereby to belief) is inescapable.[4]

Strawson argues that an analysis of meaning, even where it rests on the relationship between meaning and truth, involves belief rather than (in principle) extensionally specified relata. But his claim does not amount to a theory of communicative intentions as the basis of meaning.

Wittgenstein is one philosopher who offers an alternative to theories of meaning based on extensional conditions or truth definitions on the one hand, or communicative intentions on the other:

> Imagine that I am a strong and silent builder and you my taciturn labourer. We are looking at a pile of bricks and I hold up three fingers. You

---

[4] P. F. Strawson, *Meaning and Truth* (Oxford, 1968). Strawson here confines himself to descriptive sentences although (as he remarks) we do many things besides describing or asserting when we utter such sentences.

nod. Later I hold up those same three fingers and you go and get the
bricks. At lunch, the same gesture gets me three bacon butties.

My expression has a sense in each setting. This requires that you
and I have a set of forms of representation whose meanings vary
according to collateral features of use such as context or supple-
mentary communicative devices. A particular utterance is taken in
a particular way once informal rules govern that use. One must
then use an expression in a particular situation for one of a limited
range of purposes (descriptive, interrogative, imperative, or whatever). One could not be counted as understanding the 'language'
unless one understood how to react to any given 'utterance'.

Now this is not a million miles from a full-blooded conception
of meaning. The intentional communicative acts of thinkers
in certain situations are structured so as to have distinct functions in relation to the activities of self and others. Within this
milieu, repeated terms and recurring features of situations exhibit
regularities.

An expression has a potential influence upon the thinking or
reasoning of a subject because it exploits regularities of the practices
in which it is used. For every component of an expression there
is some 'joint' or point of articulation with what could be done
in a variety of situations. For instance, Wittgenstein asks whether
'Bring me a slab' is the actual form of 'slab' as used in certain
circumstances. He observes that "we mean the sentence as four
words when we use it in contrast with other sentences such as
'*Hand* me a slab', 'Bring *him* a slab', 'Bring two slabs', etc." Notice
that every word marks some point at which the required response
is different from other possible responses. Thus the senses of the
terms used are determinately located within a network of meanings and thereby linked in structured ways to other expressions.
Thus certain structural norms emerge and place constraints on
what makes sense and what does not. For instance, the builder
could not signal '3, 2' *simpliciter*; that combination would not be
meaningful because his helper cannot do anything with it; it has
no role in their interaction. In the same way, there is nothing one
can do with 'Green ideas sleep furiously'; such nonsense expressions have no role in our doings (even though, in certain respects,
they have the form of meaningful expressions). Wittgenstein remarks: "What does it mean to understand a proposition as a

member of a system of propositions? Its complexity is only to be explained by the use for which it is intended" (*PR* 15). Notice that this is not a claim that meaning reduces to a set of behavioural dispositions to respond thus and so.[5]

6.3. *The Normative Features of Meaning*

An account based on rule-governed use explains three normative features of meaning and representation:

1. There are normative constraints on a language-user's dispositions. Rules determining use have a role in an individual's patterns of thought but also in communication, and thus they are not merely a function of the cognitive tendencies of any individual. Similarly, content is assessable with respect to truth apart from the subject's inclination to affirm it, deny it, or incorporate it in some active propositional attitude (PA). Thus the constraints on meaning are not private to a given thinker or a function of the intentions of that thinker. Nor are they extensionally or causally 'private' because that would, prima facie, imply that there was a massive coincidence whereby just the same rules were instantiated in some way in each thinker, and an explanation of the normativity and objectivity of meaning surely cannot rest on such coincidence. By contrast public rules are, in the required way, a priori the same for all those thinkers who share the same senses and truth-related thought contents.

2. The rules governing use are structured; they prescribe *patterns* of use which can achieve a range of communication purposes (even novel purposes). The structure shown in the use of related terms captures the range of possible interactions between language-users and between them and the world in which they are acting. In fact, the structure not only expresses but also helps to form ramifying patterns of interest, action, reaction, and interaction. Structural and conceptual connections are therefore revealed by patterns of use. The rules thereby explain the connections between expressions and, in doing so, reveal both the nature of meaning

---

[5] Thus it is distinct from theories enunciated by Quine, Stich (*From Folk Psychology to Cognitive Science* (Cambridge, Mass., 1985)), and McGinn (*Wittgenstein on Meaning* (Oxford, 1984)).

and how the meaning of a complex expression is determined by its components. And these features are connected in that the rules determine both the application and the structural relations of a given component expression.

3. The normative constraints on meaning are such that a thinker can convey that meaning, whatever the relationship between it and the conditions of his utterance. Thus meaning offers a thinker resources for dealing with a situation rather than causal dispositions to respond to it. We cannot accept an account of meaning which does not make room for the thinker to exploit the structure of language in order to serve any one of a number of his present purposes.

Also, another person's response to what you say is subject to mental *ceteris paribus* clauses: 'unless he is being perverse' or 'but he always finds ambiguities' or 'if she does not believe you, she will misconstrue your words', and so on. The implications for meaning, intention, and current experience are that there is no invariant or mechanical link between extensionally specified conditions and meaning. Of course, on occasion, the demand for a certain response might be compelling, but the compulsion is essentially normative and not causal. For instance, were one to say 'Is that a banana?' when pointing to a banana, then the other person would be under some pressure to say 'Yes'. The rules prescribe how a certain expression *ought* to guide a thinker's appraisal of a situation, but the thinker may or may not respond as he ought depending on his present purposes.

Therefore, not only is there no mechanical link between conditions and the meaning of an expression, neither is there such a link between intentional or mental states and events and the meaningful use of terms.[6] Meaning and understanding provide for the formation of intentions and thoughts tailored to but not evoked by a situation. They do not have any essential connection with extra-linguistic purposes (this Davidson calls "the autonomy of meaning").

To summarize: three normative features (which cannot merely be a function of individual cognitive states) characterize meaningful transactions using a structured system of communication or

---

[6] I have already rejected the view that mental life comprises states and events with causal properties.

thought. This essential independence between individual mental
life and the determinants of meaning is, of course, damaging to a
causal account of meaning.

6.4. *Understanding and Interpreting Signs*

There is a temptation to conclude that the intentional aspects of
meaning indicate that a thinker understands a term by interpret-
ing it in a certain way. This reading of the intentional nature
of rule-following in understanding and meaning is not only phenomenologically unsound but also self-defeating. It is untrue to
the phenomenology of meaning in that it interposes in the understanding of terms a formula or key to guide usage whereas a
thinker often "obeys the rule blindly" (*PI* I. 219), which does not
mean that she does not know what she is doing or that she is not
doing it intentionally, but only that she may not have surveyable
or articulated reasons for obeying it this particular way.

   The interpretive move is also self-defeating. Even if an interpretation or formula did 'come into one's mind' to tell one what to
do, there is the further question 'How does one know to respond
to the formula in that way?' There must be "a way of grasping a
rule which is *not* an interpretation but which is exhibited in what
we call 'obeying the rule' and 'going against it' in actual cases" (*PI*
I. 201).[7] This ability to act in accordance with a rule is grounded
in training because rules governing meaning are learned in practices where terms have a use. Of course, reasoning may be involved during the training (e.g. 'He can't mean that because that
is an *x* and he is talking about *y*' or 'That must be the chartreuse
because it is not quite pale green and not quite yellow and that
is the definition he gave'), but, through training, use becomes
habitual, like riding a bicycle or tying shoe-laces. Therefore the
appreciation that there is a right and wrong way of doing these
things may not be accompanied by a mental specification of that
right way: "To understand a sentence means to understand a language. To understand a language means to be master of a technique" (*PI* I. 199). McGinn summarizes Wittgenstein thus: "understanding is not an inner process of supplying an interpretation of

---

[7] Kant made the same point at *CPR*, B172.

a sign which justifies one in reacting with the sign in a certain way; it is, rather, an ability to engage in a practice or custom of using a sign over time in accordance with one's natural propensities". But he then goes too far: "Understanding, we might say, is an unmediated propensity to act."[8] Understanding, notoriously, is not identifiable with any surveyable propensity to act.

Therefore we must reject both an intellectualist and also a behaviourist reading of the rule-following involved in meaning and understanding. The structure in thought and meaning is a structure of customary or habitual abilities which fall somewhere on the continuum between reading words or letters and reading a map, and it is related to both. We cannot reduce 'habit' to 'disposition' because meaningful signs are applied in judgements by thinkers even when correct use is automatic in practice. (One can always ask whether the present case *counts* as one which fits the rule.) Therefore the responses involved in meaning and understanding involve 'thick' information and not merely causal transactions.[9]

6.5. A Causal Account of Meaning

Can meaning, with the normative features that I have detailed, be explained in terms of causally effective states and processes? Such dispositional theories tend, explicitly or implicitly, towards a discussion of internal mechanisms and the structural complexity of the functional system they form. It is an attractive prospect. Some but not all of the causal links determining the content of thought would be to utterances, and therefore multi-tracked dispositional states with explanatory roles in behaviour could have propositional form but not be dependent upon language.

One could envisage the transactions between an individual and the world creating a store of causally structured states variously linked to input, other dispositional states, and motor output. They would together form a structure of interacting dispositions in causal contact with the world at input and output termini. The meaning of any expression or term would then be explained by the state(s)

[8] McGinn, *Wittgenstein on Meaning*, 42–3.
[9] For 'thick' information, see §5.7.

underlying the behaviour in which it was exhibited. The state(s) would be fixed by stimulus conditions to which it was linked, the causal dispositions to which it regularly gave rise, and its systematic relations within the total set. In a structured language with a core of simple expressions, some mapping function could then link environmental features (broadly construed so as to include events, properties, particulars, relations, displacements, etc.) to the appropriate causal dispositions. The dispositions, by interacting with each other, would control the behaviour of the organism and the net effect would be a response (or disposition to respond), the function of which could be linked to a proposition.[10] In this way a cognitive description of the subject could use meaningful terms and expressions to map out his mental constitution and to explicate just how he would understand different expressions.[11] The obvious advantage of such a theory is that it links thoughts to input and output conditions which can, in principle, be specified extensionally. It would therefore bypass Strawson's claims that intention is indispensable in the analysis of meaning and truth and provide a causal reading of 'use' as the source of meaning. A suitably detailed description of the dispositions of an individual and their relations to features of the situations in which he had acquired a language would then constitute an extensional theory of meaning.

If such a theory were possible, then the content of all the linguistic components within a thinker's repertoire could be systematically correlated with features of the world and the result used to predict the content of complex or composite expressions.[12] This would be an empirical interpretive theory (in Quine and Davidson's sense). But notice that it relies on mutual interpretation by thinkers for a conception of norms to which the dispositions of an individual thinker are relativized. This introduces an element into the analysis which goes beyond causal or cognitive roles and invokes prescriptive norms of interpretation.[13]

---

[10] Such a theory could follow if certain modifications were made to that offered by Fodor. A functional theory of this broad type has been elaborated by Brian Loar in *Mind and Meaning* (Cambridge, 1981).

[11] Andrew Woodfield, in his own contribution to *TO*, has taken just this view.

[12] I have discussed Gareth Evans's able exposition of this view in 'Tacit Semantics', *Philosophical Investigations*, 11 (1988), 1-12.

[13] I shall return to this in Ch. 7.

6.6. *States and Rules of Use*

I have argued that any account of what it is for a term to have meaning should explain the relation between normativity and the individuation of sense. In doing this it should preserve the inter-subjectivity of sense even if unable to secure the strong realism in Frege's view of thought and meaning. It must also show how it is that contents expressed in language are a subset of thought content in general.

Structured causal states or dispositions do not look promising; they lack the essential independence from both individual cognitive states and immediate context that is evident in linguistic meaning. In fact, the three normative aspects of meaning all cause problems.

First, the *structure* evident in linguistic meaning poses a problem. Our simple vignette of the builder and his labourer showed that the meaning of an expression is determined by the place or role that it takes in the intentional activity of those who use it. If it has no possible role (e.g. when the builder says '3, 2') because it is impossible to find an operation upon the building material, act of attending, or problem to ponder that is indicated by the composite expression used, then it is unclear what content is being conveyed and the meanings of the component terms do not combine to express a completed thought. The structural inadequacy of the expression becomes evident as soon as we try to formulate its place in the intentional activity of speakers or hearers. Therefore the meaning of what is said is revealed by the behaviour of language-users and the structure of a natural language is explained by appeal to their articulated and rule-governed activity. That is why any adequate account of meaning quickly outstrips the crude conceptual apparatus of causal contacts between organisms and the environment.

External objects and events accessible to others provide the framework for meaningful communication and thus the members of a linguistic community must share certain physical properties (for instance, they must share a range of spectral sensitivities to light if they are going to develop a colour vocabulary and, in part, share patterns of bodily reaction to injury and deprivation if their needs are to be conceptualized). But these are only enabling conditions for communication between subjects upon which a rule-governed structure of meanings can be built to provide an extensive range of possibilities for dealing with the world. These options and the structural regularities in their language might plausibly be expected to go hand in hand.

One must therefore conclude that the meaning of an utterance is given by its component terms and their uses in the activities in which the subject participates. The many uses of the component words provide an interacting set of partial determinants for the meaning of any expression. To understand this, one must conceive of language-users as people with identities, interests, concerns, and interactions. Such an understanding yields a substantive account of meaning, truth, and the link between them.[14] It is not merely a far cry but an intergalactic leap from discussion of the causal impingements of the environment on inner structures *or* the causal transactions between inner states *or* causally based mapping functions between entities and responses, however complex and ramified those structures, states, and functions are. In this vein, Peacocke remarks of his own theory of content: "The norms it outlines are norms for persons to follow" (*TEC* 50–1). He distinguishes such norms from subpersonal processes in that persons follow these norms for reasons. If meaning does involve intersubjective rules and therefore prescriptive rather than descriptive norms, there is, of course, further reason to suspect accounts based on causal or dispositional states within persons.

In addition to explaining the structure in meaning, causal theories have two further requirements to meet.

The second normative aspect of linguistic meaning is that the meaning of an utterance is *essentially independent* from the inclinations of particular thinkers. A complex of causally related processes or states provides a thinker with a relatively stable (even if modifiable) set of dispositions to respond to a given input. Such a model states only how a given thinker *tends* to react in a given situation. Any conception of a standard to be aimed at is distinct from an individual's (causally conditioned) reaction pattern and thus from what he is disposed to do; such empirically discovered causal regularities do not constitute "norms for persons to follow" (Peacocke).

[14] Just such an account is undertaken by David Wiggins in his paper 'What Would Be a Substantial Theory of Truth?', in Z. Van Straaten (ed.), *Philosophical Subjects* (Oxford, 1980).

We could introduce a teleological element into the account, but even that will not quite turn the trick. Teleological control over a disposition links it to certain goal-states. But we have already established that we need to understand linguistic meaning as a resource able to be used for a variety of purposes. It is not obvious where in a teleological account there is room for rule-governed judgements as to whether a situation warrants a certain use. A reductive teleological account specifies response types which are emitted under certain conditions so as to produce certain effects.[15] These tie meanings, if that is what they are analysing, to extra-linguistic purposes. But Davidson remarks:

a basic trait of language . . . [is] the autonomy of linguistic meaning. Once a feature of language has been given conventional expression, it can be used to serve many extra-linguistic ends; symbolic representation necessarily breaks any close tie with extra-linguistic purpose. (*ITI* 113)

He makes a similar claim for thought:

having a thought requires that there be a background of beliefs, but having a particular thought does not depend on a state of belief with respect to that very thought . . . We may say . . . that a thought is defined by a system of beliefs but is itself autonomous with respect to belief. (*ITI* 157)

The autonomy of linguistic meaning (and thought content) entails that there is a normative element to content quite distinct from one's dispositions. The meaning of any expression may *represent* the utterer as instancing a certain mental ascription (e.g. as wanting to know how many bricks there are in a pile), but whereas he is representing himself as instancing that ascription he is not necessarily caused to produce the utterance by the intentional state concerned.

A related problem for causal theories is that meaning, because it is fixed independently of the inclinations of a given thinker, has a unique role in mental explanation. The meanings of expressions are used by an individual to understand the world and others. The resulting ways of thinking and communicating direct his activity on to this or that, but they do not causally determine his behaviour given certain conditions. Thus he draws upon his grasp of certain meanings to shape his perceptions, his attitudes, and his actions

---

[15] D. Dennett, *Brainstorms* (Brighton, 1981), 73.

(including his linguistic actions of uttering and understanding), and the rules involved do not (efficiently) cause him to produce certain responses:

> It will be felt ... we are still at liberty to see somebody's understanding as determined by their dispositions of use, modulo some fixed set of assumptions about them in the other relevant parameters. ... Assume some such fixed background. Then the dispositionalist is taking it, in effect, that whatever the subject does he cannot but behave in a way that is appropriate to expressing his understanding, relative to that background. ... if, in particular, the subject correctly cognizes the relevant facts, and intends a literally informative use of the expression in question, the dispositionalist view would have it that he must then be disposed to use the expression appropriately (as far as his own understanding is concerned). Now ... the objectivity traditionally associated with meaning would have it that what sort of use of an expression is appropriate, modulo a suitable set of background assumptions, is settled independently of the subject's response.[16]

Wright's claim that the subject is not caused to make certain responses in certain situations merely in virtue of having grasped certain meanings is supported by the failure of definitional behaviourism. But if use is not analysable as output relativized to input, then rule-following and judgement do not fit a (causal) conditional analysis. We conclude that a thinker uses the meanings of words to convey certain thoughts, and that the links between his intentions and his expressions are not causal. Because meaningful use is not causally conditioned responding, it cannot be elucidated by functions which map expressions, via inner mental states, on to conditions which cause their utterance.

The third normative aspect arises because a set of interconnected inner states would not, except by massive coincidence, secure a conception of meaning which *transcends the individual*, to which he must conform, and which is intersubjective. Again, the dispositional account cannot explain the non-individualistic constraints upon a particular thinker. Wittgenstein's response overcomes this by locating meaning in public practices, where it is determined by use.

For these reasons, the normative aspects of meaning imply that the meaning of an expression is not up for subjective bids (even

---

[16] C. Wright, 'On Knowing One's Mind', 11th International Wittgenstein Symposium, 1986, 4.

those seeking safety in numbers, where the fortuitous congruence of many individual responders depends on the internal dispositions of each).

The a priori link between meaning as grasped by co-linguistic thinkers arises from competence in shared practices of use which relate different individuals to each other and to their mutual environment. An intentional agent draws on practices which are normative for the uses of those terms that determine the significance of his behaviour. Thus the practices shared by a community of thinkers articulate and inform their intentional lives and these practices are marked by terms which reflect their relations.

6.7. McGinn on Use

The present view contrasts with McGinn's suggestion that understanding is a state in the thinker:

> for Wittgenstein, meaning is use: if two people differ in their understanding of a sign then they differ in their use of it. But use is a kind of behaviour which can be described physically; so the two people must also differ with respect to the physical descriptions true of their behaviour.[17]

McGinn suggests that there must be a difference in the internal (causal) states of the two individuals and thus that understanding an utterance-type is an inner state which is the source of behaviour criterial for the ascription of that understanding. By parity of reasoning, beliefs and desires are causal states antecedent to actions so that no physical behaviour is left "nomologically dangling". He claims that epistemological independence between understanding and brain states is compatible with metaphysical dependence or "psycho-physiological correspondence" and that unless behaviour can be explained by brain events then we would be admitting a dangerous indeterminacy into our physical ontology. But our alternatives are not as limited as he seems to think.

We could claim that we do not identify behaviour in terms of physical events or sets of events. I have argued that describing the stream or totality of events purely in terms of the predicates and explanatory connections available from physical taxonomies will not reveal mental contents. There may be no physical events, states,

---

[17] McGinn, *Wittgenstein on Meaning*, 113.

or sequences which are connected in ways which correspond to mental descriptions and explanations.[18] Indeed McGinn concedes that the criteria for ascription of meaning and understanding are necessarily behavioural and thus that semantic ascriptions may be irreducible to ascriptions of other sorts (he even urges this as a powerful counter to Kripke's demand for some fact of the matter which grounds semantic ascriptions[19]).

We can therefore reject the 'causal source' theory because its posited states (the causal sources of use) can account for neither the normative aspects nor the autonomy of meaning. Meaning and understanding involve abilities which provide but do not compel certain responses. The essence or 'grammar' of these abilities (which are exercised according to the intentions of a thinker) is not that of causal states. Even if meaning and understanding depend on certain biological (and other natural) constancies so that we would not be thinking beings if we had heads full of sawdust, such conditions need not be part of a philosophical analysis of meaning. In response to the claim that "understanding may be described as a state which is the source of use", we could say that reference to such a state is *idle* in the analysis and that focusing on it obstructs a more perspicuous account of meaning and understanding. Physiological norms and the states that conform to them are not "norms for persons to follow".

A thinker uses his linguistic resources to serve certain purposes and thus meaning is understood by reference to the intentional practices of persons. Depersonalizing meaning enucleates it, and the formal and unrealistic analyses which result bear only a lifeless resemblance to the original.

6.8. Meaning and Judgement

Utterances and other acts with meaning are given form in practices where they are refined by certain rules, and a subject acts meaningfully when he draws on a whole series of such rule-governed practices. His tendency to react in a certain way or to use the sense of a certain expression in a range of situations must

---

[18] This would be a response to McGinn's argument available within Davidson's 'anomalous monism', but Wittgenstein, as I shall explain, is even more radical.

[19] McGinn, *Wittgenstein on Meaning*, 150 ff.

be sharpened until a principled difference between his being right and his thinking he is right characterizes his use. In most cases this involves others who themselves already grasp the use of an expression and, as it were, 'issue the warrant' for correct use. The individual thinker thus derives his warrant for use from participation with others in those practices where certain rules are in play. But neither the individual nor a community can just *decide* what rules are applicable; they adapt to existing practices which engage them with each other and a mutually accessible world in which they attend to things, act upon them, pick them out, and so on. (And all this is, of course, reliably imprinted on the brain.)

A meaningful act manifests mental content and usually embeds the rule-governed use of a sign. Therefore it involves "the canonical acceptance conditions for a judgment" (Peacocke). I correctly judge a sense to be appropriate when the ways in which I use a term accord with rules governing its application. We could say that sense is an internal relation between a linguistic act and the practices in which some term has a use. The (internal) relation between the use of a meaningful term and my present situation allows me to make judgements which involve the meaning of that term. The techniques, objects, and events in the relevant practices provide the links which structure my appreciation of the present experience and locate it with respect to other concepts. Shared rules individuate that conceptual locus.

In tying meaning to practices and shared human activities (or forms of life) in a public world we move from a narrow account of linguistic meaning on to a broader canvas of human discourse. Therefore the present account of meaning can be related to the account of concepts in general even if thought is not strongly dependent on language. Meanings show intentionality in the same way as representation, in that:

1. they refer beyond themselves to objects and features as picked out in the practices in which they are fixed; and
2. they help structure a repertoire of abilities to be used in intentional acts.

Moreover, meaning is intersubjective and related to truth because the practices in which use is refined are public and impose norms to which subjective responses ought to conform.

Agents act for reasons which incorporate the meanings of the expressions that they use. No doubt their activity could be described in other terms, but that would neither elucidate linguistic meaning nor help us understand thought.

6.9. *Interpretation and Understanding*

Shared meaning is a basic feature of Davidson's view that thought and language are essentially interpretive in nature. His use of Quine's radical-interpretation scenario solves a basic problem in the analysis of meaning:

> We do not know what someone means unless we know what he believes; we do not know what someone believes unless we know what he means. In radical interpretation we are able to break into this circle, if only incompletely, because we can sometimes tell that a person accedes to a sentence we do not understand. (*ITI* 27)

He concedes that "how we could come to have knowledge that would serve to yield interpretations does not, of course, concern the actual history of language acquisition" (*ITI* 125). This disclaimer prompts a reading of Davidson's account as a specification of what a language-user knows when she understands a natural language. It also absolves Davidson of any need to explain the actual development of competence in a language as part of his account of meaning and understanding. But I have suggested that the 'how' of language acquisition tells us a great deal about meaning and understanding.

Davidson does, in some places, suggest a stronger thesis than the weak claim that he is characterizing what must be known, in some form, by any competent user of a language. His account connects thought content in general to linguistic meaning and that, in turn, to a Tarski-type truth definition:

> the definition works by giving necessary and sufficient conditions for the truth of every sentence, and to give truth conditions is a way of giving the meaning of a sentence. . . . since a Tarski-type truth definition supplies all we have asked so far of any theory of meaning, it is clear that such a theory falls comfortably within what Quine terms the "theory of reference" . . . A theory of meaning (in my mildly perverse sense) is an empirical theory and its ambition is to account for the workings of a natural language. (*ITI* 24)

He also claims "all understanding of the speech of another involves radical interpretation" (*ITI* 125). His account of meaning and understanding therefore rests on:

1. the contention that "uninterpreted utterances seem the appropriate evidential base for a theory of meaning" (*ITI* 142);
2. "the attitude of holding a sentence true, of accepting it as true . . . an attitude an interpreter may plausibly be taken to identify before he can interpret" (*ITI* 135); and
3. the structured correlations between utterances and truth conditions delivered by a "Tarski-type truth definition".

Thus, it would appear that, in understanding a language, a thinker takes note of the conditions of utterance, discerns whether the utterer holds it true, and generates a theory telling her how to interpret any further utterances by that speaker in that language. There is, therefore, uninterpreted material and a scheme of interpretation. The former comprises the sounds uttered by others and the conditions under which they are uttered. The scheme comprises the propositional attitudes (PAs) to be ascribed and that theory of meaning which provides the best empirical fit to the linguistic data (i.e. makes the maximum possible number of beliefs ascribed to the thinker come out to be true). Davidson claims: "whether we like it or not, if we want to understand others we must count them right on most matters. . . . We make maximum sense of the words and thoughts of others when we interpret in a way that optimizes agreement (this includes room . . . for explicable error, i.e. differences of opinion)" (*ITI* 187).

I have argued that, in any natural language, the subject does not theorize about utterances forming an uninterpreted given but rather learns to think by using signs which mark rule-governed techniques structuring human activity in and interaction with the environment. The concepts a thinker needs in order to assign utterances to those conditions in which they are uttered, to think about those conditions, and to formulate a theory codifying the correlations therefore entail an a priori agreement with others. For this reason a developing thinker is best thought of as a novice trying to use a set of tools which will eventually provide him with a complete repertoire of cognitive and communicative devices.

Davidson is therefore wise to offer his disclaimer about language acquisition, but unwise to let the matter rest there. When one pursues what actually does happen, we find an apprentice thinker mastering a complex of abilities involving a priori agreement in the judgements basic to the meaning and understanding of utterances. Concepts are the elements enabling this activity and they are grasped as a range of terms, practices, and items become incorporated into a structured network of overt and covert responses made with the aid of linguistic guidance. It is for this reason that *thought* essentially involves operating with the signs that serve as semantic elements in a natural language.[20]

An empirical theory overlooks an essential feature of the understanding of a first language because the abilities required to formulate a truth definition and use it in interpretation involve the grasp of (a priori shared) meaning. Without these abilities the thinker is powerless to interpret but once he has them they render any empirical theory of meaning otiose. This seems to cast serious doubt on the sense in which Davidson's theory "accounts for the workings of a natural language".

I would therefore offer the following sketch of the relation between thought and language.

First, the use of signs is one of the major features of rule-governed techniques for any society with a developed language. Those signs allow the users of the language to mark their responses to various aspects of experience and link situations in a range of connected ways. Therefore the child articulates and explores the relations between events and the objects affected by them as she weaves her responses to those events in verbal form:

In other words, the facility with which a child may come to see the proper relations between such factors as volume, depth, and the identity of the object will depend on the extent to which he is subject to social influences of a certain sort and on his ability to formulate the relationships in words.[21]

This seems to impose a linguistic condition on "seeing the proper relations between things", but language is, in fact, necessary for subtle and complex beliefs about things to be formulated. For

---

[20] Hence Wittgenstein's remark quoted above (§5.9): "We may say that thinking is essentially the activity of operating with signs."

[21] D. W. Hamlyn, 'Logical and Psychological Aspects of Learning', in R. S. Peters (ed.), *The Philosophy of Education* (Oxford, 1973).

instance, imagine that a child comes in from the garden saying
'The garden is muddy. My shoes are dirty, that's why'. Now, does
she mean that the garden has caused her shoes to be muddy or
that you can infer the state of the garden from the mud on her
shoes. Perhaps she does not differentiate between causal and inferential connections (they often go hand in hand). Until she can
differentially express her thought we cannot tell, and she probably
is not clear herself about the exact relations between them.[22]

Speech obviously involves social contact and the use of words
to obtain desired ends by co-operation with other language-users.
The individuals from whom one learns how to do things form part
of a linguistically interacting community in which one grasps
concepts. Therefore language provides the child with interpersonal
and shared resources with which to understand his environment
and structure his own activity.[23]

The use of speech is, in fact, intensified when the child meets
problems which are novel or difficult—the wrong-colour pencil, the
wrong-shaped block, etc. This supports the view that language is
being used to inform and articulate the child's thought. Vygotsky
believes that language has a crucial role in cognitive development:
"Thought is not merely expressed in words; it comes into existence through them." The speech concerned is called 'egocentric
speech' and was traditionally thought to be an epiphenomenon
expressing but not having any functional role in the child's cognition. But a number of experiments and observations led Vygotsky
to conclude that egocentric speech "does not merely accompany
the child's activity, it serves mental orientation, conscious understanding; it helps in overcoming difficulties; it is speech for oneself, intimately and usefully connected with the child's thinking".[24]

Language is therefore formative in thought. It allows the child
to develop and elaborate patterns of action which are initiated in
sensorimotor activity, extended in functional play, and finally linked
to symbols. Those symbols, whose life originates from their use in
structured and articulated human activities, eventually take on a

[22] In this she would be in good company.
[23] L. S. Vygotsky, *Thought and Language*, tr. E. Hanfmann and G. Vakar (first
pub. 1929; Cambridge, Mass., 1962). I have discussed the relations between Piaget's
and Vygotsky's approaches to child psychology in 'Concepts, Structures and
Meanings', *Inquiry*, 30 (1987), 101–12.
[24] Vygotsky, *Thought and Language*, 125.

life of their own but always carry marks of their origins which can be discerned by the careful investigator.

6.10. *Summary*

I have examined the normative constraints on human mental activity as expressed in natural languages. These arise from rules governing the use of terms. Thus the structural aspects of meaning are explained by the relations between activities and practices in which the relevant terms have a use. The meaning of an expression is not just a matter of mental dispositions but is determined rather by rules. But meaning as a function of rules and practices has an essential independence from the thinking of a given subject and relates closely to our general analysis of thought content. It emerges that the person as a human user of a natural language is the central figure in the understanding not only of meaning, but also of content in general. In this spirit, I have considered one popular theory of meaning (Davidson's) and now I shall examine two vexed topics in the area.

7

Cognitive Significance

I HAVE provided an analysis of concepts and their role in representations which is based on the view that concepts essentially range over a public world and that normative and intentional features jointly determine the content contributed by a concept to any thought in which it appears. I have noted the two senses of intentionality which are relevant to cognitive significance: first (Brentano), it refers to the fact that thoughts are *of* or *about* things, and second (Dennett), it refers to the role of representations in reason-governed action. These are related because reasons are formulated in terms of concepts and their connections and the grasp of concepts rests on techniques used by thinkers to structure their activity and relate it to things around them.

Every item a thinker thinks about is represented in some particular way in each thought in which it appears. Various ways of representing a thing make use of different concepts and thus identity statements are informative by linking those different ways of thinking. To find out that the morning star is the evening star or that Peter Strawson is the slight man reading the *London Review of Books* tells us something. This is one ground for the distinction between sense and reference. Mental content, linked to the sense of an expression, determines the significance of the object for the thinker by specifying the way that the item is represented in the mental life of that thinker.

7.1. Sense, Mode of Presentation, and Cognitive Significance

The *cognitive significance* of an expression is the way of thinking about or picking out an object that is involved in a given thought about that object. That objects do figure in thought according to various distinct conceptions leads Evans to formulate an 'Intuitive Criterion of Difference' for thoughts: "the thought associated with one sentence S as its sense must be different from the thought associated with another sentence S' as its sense if it is possible for someone to understand both sentences at a given time while coherently taking different attitudes towards them" (*VR* 18–19). This criterion invokes the subject's attitudes toward the senses of expressions and thus has a natural link to propositional attitude (PA) psychology and action explanation. Because the contents of PAs are specified in terms of the senses of expressions, 'the morning star' and 'the evening star' differ in cognitive significance even though they refer to the same object.

Frege explains the sense or mode of presentation (MP) of an object as follows:

with a proper name, it is a matter of the way in which the object so designated is presented. This may happen in different ways and to every such way there corresponds a special sense of a sentence containing the proper name. (*LI* 17)

Evans paraphrases:

Frege's idea was that it may be a property of a singular term as an element of a public language that, in order to understand utterances containing it, one must not only think of a particular object, its Meaning, but one must think of that object in a particular way: that is, every competent user of the language who understands the utterance will think of the object in the same way. (*VR* 16)

He then extends the idea of an MP from singular terms to all expressions in a language.[1] This has the advantage of linking thought about particulars to a general account of conceptual thought. Whether or not Frege would agree to this move, it is clear that treating concepts as *functions* implies that objects are dealt with in a distinct way by any given concept:

Although the notion of sense is frequently illustrated by the behaviour of singular terms, Frege applies it to all meaningful expressions of the language. . . . someone who understands an utterance of the sentence "Aphla is over 5,000 metres high" must think of, or in some way or other have in mind, the concept (function) associated with the expression "ξ is over 5,000 metres high". And since, for Frege, functions are extensional entities, it becomes not merely possible but mandatory to insist that someone who understands the sentence must grasp the function *in a*

---

[1] David Wiggins makes a similar move in 'The Person as Object of Science, Subject of Experience and Locus of Value', in A. R. Peacocke and G. R. Gillett (eds.), *Persons and Personality* (Oxford, 1987).

particular way, namely as that function which maps on to the True precisely those things which are over 5,000 metres high, and not, for example, as the function which maps the following objects . . . (imagine here a list of mountains) on to the value True. (*VR* 16)

Thus each MP captures some principle of classification for items of the type in question. I have argued that the 'function' from objects to language involved in the grasp of a concept is a matter of use, practices, language games, and forms of life in which rules determine whether something counts as being of a given type. The resulting account of cognitive significance preserves the objectivity and intersubjectivity of sense:

We cannot equate an Idea (a particular person's capacity) with a Fregean sense, since the latter is supposed to exist objectively (independently of anyone's grasp of it). But there is a very close relation between them. Two people exercising their (numerically different) Ideas of an object may thereby "grasp" the same Fregean sense. What this means is that they think of the object in the same way. (*VR* 104)

Evans seeks a non-solipsistic construal of cognitive significance and thus distinguishes between 'senses' and "Ideas" (mental contents of an individual thinker).

7.2. Modes of Presentation and Mental States

Peacocke picks up the analysis in an appealing way:

I shall use the word "thought" in occurrences in which it would otherwise be ambiguous, only for the content of an attitude, and not for the mental occurrence or state which has that content. Thoughts will also be taken as structured entities: the phrase "mode of presentation" will be used relatively non-committally for whatever is a constituent of such thoughts. (*SC* 106)[2]

Therefore we need a non-solipsistic construal of MPs, so as not to contravene Frege's insistence on intersubjectivity of content for thoughts. Peacocke begins his analysis by disconnecting attitudes to demonstrative thoughts (which play a key role in his theory) from linguistic interactions. But this is problematic.[3] Of course,

---

[2] This distinction between attitudes and their contents has its roots in Hume (*A Treatise of Human Nature*, ed. E. C. Mossner (first pub. 1739; Harmondsworth, 1969), I. III. 7).   [3] See §5.9.

if content is linked to language, there is a clear relation between thought and intersubjectivity, but if an 'inner' realm of mental states has self-standing content, there is not. Peacocke's account of content links 'manner' or 'mode' of presentation to a subject's evidence for a given judgement:

Fregean thoughts are individuated by considerations of cognitive significance. If a pair of thoughts differ in the essential ways they can come to be known, it will be possible for a thinker rationally to believe one and not the other: so the thoughts must be distinct. (SC 109)

It is constitutive of a token MP being of a given type that judgements concerning that token be sensitive to evidence of the kind associated with that type. . . . The constitutive role of a demonstrative type will have three components: a sortal concept, some reference to a psychological state of a thinker, and some relation between them (a partially causal role for perceptual MPs). (SC 110–11)

Here he makes the move which later causes a tension in the analysis. Content is tied to the evidence or perceptual grounds available to a thinker and we move from 'a way of thinking of something' to relations between the thinker and patterns of evidence comprising "perceptual experiences", "memory images" and "sequences of perceptions, beliefs and memories", and, more latterly, "projection classes of . . . successive patterns of retinal stimulation" (TEC 20). Whereas a "way of thinking" stresses the active role of the thinker in grasping the sense of an expression and leaves it open for the analysis of content to draw on the relation between the subject, the world, and others, Peacocke's account is more Cartesian; it appeals to the thinker's attitudes to mental states (thus, ultimately, to relations between the mental states of an individual). However, he acknowledges that there is no simple relation between perceptual or memory experiences and thoughts:

Appeal to an undifferentiated notion of evidence in giving a theory of any sort of mode of presentation would be an unpromising strategy: for it seems to be true that anything can be evidence for a given thought in some circumstances or other, while virtually nothing can be evidence for it in all circumstances. But these truths are consistent with the existence of *canonical* evidence for a thought. A perception, a memory or a piece of information of a certain type (or a particular type of set of these) is canonical evidence for the thought that p iff it is constitutive of the thought that p that a thinker takes states or information of that type as *prima facie* evidence justifying the judgment that p. (SC 115–16)

Frege's notion of a canonical or ideal language gives each expression a place only if it bears a unique relation to conditions which make it true. Peacocke's notion is that "a thinker takes states of information of that type as *prima facie* evidence justifying that *p*" (*SC* 116).[4] Thus he retains the view that each thought relates to specifiable evidence grounding the judgement concerned. I have discussed (in §5.9) his more recent use of "canonical links" ("canonical grounds" and "canonical commitments"). A canonical ground justifies accepting some content, and canonical commitments are further judgements entailed by that acceptance. Both tie content to experience and are normative in nature although the source of their normativity is left unclear.

Peacocke claims that he does not accept the "internal notion of a conceptual role" (*TEC* 13), but he discusses content in terms of "the projection class of a given pattern of retinal stimulation", "the thinker's states", and "sets of mental states and contents" (*TEC* 19–22, 45). This implies that conscious experiential states are the basis of judgement and that the content of an MP is given by such 'inner' conditions. But I have argued that a theory combining conditions to which a thinker is exposed and internal states related (causally) to them will not do as an analysis of meaning or of concepts (which are, of course, the basis of a thinker's ability to grasp the sense of an expression).

I will therefore attempt to purge Peacocke's account of its Cartesian elements ("various sets of mental states and contents") and yet preserve something like "acceptance conditions" or even "truth conditions" so as to yield an internal relation between the senses of expressions and public objects and events.

7.3. *Methodological Solipsism*

Some philosophers are more sanguine than Peacocke about detaching cognitive or conceptual role from external things: "Descartes, Locke, Hume and indeed many great philosophers appear to have held that the specific nature of a thought or a belief is fixed by its subjective content, so that it is . . . a separate matter whether a

---

[4] It is revealing that evidence is most naturally construed as that which is presented to a subject or disclosed by him in the process of rummaging about in the world, and from which he builds or infers a judgement of the situation in question.

thought with a given content corresponds to a particular thing in external reality."[5] There are some plausible arguments for this view:

The Argument from reference mistakes:

we can imagine Alfred's believing of apple 1 that it is wholesome, and holding a true belief. Without altering Alfred's dispositions, subjective experiences, and so forth, we can imagine having substituted an identically appearing but internally rotten apple 2. In such a case, Alfred's belief differs while his behavioural dispositions, inner causal states and qualitative experiences remain the same.[6]

In this case his belief is said to have changed because its truth has changed (and the same belief cannot be both true and false). But something is constant and that is a mental property captured by the expression 'cognitive significance' which is essentially independent of the objects concerned. Of course, the fact that an ability is world-involving does not mean that it is infallible in practice and thus this argument fails to secure the solipsist conclusion.

The argument from action explanation: Actions are movements done for certain reasons and as such are causally explained by what goes on in the agent. Therefore, the components of action explanations (which are the states and events denoted by PA psychology) must be mappable on to states of the nervous system even if only on a token–token and therefore non-projectible and non-lawlike basis. This entails that the content of such states must essentially refer to what is internal to the subject, i.e. they should permit 'narrow' specification in terms of states of the organism. I have rejected the view of action underlying this argument.[7]

The argument from mode of presentation: Cognitive significance is not explained merely by picking out an object but by picking out the way a subject apprehends an object. This 'way of apprehending' must be a dynamic property of the subject and thus we get a 'dual component' theory of thought about particulars. The two components are a semantic relation and an MP, the latter of which is analysed in a way congenial to a universalist theory

---

[5] A. Woodfield, 'Foreword', in *TO*, p. vii.
[6] T. Burge, 'Other Bodies', in *TO* 97.   [7] See Ch. 3.

of content. "The universalist, remember, allows that it is quite legitimate to describe thought in the *de-re* style. This decomposes into saying that some universal thinking is going on, and that some particular object relates in the right way to that thinking."[8] But what is "the right way" within the terms of the model?

Kent Bach takes up the challenge for dual-component model of perceptual beliefs by arguing that MPs involve "percepts": "As contents, percepts constitute what perceptual states are like phenomenologically, regardless of the ontological structure of perception."[9] He then suggests, acknowledging his lack of argument, that the relation which ties a percept to an object involves "causes in the way appropriate to perception".[10]

On this view, there is a component apt for psychological explanation which is given by the subject's PAs construed as proximal states of the subject: "the causal role of a belief must depend upon and only upon those properties of representations that can be characterised without adverting to matters lying outside the agent's head".[11] The psychological states which fix this first component determine how the subject uses information. McGinn takes such an element to be implicit in the doctrine 'meaning is use'. "Meaning, on the use conception, comes to be a matter of what I shall call cognitive role—and this is an entirely intra-individual property."[12]

Second, there is a semantic relation between the internal states and the world: "We need to appeal to causality or context or some such to determine what the belief is semantically about, and hence what its truth conditions are."[13] Because "it is not true that what is in the head in the way of mental representations suffices to determine reference", McGinn elaborates a theory of meaning in terms of communication. He notes that propositional content relates both to the communicative content of sentences and the "*ofness* of perceptual representations"[14]:

This intermediate status of belief representation is perhaps not surprising in view of the location of beliefs in the causal network of psychological processes: beliefs are (typically) states caused by perceptions and

---

[8] S. Blackburn, *Spreading the Word* (Oxford, 1984), 313.
[9] K. Bach, '*De Re* Belief and Methodological Solipsism', in *TO* 144.
[10] Ibid. 145.   [11] C. McGinn, 'The Structure of Content', in *TO* 208.
[12] Ibid. 219.   [13] Ibid. 209.   [14] Ibid. 227.

subsequently expressed in speech; so their causal role with respect to input and output seems to reflect (perhaps to underlie) the conceptual status of their representational properties. The aboutness of belief stands between the more primitive (perceptual) and the more sophisticated (linguistic) ways of representing the world, and it reflects a bit of both.[15]

His account of understanding is as follows: "you understand an expression just if (a) you associate the right representation with it, and (b) the resulting states of your head are appropriately related, causally or contextually, to the referent of the expression".[16] This is the empiricist representational theory of mind (ERT) applied to meaning.

There are two internal difficulties in this account.[17] The account analyses mental content in terms of causal states and their relations to events and objects in the world, but also appeals to communication between persons and their shared (interpretive) norms. This entails that it is no longer straight forwardly causal. Interpretive and communicative activity is not merely a matter of causing states in another person, but involves judgements which obey prescriptive norms.

It is worth rehearsing why the need for co-referential items and practices bedevils attempts to provide a purely causal analysis of modes of presentation and cognitive significance. Woodfield states: "our investigation hinges upon the way inner contents are to be specified",[18] and then proceeds as follows:

a state is deemed to have content only when a certain condition holds. . . . The condition is that the psychological state in question occupies a position in a network of states whose characteristic interrelations in S qua reasoner are matched by the logico-semantic relations between the sentences of a language. . . . It is a contingent matter whether there exists a stratum of psychological states in S in which such isomorphism is to be found. . . . But when a match can be set up, it can be exploited. Each of S's states on that level can be assigned a sentence as its label or identification mark within that system of mapping. There is no need to describe its role in reasoning in tedious detail. Using the language as a model, you can identify a state simply by citing its label.[19]

[15] Ibid. 228.   [16] Ibid. 238.
[17] I have given a number of other reasons to reject it in Chs. 1–6.
[18] A. Woodfield, 'On Specifying the Contents of Thoughts', in TO 260.
[19] Ibid. 279–80.

A pre-condition of reasonably accurate communication of *S*'s content is that *A* (ascriber) and *H* (hearer) should have cognitive structures similar to *S*'s and that the contents of all three should map reasonably well on to the intensions of sentences in L_{AH}.[20]

The modelling of thought on language involves scaling the psychological structure of the individual against something public. The intensional structure of a language is determined by the rules of correct use that are created and recognized by a social community. Inevitably there will be individual psychological variations among people within a linguistic community. Consequently it is inevitable that the language will not be a perfect model of the cognitive structure of every native speaker.[21]

Although Woodfield sets out a dual component view here, he never specifies what "isomorphism" involves.[22] To account for the structure in thought, he invokes the rules, referential practices, and creativity of a social community and thus infects his account with something that is irreducible to syntactic relations between states. I would argue that the undischarged debt to conceptual rules ties the analysis to something beyond the "inner contents" upon which it is said to hinge.

This defect derives from a failure to analyse concept mastery. A concept, in Woodfield's account, is part of the "representans" and in McGinn's it is a functional or causally structured "cognitive role". But if contents are determined by rule-governed acts of judgement then:

1. they are not mere causal products of an interaction with the world but rather have normative features which ought to appear in the analysis; and
2. they go beyond individual mental mechanisms or causal dispositions and invoke "norms for persons to follow".[23]

A second defect is revealed by the claim that a subject's grasp of the senses of expressions rests on cognitive structures which for each individual contingently map on to the natural language concerned. An adequate analysis should *essentially* or a priori secure

---

[20] Ibid. 281.   [21] Ibid. 288.

[22] He suggests an analysis close to that of Brian Loar (*Mind and Meaning* (Cambridge, 1981)) in which propositions serve as indices or labels which match (or are isomorphic with) the structure of actual internal states of the subject.

[23] The phrase is from *TEC* 50–1. Saul Kripke argues this point in his criticism of a dispositional analysis of meaning in *Wittgenstein on Rules and Private Language* (Oxford, 1982).

the objectivity and potential intersubjectivity of sense or cognitive significance. The proposed link between public "rules of correct use" and understanding is by the troublesome "isomorphism" of language and cognitive states which is incomplete, allowing a certain amount of content to "slip through the social net".[24] Content or sense *is*, on this account, dependent on "men's varying states of consciousness",[25] and we have lost sight of Frege's concern to safeguard thought against any such loosening from truth.

Thus the dual component account fails because:

1. it is theoretically heterogeneous and, one suspects, may involve an immiscible set of analytic elements;
2. it does not pay sufficient attention to the normative aspects of judgement and concept-use; and
3. it loosens the connection between sense and truth by analysing the former in terms of individual mental states.

By contrast, the present account is theoretically unified and explains cognitive significance so as to secure the non-individualistic and normative aspects of sense.

7.4. *Practices, Use, and Ways of Thinking*

Wittgenstein's remark "the meaning of a word is its use in the language" (*PI* I. 43) suggests that in meaning something by an expression a thinker intentionally invokes the role that the term plays in a certain practice. In such practices people act upon or communicate about their world in articulated ways. Any term draws together a number of contexts and actions in which it has been used. Some situations are more central to the shared practice than others and therefore could be regarded as canonical, or central to the "grammar" of that term. Wittgenstein remarks: "Grammar tells what kind of object anything is" and "Essence is expressed by grammar" (*PI* I. 371, 373). Grammar refers to the informal rules which have shaped and now govern the use of a term so that it has a determinate function in discourse. This construal of meaning

---

[24] It is unclear whether this concession implies that some elements of content are essentially (i.e. not just accidentally) individualistic or merely that shared meaning determined by rules or norms is a common skeleton fleshed out by individual use dependent on cognitive structures.   [25] G. Frege, 'Thoughts', in *LI* 35.

as rule-governed use leads to a workable account of cognitive significance.

Consider the common term 'ticket'; I must think of tickets in a particular way to understand its meaning. There are many ways in which I could think of the items concerned: as pieces of paper, messages, advertisements for particular events, and so on. But to grasp the concept ⟨ticket⟩ I must think of it as a token or sign of my entitlement to some service or benefit. To take it this way is not necessarily to be aware of any perceptual feature or combination of features because perceptual evidence falls short of what is required to grasp the concept ⟨ticket⟩. In understanding the concept (and thus any thoughts of which it is a component) one must grasp the way that certain items figure in a complex pattern of human activity, and this does not depend on a physical specification of those items. An understanding of how tickets are used in human activities and the articulation of the concept ⟨ticket⟩ with other concepts jointly form the criteria which determine whether I grasp the concept. This is much richer than the notion of a pattern of evidential sensitivity, but it fits the phrase 'a way of thinking'. It shows us how the concept ⟨ticket⟩ is essentially embedded in human activity or "forms of life".

Now consider the concept ⟨handle⟩. Handles come in all shapes and sizes, and perhaps one could compile a set of examples such that someone could recognize all extant handles. Would he then grasp the concept ⟨handle⟩? I think not. To grasp the concept he needs to know what to do with a handle. Only then does he understand the cognitive significance of ⟨handle⟩ in that he can use the concept in his own intentional activity. When he has achieved this 'way of thinking' about handles he is equipped to understand a full range of thoughts involving ⟨handle⟩.

Consider next the proper name 'Peter Strawson'. I first knew of Peter Strawson as the author of *Individuals* and thought of him in that way. Among those who knew the term its cognitive significance was ⟨the author of *Individuals*⟩ and, if someone wished to build on this way of thinking about Peter Strawson, he might read the book. But Peter Strawson is also a person with whom one might have tea and who often wears a faintly bemused smile on his face. Thus there is quite a different way of thinking of him which a person visiting Oxford could acquire, if, for instance, Peter Strawson were introduced to him. This example suggests why there is a temptation to appeal to 'patterns of evidential sensitivity' to capture MPs (of course, what one takes even from a fleeting acquaintance draws on a much broader range of human activity than can be accommodated in terms of causally produced and specified states).

Now, consider the concept ⟨7⟩. A grasp of this concept involves knowing, *inter alia*, where to place the number 7 when counting, what sets it applies to, how to multiply by 7, how it figures in addition or subtraction, and so on. If I can do only one of these operations then my grasp of the concept is partial. The concept ⟨7⟩ is embedded in a series of articulated and rule-governed procedures and practices and it is my competence in some indefinite subset of these activities that constitutes understanding it. If we consider Kant's famous example '5 + 7 = 12', we see that each item in the equation has its own place in a range of practices which interact in the way given by the formula. Thus the truth of the equation could emerge from analysis of these practices. (Notice that a mathematical example makes a causal account of mode or manner of presentation look most odd.)

Finally, the concept ⟨red⟩ provides us with an example in which a grasp of the concept seems to be clearly and essentially related to sensory conditions. But what is clear can obscure other facts which are just as essential but less salient. When confronted by a red thing I must respond to its colour rather than its shape, size, or any other property, and this depends upon my attending selectively to some feature of the situation.[26] Only as I master the trick of focusing on the colour and linking my response to that feature do I master the concept. The cues given by the behaviour of others who already grasp the concept ⟨red⟩ provide me with the way of thinking in question. A "pattern of evidential sensitivity" (Peacocke) makes no reference to the techniques involved in this mastery and also blurs the distinction between criteria and evidence.[27]

7.5. Criteria and Evidence

Criteria are the basis on which mastery of a concept is ascribed. They are constitutive of a particular meaning or content rather

[26] I have discussed this in §§1.2–4 above.
[27] The complex distinctions involved have been discussed by Gordon Baker in 'Criteria: A New Basis for Semantics', *Ratio*, 16 (1974), 156–89.

than being independently specifiable items of content which serve as grounds for an inference that a given concept is instantiated. When, for instance, one is walking through drops of water falling from a cloudy sky, that is not evidence that it is raining: that is what we mean by rain. McDowell remarks:

I think we should understand criteria to be, in the first instance, ways of telling how things are ... and we should take it that knowledge that a criterion for a claim is actually satisfied ... would be an exercise of the very capacity that we speak of when we say that one can tell, on the basis of such-and-such criteria, whether things are as the claim would represent them as being.[28]

Criteria express our way of knowing that a fact pertains, and may be inexpressible apart from the judgement they support, e.g. what is meant by something being red is that it is like other red things in respect of colour. Criteria are not always so austere,[29] for instance, one can judge that a figure is square when it has four equal sides meeting at right angles. Criteria are also dependent upon certain background conditions: for instance, if it emerged that a huge fleet of Russian superbombers was dropping water on us to make us all feel miserable, we would quickly see that there was more to the judgement ⟨It's raining⟩ than 'being rained upon'. (There is a hint of verificationism in this view because the content of many concepts depends on rule-governed applications.)

Evidence, by contrast, comprises specifiable facts which may license an inference to some further fact. The further fact is detectable or at least conceivable as distinct from the evidence for it (except on a verificationist account of meaning). Evidence, we could say, is cognate or has a role in thought apart from that which it is evidence for. Certain criteria, operative in public practices, fix the content of items of evidence, and others fix that of the state of affairs to which the evidence points. I judge that it was Charles who met George on the basis of criteria for the person I saw being Charles. This judgement along with certain others enables me to infer that Charles shot George. Thus my original judgement is part of the *evidence* for the latter judgement

[28] J. McDowell, 'Criteria, Defeasibility and Knowledge', *Proceedings of the British Academy*, 68 (1983), 470.
[29] The term is borrowed from Mark Platts (*Ways of Meaning* (London, 1979), 262).

in that it has distinct content and figures in the train of thought that leads to the belief. Criteria are the basis on which I grasp what the evidence is, and inference tells me what it is evidence for. Thus to cite evidential states as the basis of meaning is to go round in circles.

A common move at this point is to invoke preconceptual evidential, informational, or causal states in an analysis of mental content. But this is suspect on two further counts:

1. there is no basis on which the requisite ascriptions can be made;[30] and
2. preconceptual matter is not evidence upon which one can make inferences because inferences involve discursive activity, namely manipulating concepts.

Criteria determine what counts as an instance of the concept forming the content of a certain judgement. The detachment of criteria from inferential activity allows that the criteria for a given judgement may be grasped non-inferentially, by training or participation in the practice in which the relevant judgements are learnt.

Thus to understand the content of ⟨red⟩ is to grasp a way of thinking based on the use of certain examples such that one can judge what 'that colour' is for a range of objects (note the connection between perception and demonstratives). It is because I have mastered a technique of selective attention and rule-governed use that I can form at will a mental image of red. Thus mental content derives essentially from public practices involving items mutually accessible between co-linguistic thinkers. These items ground the rules and criteria for the ascription of meaning and understanding and thus the content of our thoughts. Which is why, as Wittgenstein claims, "Our thought, and thus the meaning of our words, does not stop anywhere short of the facts" (*PI* I. 195).[31]

7.6. A Broad, or at least 'Non-Narrow', Account of Sense

Now we can give an *übersicht* of cognitive significance.

The sense of any expression is determined in human activities

---

[30] D. Davidson, 'On the Very Idea of a Conceptual Scheme', in *ITI*.

[31] I have discussed perceptual concepts at length in 'Learning to Perceive', *Philosophy and Phenomenological Research*, 48 (1988), 601–18.

where that expression finds a use. One grasps the sense or relevant way of thinking in appreciating and mastering that use. Therefore the cognitive significance of any expression is essentially linked to engagement in a network of interpersonal activity (which finds expression in language). The cognitive significance of a term is the way that it is interwoven with what things people do and what they encounter in situations where they use it. No doubt, in my head (or brain), there are certain 'states' which accompany its use, but to understand the cognitive significance of an expression is to become adept in certain practices which define what Wittgenstein calls the "grammar" of the expression. This excludes solipsistic or psychologistic construals of cognitive significance and safeguards the intersubjectivity of sense. It suggests that "the individuation of a given individual's mental contents depends partly on the nature (or what his fellows think to be the nature) of entities about which he and his fellow have *de re* beliefs. The identity of one's mental contents states and events is not independent of one's physical and social environment."[32]

The cognitive significance of a particular expression depends on criteria which normatively constrain its use. A way of thinking or manner of presentation associated with a term is the way an object (or set of features) figures in the use of a denoting expression. Therefore, identity statements are informative because they effect the intersection of two practices. When any thinker grasps the identity he can draw on either of the relevant practices in framing a thought. Such a contact between practices is a priori or necessary when the practices intersect solely in virtue of the rules governing both (as the practice in which one grasps that ⟨the sum of 3 and 4⟩ must intersect with those practices involving ⟨7⟩). (Of course, it may not be obvious without some reasoning that the intersection is dictated solely by the rules of the practices concerned.)

In other cases—e.g. ⟨Peter Strawson is an Oxford philosopher⟩— the intersection of the practices depends on properties of a certain individual and thus is contingent. No amount of scrutiny of the rules governing the use of terms (absent their application) will reveal the identity of their common focus; that can only be ascertained empirically.

On the present view, singular expressions (and thoughts) are

---

[32] Burge, 'Other Bodies', 107 (see also Ch. 8).

grounded in practices which involve a specifiable particular. Even an expression like 'the man' can be a singular term in this way. Imagine, for instance, that I go to a factory and say 'I am looking for a job'. I get the answer 'Aha, you need to see *the man*'. Here, 'the man' denotes just one particular because of the existence of a practice in which that expression has a certain use. Only by understanding the practice concerned do we grasp why a given particular is being unambiguously picked out (note that this understanding is of intersubjective facts).

7.7. *Résumé of Complaints about Methodological Solipsism*

I have argued that understanding the sense of a term involves competence in the practices in which it has a use. Under pressure to provide an account of action explanation which does not go beyond states of the agent, one might contend that an adequate analysis of cognitive significance *must* limit itself to proximal states of the organism. Thus action explanation would fit into the general scheme of singular causal explanations. I have already discussed this in some detail but will rehearse my general strategy.[33]

First, actions are directed towards objects in the world and therefore some specification of those objects should figure in an analysis of action. To reduce the content of such explanations to proximal states one has to neglect the fact that rules are tied to public objects which therefore have an essential role in content determination.

Second, the desire to find an internal causal grounding for mental explanation does not avoid an appeal to public practices and the objects over which they range. This point is reinforced by the fact that the structural relations between brain states are themselves explained in terms of the situations in which conceptual abilities have been developed.[34] If the brain is causally structured so that information (which can only be understood in the terms I have suggested) has a reliable role in the organization of behaviour, then the explanation of that structure rests on rules operating in the milieu in which that information has taken shape.

[33] Ch. 3.
[34] As discussed in 'Perception and Neuroscience', *British Journal of Philosophy of Science*, 40 (1989), 83–103.

Third, to frame a specification of the contents of proximal states which captured the truth and explanatory power to be found in ordinary (object-involving) mental ascriptions one would need to provide a phenomenological reduction of those objects. But thinkers deal with mental information as it is structured by concepts, and on the present analysis even universal concepts depend on those (object-involving) "situations in which language is taught and learnt".[35]

We can now return to "canonical links". Peacocke states: "A specification of the canonical links of a given content is intended to be a priori . . . The norms it outlines are norms for persons to follow" (TEC 50–1). I have argued that the norms which determine cognitive significance are determined by rules which range over items in the world. The thinker is trained to make judgements about the applicability of concepts and the truth of certain thoughts. From his contact with objects, events, people, and features in the world, and on the basis of his mastery of rule-governed practices, a thinker masters these judgements. Some of these practices are central in the grasp of a concept, and therefore one might call them 'canonical'. The contents of thoughts are thus a priori tied to practices in which thinkers communicate so as to provide truth-linked canonical grounds and commitments of the judgements made. I applaud Peacocke's introduction of canonical links and their relation to reasons, but cannot accept an account in terms of mental states. Indeed, if we take problems of private language to be at all damaging to an account of meaning, it would seem that Peacocke has detracted from his illuminating analysis by his appeal to such states.

In my dealings with the world and my engagement with certain practices, I acquire the ability to think about certain things. The practices in which I participate fix the senses of the terms that I use and thus the ways of thinking or modes or manners of presentation of objects and features of the world to which I refer in my expressions. If you are not engaged in the same practices, you will not understand my ways of thinking or be able to identify the objects to which I refer. That is why "If God had looked into our minds he would not have been able to see there whom we were speaking of" (PI II. xi, p. 217e).

---

[35] A. Quinton, 'The Problem of Perception', in G. Warnock (ed.), The Philosophy of Perception (Oxford, 1967).

7.8. Summary

The sense or cognitive significance of an expression is supposed to explain the fact that identity statements are informative. I have analysed cognitive significance in terms of the way that a given term is located within the world-involving practices in which a thinker has participated. I have examined the contention that there are two components to sense—one comprised by states internal to the subject and one which links those states to the world—and have rejected it because it does not explain the normative aspects of sense. The present account allows a distinction between identity statements which are true in virtue of the rules governing certain human abilities and those which are true because of some fact about the world. The resulting construal of sense or cognitive significance essentially rests on intersubjective features of meaning.

8

Singular Thought

I HAVE tried to rebut the most forceful reasons for analysing content in terms of states in the head. There are two reasons for discussing singular thoughts and the sense in which their content is essentially object-involving. First, any theory of thought content ought to offer accounts of general and singular thoughts which are compatible yet respect the differences between them. Second, thoughts which pick out particulars prima facie engage the mind with objects in the world rather than merely general conceptions of objects. This has crucial importance in determining the general shape of a theory of content because "No *de-re* mental state about an object that is external to the person's brain can possibly be identical with a state of that brain, since no brain state presupposes the existence of an external object" (*TO*, p. viii). But a workable account of singular thoughts must not retreat into "some special cognitive relation. . . . inspired by Russell's distinction between knowledge by acquaintance and knowledge by description, philosophers have described what they take to be this relation in various picturesque ways . . . 'rapport' . . . 'direct cognitive contact' . . . and 'epistemic intimacy'".[1] I will aim to explain the distinct nature of singular thought within the framework of the present account and without *ad hoc* additions.

8.1. *Questions of Status*

At least three distinct claims are made about singular thoughts:

1. Singular thoughts are descriptive thoughts but pick out a unique reference for the thinker concerned.
2. Singular thoughts are distinctive in nature and must be accommodated in any adequate theory of content.
3. Singular thoughts are basic to all human thought.

---

[1] Kent Bach, '*De Re* Belief and Methodological Solipsism', in *TO* 132.

There are two ways in which a singular thought could be related to one and only one particular: either by conceptual content which picked out just and only that individual, or by a constitutive relationship with an individual such that a specification of the content of the thought could not eliminate mention of that object. The first of these is compatible with attempts to specify content solely in terms of representational states of the subject (but does not entail that view).

We could call thoughts which are singular in the first sense *descriptive* singular thoughts and those which are essentially object-involving (if such exist) *de re* thoughts.[2] *De re* thoughts would fall into two classes: demonstrative and recognitional. In each case there is an intuitive sense in which the lack of an object to which the thought is related makes the thought essentially defective in that if there is nothing to recognize or demonstrate the thought goes awry. *Descriptive* singular thoughts are only controversially included here because it is a contingent matter that such thoughts concern just one item. Thus thoughts which are essentially singular (essentially involve some particular) are either *demonstrative*, involving items presented to a thinker and picked out by demonstrative expressions, or *recognitional*, involving an object that the thinker can recognize even though he may not possess any individuating description of it. He may, of course, be able to give some description which, along with his recognitional ability, does individuate the item, e.g. 'the pie I have been thinking of all day'. A coherent account of such thoughts would provide a substantive analysis of the Russellian notion of 'acquaintance'.

Geach asks "How . . . is a judgment expressible as 'that flash was before this bang', which refers to a particular flash and a particular bang, to be distinguished from a judgment with the same verbal expression which refers to another flash and another bang? What constitutes this reference to definite particulars?" (*MA* 63). Geach wants an account of how we pick out items when the *de dicto* content of our thought does not suffice to do the job. To answer him we must specify the distinction between *de re* and *de dicto* contents without invoking the problematic "special cognitive relation".

---

[2] I recognize that, arguably, there will be a possible further set of *de re* thoughts which concern natural kinds, which I will not attempt to discuss. An account could readily be forged from the materials I will provide to deal with singular thoughts.

We could say that the *res* is ineliminable in specifying the content of *de re* thoughts, by contrast with a *de dicto* thought, which is "complete" or "completely expressed" in terms of propositional content.[3] McDowell summarizes: "a belief's being fully conceptualized can mean only that it has a fully propositional content exhausted by some collection of thought symbols",[4] but then he objects to this restrictive definition:

a conceptual repertoire can include the ability to think of objects under modes of presentation whose functioning depends essentially on (say) the perceived presence of the objects. Such *de-re* modes of presentation would be parts or aspects of content, not vehicles for it; no means of mental representation could determine the content in question by itself, without benefit of context. But that does not establish any good sense in which the content is not fully conceptualized.[5]

This does not yet show how a *res* enters the specification of content. The present ('non-narrow' or "outward-looking") account does, however, provide for *de re* thought content.

8.2. *Cognition about Particulars*

The cognitive significance of any expression *E* is elucidated by appeal to the practices in which it is used. Thus the contribution of the sense of *E* to any complex thought is also determined by those practices and the rules which govern them. Suppose I think ⟨that handle is green⟩, then the content involved is determined by links:

1. to the ostensive practices where we use 'that';
2. between the term 'handle' and the use of handles;
3. to the practices where we mark present states of the objects of our concern; and
4. to those practices in which we focus on colours.[6]

My grasp of the concept ⟨handle⟩, for instance, rests both on the recognition that what is before me has a certain role and on my

---

[3] T. Burge, 'Belief *De Re*', *Journal of Philosophy*, 74 (1977), 338–62.

[4] J. McDowell, '*De Re* Senses', in C. Wright (ed.), *Frege: Tradition and Influence* (Oxford, 1984).   [5] Ibid. 102.

[6] Recall that this is not the way in which Peacocke, whose term I have adopted, characterizes "canonical links".

ability to judge, for a range of items, whether they fit that role. If someone said 'My, this magnetic paper-holder on the door looks just like a handle!', then I would have grounds for re-evaluating my use of ⟨handle⟩. I might worry, for instance, that, were I to act as if it were a handle, my action would miscarry. I can think ⟨I would have taken that for a handle⟩, can wonder whether my informant was wrong, and, perhaps, can settle things by attempting to detach it from the door. This move uses abilities developed in those practices involving the term 'handle' to reveal whether the internal relations between this item and those practices hold; in so doing, it exploits "canonical links".

Evans quotes Frege on singular thought as follows:

A sentence can be true or untrue only if it is an expression of a thought. The sentence "Leo Sachse is a man" is the expression of a thought only if "Leo Sachse" designates something. And so too the sentence "this table is round" is the expression of a thought only if the words "this table" are not empty sounds but designate something specific for me. (*VR* 12)

Frege takes names and demonstratives as paradigm cases; here there must be an object involved for the thought to be assessable as true or false. I shall discuss recognition-based thoughts, as in expressions like 'Jane Day is coming tomorrow' or 'The clown I saw yesterday looked sad', instead of names *per se*.⁷ In each case there must be an actual referent if the thought is to be grasped. If there is no 'Jane Day' or if there was no clown that I saw yesterday then there is no obvious way to take what has been said; an assessment of truth is impossible and the thought has no clear content. Demonstrative expressions such as 'That table is a bit Heath Robinson' or 'This operation is called a Smith-Robinson procedure' also depend on something being picked out by 'that table' or 'this operation'. If nothing is, then one does not know where to turn to frame a thought corresponding to the sentence. Frege himself does not analyse the denoting relation, but Evans attempts to specify what is involved by means of "information links".

---

⁷ Many names do involve recognition-based thoughts, but the examples show that not all names as understood by all thinkers do. Neither do all recognition-based thoughts correspond to names, e.g. ⟨the clown . . .⟩.

8.3. Information Links

The fact that, in thoughts expressed by sentences involving names and demonstratives, the objects or events referred to are an essential part of the content is plausibly explained if the subject requires information from the object on which to base his thought. This is Evans's view:

When a person perceives something he receives (or, better, gathers) information about the world. By communicating, he may transmit this information to others. And any piece of information in his possession at a given time may be retained by him until some later time. People are, in short and among other things, gatherers, transmitters and storers of information. These platitudes locate perception, communication and memory in a system—the information system—which constitutes the substratum of our cognitive lives. (VR 122)

Evans distinguishes information (as he uses the term) from sensations and beliefs. He rejects (as have I) the idea that sensations provide data from which states of the external world are inferred (although he does not argue for this rather short way with this idea): "the only events that can conceivably be regarded as data for a conscious reasoning subject are seemings—events, that is, already imbued with apparent objective significance and with a necessary, though resistible, propensity to influence our actions" (VR 123). He also distinguishes information from belief: "It is as well to reserve 'belief' for the notion of a far more sophisticated cognitive state: one that is connected with . . . the notion of judgment, and so also connected with the notion of reasons. The operations of the informational system are more primitive" (VR 124). But I have argued that judgement is inherent in all "seemings" and thus cannot accept his next step:[8]

We can speak of a certain bit of information being of, or perhaps from, any object in a sense resembling the way in which we speak of a photograph being of an object. . . . The sense in which a photograph is of an object is as follows. A certain mechanism produces things which have a certain informational content . . . The mechanism is a mechanism of information storage, because the properties that figure in the content of its output are (to a degree determined by the accuracy of the mechanism) the properties possessed by the objects which are input to it. (VR 124–5)

[8] See §1.6.

Evans argues that this content depends for its specification only on the properties of the representation rather than on any reference to the object itself. Therefore information *from* or *of* an object *a* need not individuate *a*. Thus he needs some complementary account of what it is that makes the epistemic relation between the thinker and the object of his thought *essentially* a relation to *a*. He notes two phenomena: first, we may have in mind an inapt description of an object we have encountered and yet still want to say that in some sense it is that particular object we are thinking about; and, second, we may have information which happens to fit an object but not the one we derived it from. In discussing these possibilities, Evans uses the term 'well grounded': "We know perfectly well which object the subject wishes to distinguish in thought . . . But he fails to distinguish it in thought; and hence his essaying of a particular thought about it is based on a mistake. In such a situation . . . the thought episode is not well grounded" (*VR* 134).

There is a slide here from an austere causal use of the term 'information', as in discourse about photographs and other mechanisms, to a use which allows us to talk about 'grounds' and 'fit' of information to objects according to "modes of identification". A purely causal imprint—(thin)[9] information—is not conceptual information; that requires a judgement that things are thus and so. Concepts (functions of judgement which unify diverse experiences (Kant) or forge internal relations between objects (Wittgenstein, *PI* 212e) are required for 'seemings'. Causal effects merely result from what causes them and questions of fit or groundedness are out of place. A seeming "fits" an object or is well or ill grounded only if there is some standard of comparison or normative aspect to what is being assessed. But this puts Evans's view under some pressure.

Causal mechanisms produce thin information but a thinker represents an object according to certain concepts which may or may not be appropriate to it depending on the rules governing them. The use of the undifferentiated notion of 'information' effects the slide between the two ways of characterizing what is going on, but should not be allowed to do so. Ascriptions of informational states which ground concepts but do not involve

---

[9] Thin and thick information is discussed in §5.7.

judgement fall foul of exactly those problems with preconceptual content that Davidson has raised.[10] How can we justify ascribing contentful states to a subject when they have no manifest conceptual role on which to ground the requisite mental ascriptions? Also, as has been noted, a photograph is assessed by subjects who know what counts as a representation of the object in question, and therefore the analogy carries an undischarged debt to what it is trying to elucidate.

If we purge Evans's account of these problems, we derive a different (analytically unified) view of information. On this view, information from an object puts one in a position to make judgements about that object. It represents the object as instancing certain concepts. Taking something to be F (say) is reliably informative if one grasps the concept $\langle F \rangle$. It is reliable because there is a relation, as Grayling has noted, between competence in basic perceptual judgements and competence in the grasp of meaning.[11] It is corrigible because to perceive is to subsume what one confronts under some rule or other, i.e. to exercise a skill, and a thinker can be in a situation which warrants a perceptual judgement about a and yet link his judgement to the wrong conceptual practices. Thus a subject "receives (or, better, gathers)" information from the object of his thought when he responds to it in some rule-governed way based on practices and the items appearing within them. This is unlike the sensation–inference–belief model because we are saying that the subject encounters and responds to an object by using conceptual abilities. He does not receive evidence or information about which he then makes inferences; rather he has information as a result of certain defeasible judgements. Note that this information is inherently apt for mental ascription and reasoning.

To be thought about is therefore to be conceived of in some way (however inchoate). Once a subject makes a conceptual response to a given item we can say there is an information link between him and that item. But notice that the link, even if it is in fact always causally mediated (by activity in some sensory system), is not a causal relation but a conceptual relation between a thinker and his world in terms of practices he has mastered. This

---

[10] 'On the Very Idea of a Conceptual Scheme', in *ITI*.
[11] A. Grayling, *The Refutation of Scepticism* (London, 1986), esp. ch. 2.

explains the close relation between perceptual information and that derived from discourse (thus elucidating how both can figure in a unified understanding of content), and it allows judgements to be defeasible without being inferential (because they involve competence in a technique or practice).

Notice also that when a subject thinks of a, the concepts in which he thinks of it are supplemented by thinking of it as something he has encountered. If he has encountered nothing then he will not frame a clear thought. If he thinks of a in a way that is not appropriate to it then, as Evans remarks, his thought will fail in a different and complementary way: "It cannot, then, be correct to suppose that the mode of identification (the Idea) employed in an information-based thought can be exhaustively given by a definite description 'the ϕ'" (*VR* 141).

8.4. *Demonstrative Thought*

Evans develops an interesting account of demonstrative thought. He remarks: "A demonstrative thought is clearly an information-based thought (one might say the mother and father of all information-based thoughts); the subject's thinking is governed by a controlling conception he derives from the object" (*VR* 145–6). The words "controlling conception" indicate that the subject's thought is tied to ongoing contact with the object. If a demonstrative Idea of an object involves ongoing sensitivity, then it requires the subject to keep track of the object that interests him and of his own position with respect to it. Evans adds a word of caution, qualifying the thin view of information here: "the sheer existence of an information-link between subject and object does not guarantee the possibility of demonstrative thought about the object" (*VR* 148). He invokes the Generality Constraint[12] to argue that any object of our thought must be open to a wide range of judgements. He claims that, in addition to information from an object, a demonstrative Idea requires the ability to locate it in space, but he does not explain how location in a cognitive map representing objective space engages that Idea in our rich conceptual structure (Campbell makes the same assertion and oversight[13]).

---

[12] The Generality Constraint is discussed in §1.10
[13] J. Campbell, 'Conceptions of Conceptual Structure'.

This deficiency must be rectified in order to put cognitive maps in their true perspective.

How do demonstratives gain significance for a subject? The present account of concepts and cognitive significance implies that we must elucidate them by appeal to the practices (or language games) in which demonstrative terms are used. These involve perception.[14]

We master demonstratives by having our attention drawn to features in our environment and by framing judgements which pick them out. Thus a judgement involving a demonstrative is linked to the information available to those using it. If I say to you 'That is a bat' you look for some perceptually accessible object to which my remark refers. You will, perhaps, light on the small animal hanging from the barn roof above us and can clarify what you see by having me use terms to illuminate it. If there is no item or feature upon which you may light for information, then you are entitled to conclude that I am using the demonstrative wrongly or using it to express a false judgement that something is suited to a practice involving mutual informational access when nothing actually is (perhaps I am having a hallucination). In any event, something is wrong if I cannot steer your attention on to an object picked out by my demonstrative. Evans is, therefore, right to focus on perception because the referent of a demonstrative expression must be in the subject's egocentric space (the space of which she is the centre and over which her perception ranges). But he neglects the internal relation between language and thought in his attempt to secure objectivity for demonstrative Ideas.

He goes on to develop an account of object identification in terms of egocentric space and public space:

... a demonstrative Idea of an object is not reducible to any other sort of Idea, and in particular cannot be regarded as a species of descriptive identification. One has an adequate Idea in virtue of the existence of an information-link between oneself and the object, which enables one to locate that object in egocentric space. (VR 173)

He claims that demonstrative ideas depend upon perceptual (and behavioural) access to objects in my egocentric space and become objective when they are more widely engaged with a range of spatial concepts:

[14] The link was suggested to me by Paul Snowdon.

the subject may be said to have an adequate Idea of a point in public space in virtue of his general capacity to impose a conception of public space upon egocentric space. (*VR* 168)

Thus an item which one knows only as ⟨something near me⟩ has an objective place in the world as one acquires the ability to locate the point near oneself in an objective or non-relativized cognitive map. This yields an individuating idea of that object:

A proposition about a material object, [*a* is *F*] where *a* is a demonstrative Idea, is conceived to be rendered true by the truth of a pair of propositions of the form [δ is *F*] and [*a* = δ] where δ is a fundamental Idea. That is to say that the object of the demonstrative thought must be conceived to be part of the objectively describable, spatially-ordered world (which is not to say that the object of the thought can be specified, in a content-giving account of the thought, other than demonstratively). (*VR* 179)

Evans thus ties the content and objectivity of demonstrative singular thoughts to a cognitive map which objectifies the relations between the places (and thus the objects) that a subject encounters. The ability to use such a cognitive map depends upon the fact that a subject can keep track of his position and locate his egocentric space with respect to it. The availability of this underpinning for the conception of an object in a demonstrative thought secures the general objectivity of perceived particulars.

I would agree that these are important aspects of our thought about things in general, but insist that it is the potential agreement with others implicit in the mutual use of demonstratives that secures the (defeasible) objectivity of a particular. The individual must have access to an object to demonstratively identify it, thus it must be in his egocentric space; but he must also conceive of that space as potentially accessible to others: both features are implicit within his grasp of the meaning of demonstratives. Therefore one's ability to keep track of things and to impose upon one's own scheme the mutual and validating perspective of others are both required to underwrite the objectivity of experience. These are (jointly) involved in the mastery of concepts within practices which focus on perceptually presented objects. Intersubjectivity is thus a normative feature of demonstrative thought even though, once we are competent in such thinking, the agreement of others is no longer necessary.

An example emphasizes the point. Imagine that Sam has a brain aberration such that whenever he sees Blackwell's bookshop on a moonlit night he imagines that the caped black figure of his old English-master is standing there. Now such a thought has, as far as Sam is concerned, an object which he can locate in both ego-centric and public space. But a moment's reassurance from his friends may convince him that it is a phantasm which does not have objective existence. Note that, once they have latched on to Sam's representation of his experience, his friends can discuss his experience despite there being no perceptual information-link between them and the figure.

How should we analyse such a case? For Sam, it is as if the canonical links for a perceptual or demonstrative MP are fulfilled, but when he attempts to initiate the standard perceptual-demonstrative language game it does not work. Thus he realizes that his judgements in this matter are ill grounded, i.e. that the criteria for (or canonical links of) the judgement he is inclined to make are not satisfied. He therefore withdraws his unconditional judgement and characterizes the situation as best he can: 'It is just as if there were the black caped figure of my old English-master standing in Blackwell's doorway'. For Sam's friends no object was picked out when he said 'Look at that man' so they concluded that his appeal to certain rules had somehow miscarried. Therefore they say 'You are not perceiving anything; that man is a figment of your own imagination'. They know that their demonstrative 'that man' has a meaning for Sam because (1) he is conversant with the normal use of demonstratives and thus the logical–conceptual form he has applied to his present experience, and (2) he is sincere in his use. In any event, Sam can rely neither on location in his own egocentric space nor on a cognitive map to identify a particular as objective. He must recognize that the ultimate criteria for successful demonstrative identification derive from the shared use of expressions where subjects would normally converge in their judgements.

We can reinforce these conclusions by further reference to Evans, who notes: "anyone who has the conception of the objective spatial world must know that no experience of his own can suffice for the truth of any . . . proposition of the form [*a* is *F*]" (*VR* 179). A subject must recognize that his mastery of the use 'that *x*' is an ability which he may exercise mistakenly and that therefore there is more to the content of ⟨that *x* is *F*⟩ than is given by his disposition to affirm the judgement. His warrant for it is not a matter of his own mental states but is rather secured by his manifest competence in following public rules of use.

8.5. Recognition-Based Thoughts

Evans makes the following points about recognition-based thoughts:
First, recognition need not involve an individuating description. An ability to recognize a particular as the same in different presentations, or, in Evans's terms, to *track* it, does not depend on some uniquely satisfiable descriptive conception. In fact the subject's representation of the object may be substantially erroneous. If he can be led to see that his information derives from a particular which does not fit his description he could well modify his representation and yet be thinking of the same particular. Neither is recognition based solely on familiarity:

> It is not enough for one to recognize an object that it strike one as familiar; one must identify it as something—usually, though not exclusively, as the object encountered on a previous occasion. In those exercises of recognitional capacities which interest us, the subject will identify the object as the object he was thinking about. (VR 270)

The subject must have a *grounded* propensity to identify the object as that of which he is thinking in order to give some conceptual substance to a recognitional thought. Familiarity with a re-encountered x is not enough because the thought ⟨this x is a⟩ is tied both to (1) some situation in which a was a source of information to which his thoughts were sensitive, and (2) some conception of what counts as an x.

A recognitional thought of a also allows reidentification of a despite changes in the subject's informational contact with it. In such thoughts some non-descriptive referring expression 'a' picks out the particular and serves as a focus for information collected about it.

Consequently, we should expect that, in any system in which information is stored about particular objects, there will be a central core of cases in which the subject has associated information with a capacity to recognize a particular individual. In this core, we should expect to find some cases in which a rich and detailed picture of an individual has been built up over an extended period of time. (VR 276)

Thus one's conceptions of a particular are controlled by repeated informational contact with it and if the particular does not exist they have no clear sense.

Evans argues that it is the spatial relations of an object that identify it as being a given particular and that these, in part, involve the non-inferential capacity of the subject to keep track of things in space and time. My view would be that we locate objects and track them through a world charted by the practices in which language is mastered.

Evans also claims that certain expressions function only as marks of recognition and need not be (though they may happen to be) individuating or definite descriptions. He notes that we may often recognize an object without having any clear recall of it which would suffice to pick it out. He rehearses Wittgenstein's rejection of the idea that comparison with an impression or representation could be the basis of recognition, remarking: "Perhaps, in some sense or other, information about the object's appearance is stored in the nervous system, but this is not information which the subject has or in any sense uses to effect an identification" (VR 288). He considers the property ⟨looks like y⟩ to be an irreducible, but in principle universal, property instantiated by y. And it is entirely plausible that different people may react to quite different saliencies in such a composite (if irreducible) property:

It might be tempting at this point to retreat to the claim that the relevant appearance property is that of looking like this to x . . . This would be a genuinely private concept, since no one other than x can be master of it, and therefore it is useless for the descriptive theorist to appeal to it. . . . A concept is something abstracted from the practice of judging . . . which is a performance assessable as being correct or incorrect. But his pseudo-concept cannot be exercised in any such performance. Whatever seems right to the subject is right, which only means that we cannot speak of "right" here. (VR 295)

Of course we do develop abilities to recognize (without checking) that, for example, this is an x, but developing such an ability requires that one's inclination to judge something to be x must be shaped into a consistent form. Only thus can there be something I aim to do correctly when I recognize x. If there were nothing to go on except my inclination, then I could have no conception of a normative aspect to my judgement and no reason to believe that there was anything regular I was doing.

It emerges that a representation or template in the mind composed of predicative or universal elements is no basis for the identification and reidentification of a particular. The only focus that a recognitional practice can have is the particular itself, to which the judgements of co-referential thinkers are answerable. Without this focus there is no controlling conception for their (essentially communicable) thoughts. However adequate a conception of some particular is as framed by any individual subject, the subject must rely on abilities which essentially incorporate a sensitivity to the agreement in judgements of those who also encounter that particular. Well-grounded information about an object depends on the competent exercise of such abilities according to rules which govern the use of a term or expression which picks out the particular concerned.

8.6. De Dicto *and* De Re

If some thoughts essentially involve particulars we must ask whether this introduces a duality into mental content marked by the distinction between *de dicto* and *de re*.

The present view is that *de re* thoughts about particulars essentially involve objects as they appear in conceptual practices and are picked out by terms with a rule-governed use. The terms include names and demonstratives, and they only have meaning when they pick out individuals. But what are the "identifying criteria to which the use of a name is answerable"?[15] A thinker must, in making a singular judgement, "know to which determinate portion of his present experience, if any, he is attempting to refer". Thus:

we must see sense, as also the general notion of the representative content of thought, as a web of knowledge consisting in a complex of dispositions and capacities. . . . to be sure there need not be one unique way in which everyone thinks of Margaret Thatcher, in the sense of some unique set of mental images or whatever. But then Frege would not wish us to take "way in which one thinks of an object" like *that*.[16]

We do, however, collect "bundles of information" (Evans) or "dossiers" (Luntley) on the particulars of which we form conceptions, but even these are normatively constrained:

---

[15] M. Luntley, 'The Sense of a Name', in Wright (ed.), *Frege*.   [16] Ibid.

The issue turns on the social character of meaning. . . . our dossiers converge in that they are generated by our intercourse with a shared practice brought into being by those whose position in the genesis of the practice gives them the right to decide whether someone really is Margaret Thatcher.[17]

(This does not, of course, confer any incorrigible status on the occurrent judgements of experts who might be as prone as anyone else to mental aberrations.) But, in addition to a thinker's use of a name, we must specify his warrant for accepting that the name applies to a given particular. This warrant rests on the fact that he is competent in the differential use of that name to denote its bearer. Although the informational contact is an individual relation between thinker and the object of his thought, it is nevertheless rule-governed within a public practice. The practice both generates and constrains the use which gives the name a role in the conceptual repertoire of the thinker. Individuation (as for 'The man' in our earlier example (§7.6)) involves using certain concepts and relying on engagement within a set of practices to supply what the conceptual specification lacks. Indeed it may be that every conceptual specification has a *de re* element.[18]

Items are identified or picked out in a distinct way in demonstrative and recognitional practices. Neither involves elements foreign to the present discussion of conceptual abilities in that both require rule-governed performances involving public criteria. Demonstrative identification is basic in that it is closely tied to the mastery of perceptual judgements and thus needs no descriptive sophistication on the part of the thinker. For instance, imagine the following conversation:

A. What is that?
B. That what?
A. Well, that . . . er . . . thing over there.
B. Oh, that.
A. Yes, that; I don't understand it at all.

Here A has perceived some object which he wishes to think about. What is important is that A's contact with the object (or putative object) and the interactions within which he will fill out its conceptual specification are both embedded in the practices where

[17] Ibid.   [18] See §8.6.

concepts are learnt. He latches on to some item by directed attention, thus using an ability that is primitive in thought but is transformed and informed by linguistic interactions to form part of the web of activity which is our grasp of concepts.[19]

Recognitional thought also and essentially picks out objects within the framework of concept-use. Every time I recognize the colour red or a dog I make use of a capacity which has a natural place in my mental activity and structure. We can therefore specify the type of normative constraints which govern recognition: they tie our judgements to items picked out in practices where certain terms are mastered. Appeal to the item or *res* is permissible because all mental abilities involve responses to such items. Thus singular terms and their senses, like concepts, involve functions of judgement conforming to the rules of world-involving language games, but these functions track particulars rather than assimilating objects on the basis of general features.

8.7. *Foundational Matters*

I will now turn to the three stances toward singular thought noted above (§8.1). These are:

1. All singular thoughts are descriptive thoughts.
2. Singular thoughts are a distinctive range of thoughts along with other types.
3. Singular thoughts are basic or primary in the understanding of human thought in general.

I have argued that there is a range of singular thoughts which essentially involve a specification of the subject's contact (either perceptual or through an individuating sign or device used in practices in which he participates) with the particular concerned. If there is no individual apt to figure in this specification, then these thoughts are (at least) indeterminate.

We can now attempt "an illuminating account of the role of singular ideas in our conceptual scheme". Campbell suggests that "possession of the idea of oneself as in an objective world is required for the possession of concepts. . . . possession of a conceptual repertoire can only be explained as consisting in possession

---

[19] Directed attention is discussed in Ch. 1.

of that idea".[20] In possessing this idea the thinker depends on the ability to locate himself in relation to an understandable order of items whose properties (particularly spatio-temporal properties) are not dependent on his own thoughts about them: "the process of self-location is existence dependent: if one is to identify one's route by reference to encountered objects, the objects must really be there to use them to identify one's position".[21] Campbell claims that, in addition to positional knowledge, we grasp an intuitive mechanics by which we make sense of the events around us:

The idea of the temporal order of past states of affairs depends upon one's grasp of the relevance of causal regularities. One has to have the idea of the *right* causal regularities . . . in establishing the order of past states, however. But *that* conception is provided only by the anchoring which one's intuitive physics has in the real world, by being applied to objects which one recognises as the same again from time to time. Unless the objects are actually there, that anchoring is lost, and there is no saying what would make a set of causal regularities the right set; in that case, one has lost one's grip on what would make a particular way of temporally ordering past states of affairs the right way.[22]

Campbell appeals to the need for order in one's experience and opts for an empiricized version of Kant's account. His account rests on singular thoughts, where Kant talked about "permanence of substance" and causal interactions. It is highly plausible that, if we conceive of the individual thinker as needing to impose some objective order on a series of states which he enjoys, then just this kind of view is the only way to allow a notion of the way things are independently of my thought of them. But I have urged that the possession of concepts essentially locates the subject in a system of rule-governed uses. Even a solitary subject like Robinson Junior must develop practices which regulate, and do not just shift with, his own mental states, and only thus can a normative influence upon his judgements be secured.[23] It remains plausible, indeed almost irresistible, that there will be an important role for recognizable individuals in the thought life of any given human being. Although co-referential thinkers orientate and direct much of a given person's thought, practices involving perceptual

---

[20] J. Campbell, 'The Possession of Concepts', *Proceedings of the Aristotelian Society*, 85 (1985–6), 135.
[21] Campbell, 'Conceptions of Conceptual Structure', 4.
[22] Ibid. 5.   [23] This is discussed in 4. III.

judgements and recognition (rule-governed responses to particulars) must have an important and continuing place in the articulation of his thought. These, of course, require him to keep track of his position and so on. When he attempts to develop his understanding of the actions and interactions he sees around him, he will again and again appeal to the landmarks and signposts provided by particulars which figure in such practices. His grasp of the rules and his ability to identify recognizable objects will bring order when he is confused and will be part of making good use of the cues and clues that a conceptual repertoire provides.

I differ from Campbell in that I have begun with concepts and the practices in which they are mastered as the basis of all representational content and have not accepted that there is a 'given' of any kind awaiting an organizing scheme informed by intuitive physics or any other system. I would agree that an intuitive understanding of the way that things work plays an important role and that the structure of our concepts reflects this. But the understanding concerned is part of the shared resources we gain when we learn concepts and is therefore implicitly informed by the viewpoints of others. Even if a mental map, an intuitive mechanics, and recognition-based ideas of objects are important (especially in the assessment of one's own thoughts), they must not obscure the a priori public and interactive nature of concepts.

8.8. Thought Can also Be of What Is Not the Case

It remains to sketch out an approach to the vexed topic of empty singular terms. Consider two cases:

(1) James Goldberg thinks ⟨Moses did not exist⟩.
(2) Tom is walking home one night and observes a 'figure' moving through Mrs Dag's garden. He thinks ⟨that man might be a burglar⟩. Unbeknown to him the figure is a shadow cast be a leafy branch waving across a street light.[24]

In addressing the first case Wittgenstein's strategy is to tie down the use of the term at the heart of the puzzle (i.e. 'Moses') in order

---

[24] I shall not discuss a case of hallucination, as the phenomena and the mental contexts of these experiences are so different from normal cases that our basis for mental ascriptions is undermined.

to disambiguate the thought. If 'Moses' is being used to denote the literary character described in the Bible, then the thought may be that there is no historical character who fits the description given and that thoughts about Moses involve a figure in literature and are confined to that context. If 'Moses' is used to assert something about "the one who led the Israelites from captivity", then James might think that such an Exodus did not occur or that it had no one leader. The content of his thought can be identified once we understand James's use of the term or the 'way of thinking' it marks. We also get some clue to where information is to be sought when no particular fits his use, and so can decide what, if anything, would count in assessing the truth of the thought.

The practice–use–language game approach shows that we cannot say that every sentence-type expresses just one idea nor that every thought 'maps' on to just one state of affairs or item in the world. But we can preserve the intersubjectivity of truth. We can say that all thought 'gets to grips' with reality through conceptual abilities and the rule-governed uses of terms, and essentially involves public determinants.

Empty demonstrative thoughts submit to a similar analysis. In the second case, Tom invoked the language games where the term 'that man' is normally in play. There are criteria which determine the meaning of this term, but in the situation in question (the shadow falling on the wall) he is mistaken about what he sees. There is no man to ground the use of the term and his speculations about 'that man' are empty. We can understand what he is thinking because we also engage in the practices upon which he is drawing and use the same skills. Thus, even if he *is* mistaken, his demonstrative draws on 'informational contact' with *something* and responds to some perceptual presentation. His thought mistakenly locates his experience in one language game, with internal relations to one set of objects, but would only be represented correctly in another language game or set of practices.

8.9. *Summary*

The present analysis of singular thought is continuous with that given for concepts in general. The content of singular thoughts involves practices in which individuals are picked out for and by a subject who grasps certain concepts. I have again complained about an analysis in terms of 'informational states' and their causal roles. I have outlined the sense in which singular thoughts are essentially object-involving. On this view neither perception nor recognitional abilities introduce mystery into the determinants of content, and an analysis of empty singular thought is possible. This portrays the subject as exercising a skill that normally functions to assign a presented object to a place in his conceptual system.

9

Mind-Dependence and Reality

I HAVE outlined an account of thoughts in which content is shown to be intersubjectively available, cognitively significant for a given individual, and intentional in two senses (directed upon items in the world and used in intentional activity). I have linked content to rule-governed techniques of use which provide the thinker with a repertoire of mental acts (be they overt or covert). I have argued that concepts, for the most part, involve terms and expressions in a natural language and thus, in essence, incorporate distinctive features of the interactions and language games in which a thinker is engaged. Rules structure his conceptual activity and link his operations with signs to the milieu in which those signs have life and in which he is a participating subject. This has definite implications for certain forms of scepticism.

9.1. Copernican Revolutions

John Locke expresses an abiding philosophical worry about perception and knowledge of the real world as follows: "We are further to consider concerning perception, that the Ideas we receive by sensation, are often in grown People altered by the Judgement, without our taking notice of it."[1] His response to this worry appealed to the unmediated nature of simple ideas which directly reflected the properties of things in the world via causal links.

Kant, in his 'Copernican revolution' in philosophy, reformulated the relation between representation and reality:

Hitherto it has been assumed that all our knowledge must conform to objects. But all attempts to extend our knowledge of objects by establishing something of them *a priori*, by means of concepts, have, on this

---

[1] J. Locke, *An Essay concerning Human Understanding*, ed. P. Nidditch (first pub. 1689; Oxford, 1975), II. ix. 8.

assumption, ended in failure. We must therefore make trial whether we may not have more success in the tasks of metaphysics, if we suppose that objects must conform to our knowledge. (*CPR* Bxvi)

Stroud explains: "Kant's 'Copernican' point is that perception must be seen as necessarily involving thought or the understanding, and the principles of the understanding that are required to 'constitute' objects for us must be seen as 'in us' independently of our having any experience."[2] But if the mind dictates the form of knowledge, and the objects of experience must conform to it, then how can we have an idea of what reality is really like? We seem bound within the appearances that the mind presents to us because all our thoughts relate to 'the-world-as-the-thinker-conceives-of-it', or what Dennett calls a "notional world".[3] On such a conception, thoughts of the world are "mind dependent—not really describing a mind-independent reality at all, but in some sense creating the reality they describe".[4] This idea leads us either to a platitude—"that if we did not have minds of a certain kind we could not possess the concept of a tree", or a paradox—"that 'objects' do not exist outside our conceptual schemes or that we 'create' objects".[5] The difficulty is to acknowledge that human judgements make sense of experience and yet retain some objectivity for that experience.

Before I try to meet this challenge I will need to distinguish two views of mind-independence. The first is that a thinking subject can be justified in thinking he is in touch with a reality which stands over against his own thoughts about it. The second is that reality stands over against and may be related to our ways of thinking in general. I shall attempt to justify the first but deny that the second makes sense. I shall develop a dialogue between the sceptic and realists of various kinds. In each case, the sceptic will be allowed to occupy only the conceptual ground which is coherent within the account he is attacking; thus some sceptics have more purchase for their attacks on realism than others.

9.2. *Kant Schemata and Experience*

The mind's contribution to experience runs throughout Kant's extended theoretical treatment of experience, perception, and

[2] B. Stroud, *The Significance of Philosophical Scepticism* (Oxford, 1984), 155.
[3] D. Dennett, 'Beyond Belief', in *TO*.
[4] S. Blackburn, *Spreading the Word* (Oxford, 1984), 146.   [5] Ibid. 219.

knowledge. His notion of *synthesis* fills a gap in empiricist theory by accepting that perception involves actively taking things to be thus and so.[6] To appreciate that a given experience instances a certain concept or complex of concepts requires synthesis, a creative function of judgement which either subsumes the particular experience under a general concept or composes the elements of present experience into a conceptual whole so that the mind judges that an experience counts as being of a certain kind. But the difficulty arising from the mind's role in *generating* experience is made acute when Kant contends: "Synthesis in general, as we shall hereafter see, is the mere result of the power of imagination, a blind but indispensable function of the soul, without which we should have no knowledge whatsoever, but of which we are scarcely conscious" (*CPR* B103).

The *imagination* is the faculty which provides *schemata* by which our perception incorporates rules which determine perceptual types (*CPR* B179–80). The schemata take the synthetic rules dictating the form that an experience must have in order to fit a concept and provide an empirical form or 'perceptual prescription' which sets out what counts as an instance of a given concept. "The question therefore arises, how it can be conceivable that nature should have to proceed in accordance with categories which yet are not derived from it, and do not model themselves upon its pattern: that is, how they can determine *a priori* the combination of the manifold of nature" (*CPR* B163). This is the epistemic paradox: if the mind *imposes* form on experience how can it discern what is really there?

Ulrich Neisser, a cognitive psychologist, also wrestles with this problem. He asks how the perceiver, who must bring schemata to his experience of the world, can nevertheless have experiences which are constrained by sensory input and not merely determined by his own cognition:

I suggested that the internal flow of perception involves two consecutive stages. In the first pre-attentive stage, features are detected and analyzed. This automatic process is usually followed by an act of construction, in which the perceiver "makes" one perceptual object rather than another. . . . [But this] fails to explain the veridicality of perception. If percepts are

---

[6] P. F. Strawson, 'Perception and Imagination', in *Freedom and Resentment and Other Essays* (London, 1974).

constructed, why are they usually accurate? Surely perceiving is not just a lucky way of having mental images![7]

Neisser tries to overcome the difficulty by characterizing the "perceptual cycle", which engages the perceiver in an ongoing perceptual interaction with the world:

although the schema plays a critical role in every perceptual act, it is not a "percept", nor does it produce one anywhere in the perceiver's head. The act of perceiving does not terminate in a percept at all. The schema is just one phase of an ongoing activity which relates the perceiver to his environment. The term perception applies properly to the entire cycle and not to any detached part of it.[8]

Berkeley, of course, would attack such a basis for realist claims. His own coherent but totally unpersuasive view is that all experience is based on ideas and thus that objects are just complex ideas constructed out of simple elements. Interactions between objects and perceivers comprise longitudinal patterns of complex ideas, some of which concern the movements of the thinker's own body. But, if Berkeley's denial of validation within experience is combined with Kant's imposition thesis, then an appeal to experiential states cannot overturn the 'mind-dependent' conception of reality that emerges.

Stroud discusses Kant's appeal to the categories of judgement as the warrant for believing that an experience is objective; he complains: "categories might be no more than 'an artefact of our subjective constitution', with no essential connection to the way things are or must be".[9]

So, the philosophical problem remains:[10] How do mental representations capture the way things are in the real world? We must find a path through the thicket of issues surrounding "an artefact of our subjective constitution" and "the way things are or must be". How *can* we say that we do not merely construct a hypothesis of perception which, as it turns out, is remarkably

---

[7] U. Neisser, *Cognition and Reality* (San Francisco, Calif., 1976), 19.

[8] Ibid. 23.

[9] B. Stroud, 'The Disappearing We', *Proceedings of the Aristotelian Society*, 84 (1983), 244.

[10] The problem for cognitive science may well be solved by Neisser's adaptation of Gibson's views, because cognitive science need not account for truth and epistemological justification, but merely trace the causal transactions between thin informational pick-up and adaptive movement.

useful to us? If a perception at time t_1 is merely part of a mind-dependent construct with an unspecified relation to what is 'outer', then a sequence of such perceptions, however they are related to each other, merely multiply our evidence at the same level and cannot validate it.[11]

We can approach this problem in several ways. A claim for the mind-independence of the perceived world could be based on a 'given' element in perception which impinges upon the mind. Alternatively, we could argue that the regularities and relations within experience secure the objectivity of perception. Lastly, the mind-independence of the world could be grounded in the intentionality of perception according to which "An intentional object is given by a word or phrase which gives a description under which".[12]

9.3. Scheme and Content

According to the first approach it is the given matter of experience which we receive from the world that assures us of something beyond the mind. Kant puts it thus:

Our knowledge springs from two fundamental sources of the mind; the first the capacity of receiving representations (receptivity for impressions), the second is the power of knowing an object through these representations (spontaneity [in the production] of concepts). Through the first an object is *given* to us, through the second the object is *thought* in relation to that [given] representation (which is a mere determination of the mind). (*CPR* B74)

He also remarks: "appearances are only representations of things which are unknown as regards what they may be in themselves" (*CPR* B164), and "the understanding is itself the source of the

---

[11] This appears to be the position occupied by A. J. Ayer in *The Central Questions of Philosophy* (Harmondsworth, 1981).

[12] G. E. M. Anscombe, *Metaphysics and the Philosophy of Mind* (Oxford, 1981), 9. Dummett, commenting on the fact that intentionality is an essential feature of contentful experience, coins 'Kant's principle': 'Every object is given to us in some particular way' (Lectures on Gareth Evans's *Varieties of Reference*, Oxford, Trinity Term, 1986). I shall not discuss here two other aspects of intentionality which Anscombe mentions, viz. the vague or indeterminate nature of some intentional objects by contrast with material objects, and the fact that an intentional object may have no material counterpart.

laws of nature". But the conclusion that reality "as it is in itself" is unknowable and therefore that all that we can have is a coherent set of ideas seems to threaten that thinkers might "cut themselves off from reality".[13] This threat depends on a distinction between representations and what they represent such that the ties between the two can be cut. In response one can either strengthen some of the ties so as to prevent wholesale sceptical disruption or recast one's view of representations so that they cannot be prised apart from reality.[14]

However, there is an internal problem in this position: How does one specify what lies 'beyond' our system of representations to provide the 'given'? To conceive of this mysterious reality is to represent it in some way, so that it cannot stand over against our representations *in toto*. Thus we seem to be left with the nihilism of the *Tractatus*:

The limits of my language mean the limits of my world. (5.6)

and

What we cannot speak about we must pass over in silence. (7)

But elsewhere we find:

Reality is compared with propositions. (4.05)

A proposition can be true or false only in virtue of being a picture of reality. (4.06)

The latter remarks capture our deep intuition that our thought must shape itself to *fit* reality and that perception gives us knowledge which stands in contrast to spontaneously created ideas. This intuition is directly counter to the 'imposition' view and demands an account of representation in which we grasp reality as it is, independent of us. We want to understand how we can be engaged with things and not be confined to "problematic" conjectures about them.

But the objectivity and validity of our thought cannot be secured by 'given' material the content of which we do not apprehend in thought. Such material cannot figure in mental ascriptions and self-ascriptions, as it is pre-conceptual; it is therefore quite mysterious

---

[13] R. Walker, 'Empirical Realism and Transcendental Anti-Realism', *Proceedings of the Aristotelian Society*, 83 (1982), 167.

[14] It takes no philosophical sleuth to discern that I opt for the latter path.

how we could ever sketch an epistemological role for it. In fact, it is unclear how such material could be mental content at all.[15]

Davidson claims that scepticism of this scheme-content-type and even significant relativism is ruled out by the need for us to be able to interpret what another thinker says in order to understand her. But even if we could justify a claim that every thinker must, to a large extent, be interpretable by us and have a conceptual system commensurate with ours (so that we can discern that they have beliefs of some sort), we still want to know in what sense the mutually interpretable beliefs are about something independent and thus in what sense they can be assessed for their adequacy in general. Davidson uses a Quinean move and relativizes interpretation to conditions of utterance. I have eschewed that path, which, one might briefly note, seems merely to shift the problematic cognizing on to the conditions which are correlated with the utterances in question to form Tarskian T-sentences.[16]

If the pre-conceptual 'given' cannot supply material for thought (and thus be mind-independent) because, *ex hypothesi*, it escapes the grasp of our conceptual system, neither can it be in the mind because it is prior to our (conceptual) ascriptions. So we lack any conception of what it is that engages with our conceptual structure. Having begun with the empiricist notion that there is 'something there' which gives rise to thoughts, we find that the 'something' which ought to be there is not captured by scheme-content dualism ("the third dogma of empiricism"—Davidson).

9.4. *Subjective and Objective Representations*

A second approach divides representations into subjective and objective on the basis of their interrelations:

---

[15] D. Davidson, 'On the Very Idea of a Conceptual Scheme', in *ITI*.

[16] A T-sentence has the form: 'P' is true if and only if P, e.g. "Grass is green" is true iff grass is green. Tarski suggests that we can define "true" for any given language by assembling a comprehensive list of such T sentences. Other writers have then used this to give an account of what it is to understand the language concerned. I have merely argued that we lack an account of what it is to cognize the conditions forming the truth conditions for a T-sentence in a way sufficient to underpin intersubjectivity unless we focus on the multiple subjects involved and their convergence in judgements.

What we may say is that our way of having the notion of an objective world is by having the notion of a spatial world and there is no level of our conceptual thought more basic than that.

In order to have the conception of an objective world, the subject must think of his successive perceptions as explained jointly by the objective temporal order and his own changing position. This requires that he be able to distinguish a succession of perceptions from perception of a succession. It is in applying this distinction . . . that a rudimentary mechanics is employed. . . . This means that one must take one's perceptions of the objective world to have a certain systematicity, a systematicity which consists in the fact that they can be regarded as, in the main, perceptions of a world governed by such a mechanics.[17]

A version of this view is found both in the 'Analogies of Experience' (*CPR* B218–65) and in Strawson's *Individuals*. Kant claims that (a priori) mechanical and spatio-temporal principles order experience and secure its empirical objectivity. He could be seen as basing the spatio-temporal scheme on "recognition-based thoughts" of those objects which are relatively enduring.[18]

On this view spatio-temporal and causal relationships between perceptual contents create a framework in which we can have objective reference and world-related thoughts assessable for truth. The distinction between "two sets of relations: (1) the time relations between the objects which the perceptions are to be taken as perceptions of; (2) the time relations between the members of the subjective series of perceptions themselves",[19] is said to allow the subject to correct his percepts. It is not clear that it does so:

in contradistinction to concepts of simple sensory qualities . . . concepts of objects are always and necessarily compendia of causal law or law-likeness, and carry implications of causal power or dependence. Powers, as Locke remarked—and under 'powers' he included passive liabilities, and dispositions generally—make up a great part of our idea of substances. More generally, they must make up a great part of our concepts of any persisting and reidentifiable objective items. And without some concepts such as these, no experience of an objective world is possible.[20]

[17] J. Campbell, 'The Possession of Concepts', *Proceedings of the Aristotelian Society*, 85 (1985–6), 136.

[18] Cf. ibid. 151. This involves a certain reading of "substance" in the first analogy (B224 ff.); it is not, I am sure, Kant's view.

[19] P. F. Strawson, *The Bounds of Sense* (London, 1966), 124.

[20] Ibid. 146.

We may need concepts of this nature to conceive of an objective world, but it is not clear, from either Kant, Strawson, or Campbell, that mental states systematized on this basis will secure the distinction between subjective and objective. That we need something *more* is suggested by the fact that these regularities characterize our experience (more or less) even in a dream or fancy.

Kant claims that "we can also, however, know the existence of a thing prior to its perception, if only it be bound up with certain perceptions, in accordance with the principles of their empirical connection (the analogies)" (*CPR* B273). Thus he sees a distinction between mind-dependence of the type found in imagination and what we find in perceptual experience. But this only entails that perception is not subjective in the same sense as creative imagination, and we remain tied to a conception of knowledge as something based on mental states and events which we "enjoy" (*SC* 112). The persistent worry is that, if perception is a matter of a succession of mental states showing relations which mark some off as being 'objective', then we still have no assurance that even the preferred subset captures reality. It is open to us to *assume* that they are ordered as they are because they are caused by the impingement of a reality to which we are sensitive, but we cannot justify that assumption.

9.5. *The Problem of Co-Reference*

Neither a duality of scheme and content (or concepts and given), nor a set of relations between representations, grounds a clear response to Neisser's worry that perception might be "a lucky way of having mental images". And our troubles do not end here; there is a further sceptical problem about multiple 'notional worlds'. I have a representational world which I take to reflect something beyond my mind because of certain relations within it. You have a similar world, but no basis exists for me, in my world, to refer to an item I take to be apparent to you and about which we might converge in judgements. It may be that the structure which secures the stability of my experiential world and that which secures yours are alike and that thus we enjoy 'token' experiential worlds of the same type. But I have no reason to believe that the objects over which my thoughts range are available to you in such a way as to secure that you and I have *de re* thoughts about the same particulars and identifiable features. Kant claims that the "world whole" for any thinker must be an a priori unity on the basis of principles of permanence, causal connectedness, reciprocity, and the a priori (mathematical) unity of space and time (as forms of experience in general). But nowhere does he justify belief in a common ground for the assessment of truth as held by you and me.[21]

There is a similar failing in McGinn's analysis.[22] He begins with the distinction between primary and secondary qualities, noting the observer-dependence of the latter: "for an object to be red is for it to present a certain kind of sensory appearance to perceivers. On the other hand, being cubical is recognised not to consist in such a disposition but in some intrinsic feature of the object."[23] He argues for a conceptual difference between the way things seem and the way they are and concludes that the way they seem, replete with secondary qualities, is an inseparable part of perception, but that this inseparability does not apply to our *conception* of how things are. "Thought is not constrained by the same principles that determine the possibilities of perception. And thought is what represents how things are objectively, not perception."[24] He rejects the intrusion of a 'veil of perception' between the thinker and reality although it is quite unclear how he means to avoid it. The subject discerns that colours and perspectival content depend on his relation to the object in a special way, but these aspects are like all perceptual input in being derived from states caused in him. McGinn's conclusions about the notion that concepts are abstracted from sensory experience is, in fact, the same as Kant's (in the Analogies of Experience):

I do not have an alternative theory of how the concepts of the scientific image are come by, but it does seem to me that . . . the manufacture of concepts must be thought of as the province of more intellective functions of mind. . . . We think of the world purely objectively when we employ

---

[21] The possible exception is his discussion of the a posteriori fact that you and I can mutually assess the truth of our judgements about a third item because we are both thinking about that item (B848). This is neither reconciled with his earlier ideas nor pursued.

[22] C. McGinn, *The Subjective View* (Oxford, 1983).

[23] Note that the present account has rejected a distinction expressed in these terms.   [24] Ibid. 90.

primary quality concepts in judgments which are not made in response
to what is perceptually presented—but in the formulation of physical
laws and the like. Concepts suited to the objective conception are thus
neither derived from, nor restricted in their application to, the contents of
experience.[25]

The problem remains to justify the objectivity attached to the
scientific concepts of an individual thinker. Where do such concepts get their normative and privileged status from, and what is
their relation to perception?

I will not stray into the philosophy of science save to suggest
that the authority of such statements is to be found in the same
place as other normative influences on thought. If the source of
standards for judgement in general is rule-governed practices which
provide us with conceptual tools to deal with experience, then that
same source will provide the epistemological weight we attach to
scientific truth.

McGinn later notes the link between primary-quality judgements
and action, claiming that such judgements reveal the causally
efficacious features of experience of which we must take account
when we act.[26] On the present account, the link emerges from
one's activity within those interactions and forms of life where
concepts are learned and a conception of the world evolved. But
if a solipsist takes a 'narrow' view of these interactions so that the
individual activity of the subject (even if it is dynamic, as Neisser
suggests) is seen as itself a matter of relations between representations, he can still deny that there is any connection between
objectivity, reference, and intersubjectivity such as to link thought
to truth. Thus the view of 'objectivity' which emerges remains, by
Frege's standards, deficient.

9.6. Causal and Intentional Foundations

There are at least two ways in which one could secure co-referential
underpinnings for meaning and truth. One could accept representational worlds and import a causal theory in which perceptions
as of things being thus and so are caused by objects (or events).
On the other hand we could opt for a view based on the intentionality of perception.

[25] Ibid. 126–7.   [26] Ibid. 142 ff.

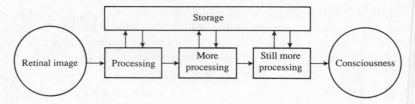

FIG. 9.1. The internal information-processing model of perception.
Source: U. Neisser, *Cognition and Reality*, 17.

On a causal view, token presentations of the same type would
be secured as being of that type by their common causal origin.[27]
I have already argued against such an account. First, I am not sure
that an object causes me to see it, nor by parity that the absence
of an object could cause me to see it was missing. Second, if concepts structure our perceptual experience, then it is clear that
perception is not merely a matter of a causal chain leading from
an object to me. Attempts to get concepts into the causal chain by
some processing model of perception leave us with a theory which
Neisser whimsically caricatures as in Fig. 9.1. He complains about
the 'woolly' understanding of perception evident in this model and
notes that, *inter alia*, it does not accommodate the interrelation
between perception and action. The model is, in fact, implicit in
the empiricist representational theory of mind (ERT) (which has
causal impingements on receptor surfaces initiating a series of
states and events culminating in conscious experience). But if the
input for conscious experience is a range of proximal states, then
we still have an epistemic gap between the contents of the mind
and the world. Thus we are back where we started.

I have pursued the analytic route indicated by Frege when he
rejected the idea that thought content essentially was a matter of
occurrent conscious or cognitive states of individual thinkers. On
the causal view, mental activity with conceptual content bears
exactly the indirect relation to its referents that undercuts knowledge
of the fit between our thoughts and reality. I suspect that similar
problems attach to any theory which bases thought on information states of the subject because these tend to lock the thinker

---

[27] This, of course leads to the problem of what counts as a type and how we
set up the criteria of classification.

within the veil of the senses rather than allow his mind to directly engage with the real world. This was both the starting-point and a persistent weakness of Kant's position.

A way out is indicated by a comment of Strawson's:

We should remember that all Kant's treatment of objectivity is managed under a considerable limitation, almost, it might be said, a handicap. He nowhere depends upon, or even refers to, the factor on which Wittgenstein, for example, insists so strongly: the *social* character of our concepts, the links between thought and speech, speech and communication, communication and social communities.[28]

9.7. *Intentionality and Objectivity*

Perception is the ability to derive conceptual knowledge from sensory contact with the world. In perception, a subject engages what he encounters with the structure of his thought system. To do this he uses the fact that his mastery of concepts has been developed in situations internally related to the one he is in. For instance, imagine a townsman and a deerstalker observing a certain patch of forest. The deerstalker whispers 'Can you see the deer?' and the townsman replies 'No, I can only see a bush'. The deerstalker tries to direct his companion's attention and appreciation so that the applicability of ⟨deer⟩ to what is before him becomes apparent. It may take a number of such experiences before the townsman develops the ability to see (i.e. learns to perceive) a deer in those circumstances. He then becomes sensitive to criteria which justify the application of the concept ⟨deer⟩ in a difficult context. I have argued that concepts like ⟨deer⟩ are not solipsistic. Thus we must explain what it is to master the ability to see items as being thus and so in a way that does not appeal to inner states.

When Wittgenstein discusses perception he spends a great deal of time on "seeing as" or "aspect seeing". This is relevant to our present problem because it concerns our justification for the conviction that what we perceive are actual objects and features in the world. Notice that we cannot always be said to see x as y when we see something; Wittgenstein remarks that it makes no sense "to say at the sight of a knife and fork 'Now I am seeing

---

[28] Strawson, *The Bounds of Sense*, 151.

this as a knife and fork'. One doesn't *'take'* what one knows as the cutlery at a meal for cutlery; any more than one ordinarily tries to move one's mouth as one eats, or aims at moving it" (*PI* 195e). We must be careful not to import theories about what *must* be going on (despite the phenomenology) into an analysis of perception. The fact that we see some things now as this and now as that suggests that we do so by means of representations which are distinct from those things. We can approach this more general question by discussing whether a valid reading of 'perceiving *x* as *y*' substitutes a 'percept' or similar for *x* and something in the world for *y*.

The arguments so far have established that concepts apply to objects which are intersubjectively accessible, and also that perception as the apprehension of the world by means of concepts does not rest on pre-conceptual information states. Therefore we *can* insist that in perception our thought latches directly on to the world (because the world and its contents are what concepts range over). This noted, what happens when one perceives something as being thus or so? Consider the 'duck-rabbit':

The duck-rabbit. One asks oneself: how can the eye—this dot—be looking in a direction?—"*See, it is looking!*" (And one "looks" oneself as one says this.) But one does not say and do this the whole time one is looking at the picture. And now, what is this "See, it's looking!"—does it express a sensation? (*PI* 205e)

What does make it an eye perceived as looking this way rather than that? We assimilate the picture to something that *is* a certain way and is enmeshed within practices of using terms and expressions to mark it as such. We see the eye as looking this way or that because we grasp the possibility of an internal relation between the figure and either a duck's or a rabbit's head. Such a relation carves out conceptual niches for the various elements of the array to which it is applied, and one of these niches determines that the dot is taken to be an eye. Once we take the dot as an eye, then it must be thought of as looking in some direction (we could say that this was a canonical commitment of judging it to be an eye). We see a thing as thus and so when we place it in our conceptual structure, or apply a technique linking it to other objects through rules for the use of certain terms: "'Now he's seeing it like this', 'now like that' would only be said of someone capable of making certain applications of the figure quite freely. The substratum of this experience is the mastery of a technique" (*PI* 208e). The technique, *inter alia*, enables one to perceive (by actively attending to this and then that) that a figure has certain characteristics.[29] We apply concepts by engaging what confronts us with a structure of uses and practices so that "seeing it like this" relates the figure to items and features which are part of our rule-governed activity. When we do this we may isolate one feature of a scene as the object of our thought, or assimilate the presentation to some significant type of item marked by the use of a term or sign. By seeing figure x as y—say as a duck or as a rabbit, or (in another case) as a black vase on a white ground rather than as two white profiles against a black ground—we respond to a feature or set of features as falling under some rule. The rule governs a way of dealing with things in a variety of situations. For instance, when I identify a colour as red, I obey a rule which has been imparted by isolating for my attention *red* as a feature of public things. They must be public so that others can correct my use of a term by tying it to conditions recalcitrant to my inclinations to use it any old how. There must be a principled distinction between my being correct and my seeming to be correct (even about secondary qualities) and this is given by the agreement in judgements fundamental to meaning (*PI* I. 242).

The techniques applied in seeing, selecting, attending to, becoming aware of, noting or noticing something, or judging of something that it is x determine what it is to perceive an x, where x might be a colour, object, shape, movement, quality, expression, smell, warning, difficulty, and so on. The techniques are internally related to the informal rules of use which constitute the meaning of my words. Therefore 'grammar' or essence involves objects or items which figure in co-referential linguistic practices (*PI* I. 371). Thus, most of the time, I see objects presented (actually or potentially) to me and to others, and there is (as Grayling has noted) an essential relation between the meaning of my words, or the very possibility of making sense of my experience, and competence in perceptual judgements.[30]

[29] In cognitive science this is evident in the selectivity of attentional scanning of complex stimuli.
[30] A. Grayling, *The Refutation of Scepticism* (London, 1986), 30.

Perceptual judgements are not just the result of impressions arising from what impinges upon a thinker, but also rest on her competence in certain conceptual practices which exploit her causal contact with the world. Perception is paradigmatically a direct engagement with things as they are according to the ways that they figure in conceptual practices.

Although most of the time what I perceive is what is there (this is entailed by my grasp of the meanings of words), at times I can perceive an aspect of something which involves assimilating that object, in an imaginative way, to other (equally public) objects of experience. By so doing I *forge* an internal relation (based on the practices in which a term is used) between the x I am seeing and examples of y. The assimilation essentially involves the application of the concept $\langle y \rangle$, to x so that we see it as y. When I see an aspect, I locate what I am seeing in a conceptual practice, the specification of which involves concrete situations and what people say and do in them. To see an aspect is thus to draw upon a technique (or rule-governed habit or custom) which ties sensory contact to action and discourse.

This view severely restricts the space for the sceptic to occupy. If thought is an activity which constitutively involves operating with signs whose function is tied to public rule-governed use, then perception cannot involve a veil or array of proximal states between the thinker and the world in which he is co-referentially engaged.[31]

9.8. *The Objective Conception of Reality*

We are now in a position to link together perception, mind-dependence, correspondence, and reality, and to show: (1) the role of primitive mechanics in particular identification; and (2) why we do not have an indirect or merely representational apprehension of an unknowable reality.

We are justified in thinking that we perceive features of a public world, for only thus can our concepts have rule-governed (and thus determinate) content. Rules of use tie the meaning of our words to features accessible to multiple thinkers. We perceive things

---

[31] That it is thought to do so is based on a mistaken view of the import of neuroscience; on this see my 'Perception and Neuroscience', *British Journal of Philosophy of Science*, 40 (1989), 83–103.

in terms of the way they figure in meaning-giving practices, and in this sense our conception of the world is selective and dependent on our forms of life. But this locks the things we perceive firmly into the physical world rather than lifting them into a 'representational' or 'mind-dependent' realm. It is truistic to echo Wittgenstein's words: "What we cannot think we cannot think" or even "The limits of my language" (or, more properly, the language that I could learn) "are the limits of my world." These remarks do not in any way undermine the fact that representations are tied to the mind-independent reality in which I and others use mutually intelligible concepts. Reality is mind-independent in that it is not a function of what happens in a single mind or even a set of minds. It is apprehended by any thinker or series of thinkers as having a normative role independent of the concepts applied to it on any given occasion. There is, therefore, a link between content and truth, and my words *correspond* to reality in the sense that the practices in which they are used are either appropriately or inappropriately related to a given situation by my use of them.

However, the content of my thought necessarily draws upon the elements of my world as they figure in conceptual practices so that the idea of intelligible representations which suspend all or part of the actual world nature of those things about which we think is suspect (and thus certain thought experiments are flawed, as Seddon has noted).[32] Certain general facts of nature underpin, in a readily understandable way, the concepts that we use (*PI* II. xii). For instance, if the world were iridescent we could not grasp colour concepts, or, if sound wavered unpredictably in pitch we could not have most of the musical concepts that we do. If each human body were associated with multiple (perhaps even two) sets of cognitive processes which maintained a variable and capricious relationship, then it is unclear whether we would have our present concepts of persons, mental states, and personal identity.[33] If facial expressions changed through a pattern of random muscular contractions which varied in frequency depending on the state of the moon rather than our emotional reactions, we would not call them expressions and have concepts like ⟨smile⟩, ⟨frown⟩, ⟨shifty⟩, and so on. Thus the general laws of nature underlie our possession

---

[32] G. Seddon, 'Logical Possibility', *Mind*, 81 (1972), 481.
[33] This observation, if true, has devastating effects for a theory such as Parfit's view of personal identity.

of concepts in that those concepts derive from activities in which items and features in the world are stable enough to be usable, identifiable, and mutually accessible. One cannot build reliable practices of use and thus meaningful discourse around foci which do not remain sufficiently constant and accessible for different thinkers to be able to agree in judgements and for those judgements to track significant changes in the environment.

It is interesting to note how little we can do to the regularities of the mechanical or spatio-temporal framework before we become conceptually insecure. Try, for example, undermining one of Kant's analogies of experience by imagining a world in which the co-existence of bodies did not reveal itself in mutual reciprocity of effects (CPR B257). Two bodies arriving together at the same point would then . . . what? Could they interpenetrate, but not bounce off one another? Neither could interfere with the other because this would evince a reciprocity of activity. What would happen to the notions of solidity and substance, of extension, causality, or the principle of sufficient cause for changes in properties? How far can one consistently order one's thoughts about a world where two bodies inhabiting the same region of space-time have no effect on one another? How, for instance, could one expect to act on anything if putting one's hand to it had no effect? And would photons constitute an exception to the lack of reciprocity or just not be reflected from surfaces; but if that were the case, how would we see anything? Perhaps the lack of reciprocity would not affect subatomic particles? The more questions one asks, the more of a conceptual mess one gets into, which implies that something fundamental has gone wrong with our thought. Thus a primitive mechanics *is* basic to our conceptual system. But the structure of that system also reflects an interpersonal milieu; so perhaps it also requires a primitive biology, psychology, and sociology. Where stable items figure in the grammar of a term they will be identifiable as particulars, perhaps by their places in a spatio-temporal framework, but at least in such a way that recognition-based thoughts are important in a consistent world picture. Thus the two basic features of Campbell's account are put in perspective.

There is always the possibility of going wrong in a perceptual judgement or of introducing an item into one's conceptual structure in a tentative and perhaps even experimental way. Thus there are intentional objects which are vague, mistakenly identified, or even turn out not to exist. In any of these circumstances the intentional features of perception provide ways of finding out more by using techniques that cluster round the point at which the item concerned has been engaged with one's conceptual system. These techniques involve calling to mind the criterial or canonical uses of certain terms so as to explore one's present experience. Because the judgements concerned depend on abilities which answer to norms, the indeterminacy or non-existence of the intentional object is a possibility; it may seem that one is seeing an x without the criteria for doing so being satisfied. Inclinations to apply certain concepts, although reliable, are corrigible, and therefore one should reserve judgement where the standards applicable to one's practices dictate it. Only a normative element allows such a conceptual 'joint' in perceiving to be understood. Hamlyn remarks:

There is nothing subjective about this. In fitting something to a concept we are not imposing on it a subjective point of view; for ... to have a concept can be as much an objective matter as anything else. The objectivity of a concept is bound up with the idea that it must be inter-subjective, interpersonal, just as knowledge is.[34]

The vagueness and indeterminacy or even non-existence of intentional objects are necessary correlates of the fact that perception is not just a causal process happening within a given perceiver; it involves making judgements in the light of rules or (public) norms which transcend the workings of individual minds. These rules determine what counts as fulfilling the concepts which articulate perceptual judgements.

9.9. 'Direct' Perception

Some terms capture what one perceives in a way that is austere or irreducible with respect to other properties. I might, for instance, recognize Mary Fugle but not be able to describe any basis for that recognition (as some folk perceive the sex of chickens or the distinctive style of a Citroën). There is therefore no warrant to ascribe prior or primitive mental content upon which my perception

[34] D. Hamlyn, 'Logical and Psychological Aspects of Learning', in R. S. Peters (ed.), *The Philosophy of Education* (Oxford, 1973), 210.

of these things depends. Lacking any mental precursor, I can be said to perceive these things *directly* (given my prior arguments that the causal process involved is not part of the analysis of mental activity).

The idea that perception comprises the enjoyment of a succession of mental states has now slunk quietly out of the back door. Perception involves an interaction with the world in which a subject picks out features and objects according to the way in which they are apt to figure in conceptual practices and thus engages her mind both creatively and receptively with objects accessible to co-referential thinkers. There is therefore no gap (between the mind's perceptual activity and the world) into which a range of representational or informational states can insinuate themselves. Perception is, in this sense, a direct apprehension of the way things are with a public world, and thought does not stop short of the objects, properties, and events to which concepts apply (*PI* i. 95). Neisser's haunting concern is thus laid to rest and we *can* be sure that in the perceptual cycle we are directly involved with what is 'out there'. Mental content, one might say, constitutively embraces things we perceive in the world, and it is within its structure that we live and move and do our seeing.

9.10. 'Reality in Itself'

I have argued that a subject is entitled to regard himself as being in epistemic or experiential contact with a reality independent of his own mental acts and inclinations and essentially shared with other co-linguistic thinkers. But can thought, in any sense, be contrasted with reality 'as it really is' and so, in principle, be tested for validity *in toto*? This would involve a transcendental justification of our ways of thinking in relation to "the way things are or must be" (Stroud), which is a highly suspect undertaking. If we return to 'Kant's principle': 'Every object is given to us in some particular way',[35] and combine this with the fact that our concepts are grounded in rule-governed practices in which we make judgements about things, then:

---

[35] See n. 12.

intelligible thought is . . . possible only within the limits of possible experience. The concepts that enable us to make sense of our world must have an empirical application. How then could there be intelligible thought and discourse in terms whose employment is not determined by empirically ascertainable conditions we can discover to hold in our experience?[36]

If meaning not only embraces the things we perceive but is tied to them, then any general validation of our ways of thinking is unattainable in principle. This can be brought out by examining the five strands of antisceptical argument in Wittgenstein's *On Certainty*.[37]

First, we do not understand the use of 'know' that is in play in global doubt (*OC* 260, 589). We flounder about not quite sure which epistemic warrant is to be met and therefore unsure what exactly is required. What would count as the knowledge we are said not to have? A proper answer, we could say, can only be given to a proper question.

Second, there is a relation between meaning and truth (*OC* 61, 62, 80, 114). Thought involves concepts which engage us with a shared world and are grasped as one learns to make a number of true judgements about things. Because getting a large number of things right is therefore a requirement of knowing what one thinks, global doubt looks nonsensical (*OC* 383).

Third, beliefs form a system in which doubts may take form (*OC* 105, 141, 144). We use a ramifying structure of meanings which interconnect to illuminate and guide our experience and actions. Within this structure we can deliberate and argue, correct one another, and refine our ways of thinking and acting, and we can also entertain meaningful doubts. So can we entertain the doubt that we might have, in the most basic way, got it all wrong? "Would that not be like the hypothesis of our having miscalculated in all our calculations?" (*OC* 55). If a doubt threatens to unhinge our cognitive system so totally, we know neither how to formulate the question nor how to recognize a right answer. Such a doubt is therefore vacuous.

Fourth, active engagement with the world is the basis of thought, not contemplation (*OC* 204, 229, 259, 534, 601). Representing,

[36] Stroud, *The Significance of Philosophical Scepticism*, 160–1.
[37] The following arguments sketch the outlines of my piece 'An Antisceptical Fugue', *Philosophical Investigations*, 13 (1990), 304–21.

operating with signs, is derivative from the use that those signs have and that means that "how things are or must be"[38] comes down, in the end, to interacting with and reacting to things.

Fifth, we act in the world in very natural and shared ways (OC 156, 220, 271). A person who cannot go right in terms of rule-governed abilities cannot think or (cognitively) be one of us. To think just is to latch on to certain shared or potentially shared rules and learning to apply them in experience. Thus experience involves "judging in conformity with mankind" (OC 156).

So we come to the transcendental validity of our thought. Is there a reality which stands over against our ways of thinking in general? One must ask what sense is being given to the term 'reality' here. But of this nothing can be said, not because it is mysterious, but rather because there are no terms which make a formed thought available. Thought and language are activities conducted by interacting beings with signs which have meaning in certain forms of life. Those meanings can be shared by all who can enter into the forms of life concerned. Beyond their applications, actual and hypothetical, within this milieu, the terms, and their meanings, will not go. The attempt to make them go further is just confused. Kant argued this, but Wittgenstein supplied the aphorism "That whereof we cannot speak, thereof we must be silent". To attempt to discuss a conception of reality which outstrips the meaning in which conceptions have their life is to attempt nothing. It is a mistake of a similar order to that which one commits when one is told that nobody is walking down the road and goes to look for him.

9.11. Summary

I have discussed a problem which dogs the steps of neo-Kantian views of thought content. How can the mind apprehend an objective world when it has an active role in conceiving of that world? The response in terms of scheme-content dualism is wanting because it lacks a coherent notion of the 'given'. A response based on the order in experience cannot provide a co-referential or truth-based conception of meaning. However, the intentionality of

[38] Stroud, 'The Disappearing We', 244.

perception links content and intersubjectivity through rule-governed practices of use which involve public items. Wittgenstein can be read as offering an antisceptical argument based on the fact that meaning essentially locates us in a shared world of human activity. The grander question of whether we could have any conception of objective reality against which the totality of our thought might be gauged is meaningless.

Conclusion

I HAVE set out to sketch a theory of content which is adequate to fulfil the needs both of mental explanation and of the theory of meaning. The account I have given builds from an analysis of concepts which draws together a multitude of characterizations under a unitary view of mental ascriptions. The subject is seen as responding differentially to things about her in ways that are determined by prescriptive norms. These norms dictate what counts as instancing a given concept such as ⟨red⟩. Once the subject has become adept at characterizing things in the many connected ways that go to make up a system of concepts, she can then use these characterizations to predict and explain the course of events around her. She learns to do this by latching on to the myriad ways in which others both respond to the world and mark the regular and repeatable aspects of their responses by the use of signs.

These facts about mental content entail that any view of personal identity must acknowledge that the mind and brain of an individual realize competencies based on a myriad of judgements over time which cumulatively produce a mental life. At the centre of these judgements, and thus crucial to the unique mental economy that results, is the subject. The subject is therefore both *unitary*, in the cumulative activity comprising her mental life, and *an object* who experiences the normative responses of others to her manifest activity. This entails that, even if we reject an immaterial (Cartesian) essence or 'self', we can identify the concept-using subject—a transcendental unity of apperception—at the centre of an individual mind.

On the present view, to explain the behaviour of a given person is to map it on to the rules and practices of a communicating group. That mapping reveals points at which the individual's activity is sensitive to things around him, but also reveals the underlying structure of the actions exhibited. This explains several puzzling features of mental explanation. Because the connections involved are linked to the subject's intentional activity and the norms operating in a group of concept-users, they are not causal but they do necessitate behaviour. The subject thinks thus and so and acts thus and so on pain of falling into nonsense or of disintegration of his structured, purpose-driven activity. This embodies a weak variety of naturalistic pragmatism, but, as the dependence of a complex and flexible cognitive structure hinges on accuracy in representing things in the world, it also embeds a norm of truth for thought.

The brain also reflects an increasing organization in and by the conceptual system of the human group in which a subject is raised. It lays down processing structures to deal with incoming information which reflect the ways in which that information has been gathered and weighted. Because of the formative effect of rules on techniques of information-gathering and classification, the structures that an individual's brain realizes depend on the rules governing the concepts used by that individual.

It emerges from this approach that representations are complex structures which build on the conceptual competence of the subject to guide and direct his behaviour and his search for knowledge. Thus the representations used by an individual to structure his own behaviour are essentially linked to intersubjectively determined forms of and norms for representation.

Linguistic meaning is seen as follows: The sense of an expression is given by the shared rules which govern its use, and thus there is an a priori agreement in meaning between different language-users. The use of a given term is thereby tied to certain situations because they are part of the (normatively determined) understanding of that term—they structure one's grasp of it. The intersubjective norms governing meaning also secure the fact that meaning is independent of the extra-linguistic purposes of any speaker or hearer (the autonomy of meaning). The cognitive significance of a term thus depends on the techniques required to master its use and the conditions under which a thinker feels comfortable using those techniques. The public and non-causal contribution to this component of sense avoids the anomalies of methodological solipsism and dual component theories of meaning.

Singular thoughts are accommodated well in the account of content because all thought essentially involves items in a public world and the signs used to codify both them and our relations to them. There is therefore no mystery to the idea of introducing an object essentially into the content of a thought because one can appreciate that certain techniques and shared practices only function if there is an object on which they can focus.

This view has profound implications for various kinds of scepticism. It forges a close link between public and intersubjective norms which govern the responses of a thinker and the content of that thinker's thoughts and experiences. This means that we cannot make sense of the idea of intra-individually meaningful mental states because the individual *sans* norms which impart consistency and some independent check on her activity (an idea of right and wrong as distinct from what seems to her to be right or wrong) is at the mercy of shifting inclinations to respond thus and so. Even the fact that there is a contentful 'thus and so' implies some regularity or re-presentational component to what is going on.

Thus representation—the ability to recover and use certain identifiable features of what is presented to one—is built on there being consistency, structure, and order in the responses of a thinker. These features derive from prescriptive norms which one implicitly obeys and which determine what counts as what. The norms take the form of rules governing patterns of manifest reactions and responses which human beings find natural to develop and share. This structured activity with signs is what we call thought.

BIBLIOGRAPHY

See also the Notes on References.

ANSCOMBE, G. E. M., *Metaphysics and the Philosophy of Mind* (Oxford: Blackwell, 1981).

ANTONY, L., 'Anomalous Monism and the Problem of Explanatory Force', *Philosophical Review*, 98 (1989), 153–87.

AYER, A. J., *The Central Questions of Philosophy* (Harmondsworth: Penguin, 1981).

BACH, K., '*De Re* Belief and Methodological Solipsism', in *TO*.

BAKER, G., 'Criteria: A New Basis for Semantics', *Ratio*, 16 (1974), 156–89.

—— and HACKER, P. M. S., *Meaning and Understanding* (Oxford: Blackwell, 1983).

BAKHURST, D. J., 'Thought, Speech and the Genesis of Meaning: On the 50th Anniversary of Vygotsky's *Myslanie I Rec*', *Studies in Soviet Thought*, 31 (1986), 189–209.

BLACKBURN, S., *Spreading the Word* (Oxford: Oxford University Press, 1984).

—— 'Finding Psychology', *Philosophical Quarterly*, 36(143) (1986), 111–22.

BUHLER, C., *From Birth to Maturity: The Child and his Family* (London: Routledge, 1935).

BURGE, T., 'Belief *De Re*', *Journal of Philosophy*, 74 (1977), 338–62.

—— 'Other Bodies', in *TO*.

CAMPBELL, J., 'Conceptions of Conceptual Structure', 1985.

—— Critical Notice of C. Peacocke, *Sense and Content*, *Philosophical Quarterly*, 36(143) (Apr. 1986), 278–91.

—— 'The Possession of Concepts', *Proceedings of the Aristotelian Society*, 85 (1985–6), 135–57.

CHURCH, J., 'Reasonable Irrationality', *Mind*, 96 (1987), 354–66.

CHURCHLAND, P., *Neurophilosophy* (Cambridge, Mass.: MIT Press, 1986).

CLAXTON, G., *Cognitive Psychology: New Directions* (London: Routledge & Kegan Paul, 1980).

DANTO, A., 'Basic Actions', *American Philosophical Quarterly*, 2 (1965), 141–8.

DENNETT, D., 'Beyond Belief', in *TO*.

—— *Brainstorms* (Brighton: Harvester Press, 1981).

DONALDSON, M., *Children's Minds* (London: Fontana, 1978).

EVANS, G., 'Semantic Theory and Tacit Knowledge', in S. Holzmann and

C. Leich (eds.), *Wittgenstein: To Follow a Rule* (London: Routledge & Kegan Paul, 1981).

FODOR, J., 'Fodor's Guide to Mental Representation: The Intelligent Auntie's Vade-Mecum', *Mind*, 94 (1985), 76–100.

—— *Psychosemantics* (Cambridge, Mass.: MIT Press, 1987).

FREGE, G., *Collected Papers on Mathematics, Logic and Philosophy*, ed. B. McGuinness (Oxford: Blackwell, 1984).

GILLETT, G. R., 'Actions, Causes and Mental Ascriptions', in H. Robinson (ed.), *Objections to Physicalism* (Oxford: Oxford University Press, 1992).

—— 'An Anti-Sceptical Fugue', *Philosophical Investigations*, 13 (1990), 304–21.

—— 'Concepts, Structures and Meanings', *Inquiry*, 30 (1987), 101–12.

—— 'Consciousness and Brain Function', *Philosophical Psychology*, 1(3) (1988), 325–41.

—— 'Consciousness, the Brain and What Matters', *Bioethics*, 4 (1990), 181–98.

—— 'Learning to Perceive', *Philosophy and Phenomenological Research*, 48 (1988), 601–18.

—— 'Multiple Personality and Irrationality', *Philosophical Psychology*, 4(1) (1991), 103–18.

—— 'Neuropsychology and Meaning in Psychiatry', *Journal of Medicine and Philosophy*, 15 (1990), 21–39.

—— 'Perception and Neuroscience', *British Journal of Philosophy of Science*, 40 (1989), 83–103.

—— 'Reasoning about Persons', in A. R. Peacocke and G. R. Gillett (eds.), *Persons and Personality* (Oxford: Blackwell, 1987).

—— 'Representations and Cognitive Science', *Inquiry*, 32 (1989), 261–76.

—— 'Tacit Semantics', *Philosophical Investigations*, 11 (1988), 1–12.

GJELSVIK, O., 'Dretske on Knowledge and Content', *Synthese*, 86 (1991), 425–41.

GRAYLING, A., *The Refutation of Scepticism* (London: Duckworth, 1986).

HALDANE, J., 'Naturalism and the Problem of Intentionality', *Inquiry*, 32 (1989), 305–22.

HAMLYN, D. W., 'Epistemology and Conceptual Development', in T. Mischel (ed.), *Cognitive Development and Epistemology* (New York: Academic Press, 1971).

—— 'Human Learning', in Peters (ed.), *The Philosophy of Education*.

—— 'Logical and Psychological Aspects of Learning', in Peters (ed.), *The Philosophy of Education*.

HAMPSHIRE, S., 'Some Difficulties in Knowing' in Honderich and Burnyeat (eds.), *Philosophy As It Is*.

HARRÉ, H. R., *Personal Being* (Oxford: Blackwell, 1984).

HONDERICH, T., and BURNYEAT, M. (eds.), *Philosophy As It Is* (Harmondsworth: Penguin, 1978).

HUME, D., *A Treatise of Human Nature*, ed. E. C. Mossner (first pub. 1739; Harmondsworth: Penguin, 1969).

KANT, I., *Foundation of the Metaphysic of Morals*, tr. L. W. Beck (first pub. 1785; New York: Bobbs-Merrill, 1959).

KENNY, A. J. P., *Will, Freedom and Power* (Oxford: Blackwell, 1971).

KRIPKE, S., *Wittgenstein on Rules and Private Language* (Oxford: Blackwell, 1982).

LOAR, B., *Mind and Meaning* (Cambridge: Cambridge University Press, 1981).

LOCKE, J., *An Essay concerning Human Understanding*, ed. P. Nidditch (first pub. 1689; Oxford: Oxford University Press, 1975).

LUNTLEY, M., 'The Sense of a Name', in Wright (ed.), *Frege: Tradition and Influence*.

LURIA, A. R., *The Working Brain*, (Harmondsworth: Penguin, 1973).

MCDOWELL, J., 'Criteria, Defeasibility and Knowledge', *Proceedings of the British Academy*, 68 (1983), 455–79.

—— 'De Re Senses', in Wright (ed.), *Frege: Tradition and Influence*.

—— 'Non-Cognitivism and Rule-Following', in S. Holzmann and C. Leich (eds.), *Wittgenstein: To Follow a Rule* (London: Routledge & Kegan Paul, 1981).

—— 'Virtue and Reason', *Monist*, 62(3) (1979), 331–50.

MCGINN, C., 'The Structure of Content', in *TO*.

—— *The Subjective View* (Oxford: Oxford University Press, 1983).

—— *Wittgenstein on Meaning* (Oxford: Blackwell, 1984).

MELDEN, A. I., 'Action', in D. F. Gustafson (ed.), *Essays in Philosophical Psychology* (London: Macmillan, 1964).

MORRIS, M., 'Causes of Behaviour', *Philosophical Quarterly*, 36 (1986), 123–44.

MORSS, J., 'The Public World of Childhood', *Journal for the Theory of Social Behaviour*, 18 (1988), 323–44.

MORTON, A., 'Because he Thought that he had Insulted him', *Journal of Philosophy*, 72 (1975), 5–15.

NAGEL, T., *The View from Nowhere* (Oxford: Oxford University Press, 1986).

NEISSER, U., *Cognition and Reality* (San Francisco, Calif.: Freeman, 1976).

NOONAN, H., 'Fregean Thoughts', in Wright (ed.), *Frege: Tradition and Influence*.

PALMER, A., *Concept and Object* (London: Routledge, 1988).

PETERS, R. S. (ed.), *The Philosophy of Education* (Oxford: Oxford University Press, 1973).

PIAGET, J., *Psychology and Epistemology*, tr. P. A. Wells (Harmondsworth: Penguin, 1972).

—— and INHELDER, B., *The Psychology of the Child*, tr. H. Weaver (London: Routledge & Kegan Paul, 1969).

PLATTS, M., *Ways of Meaning* (London: Routledge & Kegan Paul, 1979).

PRICE, H. H., *Perception* (London: Methuen, 1932).

QUINTON, A., 'The Problem of Perception', in G. Warnock (ed.), *The Philosophy of Perception* (Oxford: Oxford University Press, 1967).

RUMELHART, D. E. and MCCLELLAND, J. L., *Parallel Distributed Processing: Explorations in the Microstructure of Cognition*, i (Cambridge, Mass.: MIT Press, 1986).

SARTRE, J.-P., *Being and Nothingness*, tr. H. E. Barnes (first pub. 1943; London: Methuen, 1958).

SEARLE, J., *Minds, Brains and Science* (London: BBC Publications, 1984).

SEDDON, G., 'Logical Possibility', *Mind*, 81 (1972), 324, 481–94.

STICH, S., *From Folk Psychology to Cognitive Science* (Cambridge, Mass.: MIT Press, 1985).

STRAWSON, P. F., *The Bounds of Sense* (London: Methuen, 1966).

—— *Meaning and Truth* (Oxford: Oxford University Press, 1968); repr. in T. Honderich and M. Burnyeat (eds.), *Philosophy As It Is* (Harmondsworth: Penguin, 1979).

—— 'Causation and Explanation', in B. Vermazen and M. B. Hintikka (eds.), *Essays on Davidson* (Oxford: Oxford University Press, 1985).

—— *Freedom and Resentment and Other Essays* (London: Methuen, 1974).

STROUD, B., 'The Disappearing We', *Proceedings of the Aristotelian Society*, 84 (1983), 219–58.

—— *The Significance of Philosophical Scepticism* (Oxford: Oxford University Press, 1984).

VYGOTSKY, L. W., *Thought and Language*, tr. E. Hanfmann and G. Vakar (first pub. 1929; Cambridge, Mass.: MIT Press, 1962).

WALKER, R., 'Empirical Realism and Transcendental Anti-Realism', *Proceedings of the Aristotelian Society*, 83 (1982), 131–77.

WIGGINS, D., 'The Person as Object of Science, Subject of Experience and Locus and Value', in A. R. Peacocke and G. R. Gillett (eds.), *Persons and Personality* (Oxford: Blackwell, 1987).

—— 'What Would Be a Substantial Theory of Truth?', in Z. Van Straaten (ed.), *Philosophical Subjects* (Oxford: Oxford University Press, 1980).

WITTGENSTEIN, L., *Remarks on the Philosophy of Psychology* (Oxford: Blackwell, 1980).

—— *Tractatus Logico-Philosophicus*, tr. D. F. Pears and B. F. McGuinness (London: Routledge, 1961).

WOLFF, R. P., *The Autonomy of Reason* (New York: Harper & Row, 1973).

WOODFIELD, A., 'On Specifying the Contents of Thoughts', in *TO*.

WRIGHT, C., 'On Knowing One's Mind', 11th International Wittgenstein Symposium, Kirchberg, Austria, 1986.

—— (ed.), *Frege: Tradition and Influence* (Oxford: Blackwell, 1984).

YOUNG, J. Z., *Philosophy and the Brain* (Oxford: Oxford University Press, 1987).

INDEX